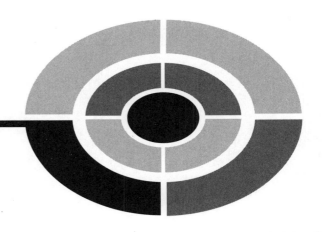

FINANCIAL PLANNING
DEMYSTIFIED

Other Titles in the Demystified Series

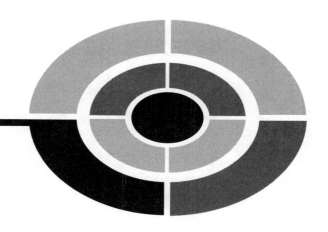

FINANCIAL PLANNING
DEMYSTIFIED

PAUL J. LIM

New York   Chicago   San Francisco   Lisbon   London
Madrid   Mexico City   Milan   New Delhi   San Juan
Seoul   Singapore   Sydney   Toronto

1 2 3 4 5 6 7 8 9 0   FGR/FGR   0 9 8 7 6

ISBN-13: 978-0-07-147671-3
ISBN-10: 0-07-147671-7

This publication is designed to provide accurate and authoritative information in regard to the subject matter covered. It is sold with the understanding that the publisher is not engaged in rendering legal, accounting, or other professional services. If legal advice or other expert assistance is required, the services of a competent professional person should be sought.
—*From a Declaration of Principles Jointly Adopted by a Committee of the American Bar Association and a Committee of Publishers and Associations*

McGraw-Hill books are available at special discounts to use as premiums and sales promotions, or for use in corporate training programs. For more information, please write to the Director of Special Sales, Professional Publishing, McGraw-Hill, Two Penn Plaza, New York, NY 10121-2298. Or contact your local bookstore.

This book is printed on acid-free paper.

Library of Congress Cataloging-in-Publication Data

Lim, Paul.
   Financial planning demystified / by Paul Lim.
      p. cm.
   Includes index.
    ISBN 0-07-147671-7 (pbk. : alk. paper) 1. Finance, Personal. I. Title.
HG179.L497 2007
332.6–dc22

                                2006028078

For Shirley

CONTENTS

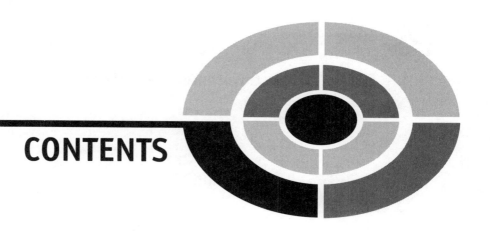

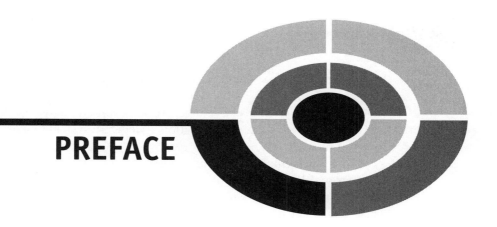

PREFACE

This book is geared for anyone and everyone who earns, spends, borrows, saves, invests, needs, and (most of all) *wants* money. In today's day and age, that's pretty much all of us.

Why is it necessary for all of us to plan for our financial futures? Here's the simple answer: It costs more than $200,000 to send 2.1 kids to private colleges for four years. To buy a home, you may have to spend close to $300,000. And if you want to be able to fund a long and comfortable retirement (with an emphasis on long, as we're living longer than our parents did), you may need to save anywhere from $500,000 to $1 million or more, depending on how and where you plan to live in your golden years. In fact, recent studies show that a retired couple turning 65 will need to save $200,000 just to cover out-of-pocket medical expenses in retirement—and that's with health-care coverage.

The fact is, we are constantly being reminded of a singular truth: When it comes to money-related matters, such as paying for college, paying to keep up with the Joneses, and saving for retirement, we are on our own.

True, the government says it will be there for us. But the safety nets that Uncle Sam created generations ago, such as Social Security and Medicare, are clearly fraying at the edges. At the very least, younger Americans don't trust the integrity of such programs.

Recent surveys, for instance, have shown that two thirds of younger workers do not think Social Security will be a viable or significant resource for them by the time they retire (even though Social Security checks took care of half or more of their parent's retirement needs). In fact, a large majority of so-called Generation X workers, those in their mid 20s to early 40s, now believe that they will have to

rely primarily—if not solely—on their own savings and retirement funds to pay for their golden years.

Meanwhile, two thirds of younger workers don't think that the U.S. government will make necessary fixes to the nation's Medicare system to meet their healthcare needs in retirement.

What's frightening is that this comes at a time when retirement is becoming a longer and longer phase of life. The average American male, for example, is expected to live to 74, while the average U.S. woman may live until almost 80. This means that if you retire at the traditional age of 65, you could easily have another 10 to 15 years worth of living expenses to cover. In fact, chances are, you'll have more. That's because if you're lucky enough to make it to 65, chances are, you'll live another 18 years. That's a whole lot of years of bills to pay.

As for our employers, the safety nets that they used to provide—such as guaranteed traditional pensions and retiree healthcare benefits—are also being torn asunder. Everyday, we read about yet another Fortune 500 company that is doing away with guaranteed retirement benefits for its workers because they can no longer afford to take care of us in our old age. Yet many Americans entered the workforce with these guarantees in mind. Now, only a small minority of us will be lucky enough to enjoy a guaranteed pension in retirement.

What has replaced these safety nets? Self-directed accounts and plans such as 401(k) retirement accounts, individual retirement accounts (IRAs), and health savings accounts that make *us* do all the work. This explains why today more than 90 million of us—representing about half of all U.S. households—invest in mutual funds, primarily through our 401(k)s and other employer-sponsored retirement accounts. Compare that to a half a century ago, when only around 6 million people had to invest.

But it's not just 401(k)s. Nearly 40 million of us invest in IRAs. And don't forget the growing popularity of 529 college savings accounts and Coverdell education savings accounts, which are both self-directed tax-deferred college savings plans that force parents to make their own investment decisions.

"Self directed" has become the new catch phrase for our financial planning system. No longer are things guaranteed and done for us, as pensions are. Instead, we have to do all our own savings and investing and planning. And there are no guarantees that at the end of a long, hard working career that our efforts will be enough to cover our needs.

Of course, the trade off in this new do-it-yourself system is that if we save, spend, and invest wisely, some of us may actually come out better than we would have under the old system of government and corporate guarantees. Some of you may like this. Others won't. Either way, this is the reality we live in today.

* * *

The term *financial planning* gets thrown out a lot, but there's some confusion about what it really means. Let's address this front and center. For starters, financial planning is not simply investing, though investing is a major component of a long-term financial plan. Financial planning refers to a life-long process of organizing the things that work for you—like your job, your income, your assets—while simultaneously controlling and diminishing those things that work against you. These would include your liabilities, such as debts and loans. It's about controlling what you can, like your savings and investment decisions, while doing the best unnecessary fees and expenses and taxes.

In this book, I will try to touch on several aspects of financial planning. In Part I, I will focus on **your assets and liabilities** by discussing ways in which we can save money and avoid debt. In this section, I will also address an often-overlooked asset that households need to be mindful of—their credit profile. Indeed, your credit profile and score can end up either saving (or costing) you tens, if not hundreds of thousands of dollars over the course of a lifetime of borrowing. Yet many families often ignore this valuable asset.

Next, in Part II, we will turn our attention to **your investments**. One of the biggest challenges for families as they attempt to create a financial plan is deciding which buckets to place their hard-earned savings into. Does the money belong in stocks, for instance, or bonds or cash? Or are you better off investing additional money in real estate? We will go over the ins and outs of all the major competing investment vehicles in this section of the book.

Then in Part III, we will focus on how to organize those buckets of stocks and bonds and cash that you've just put your savings into. In other words, we will talk about **your financial accounts**. For example, households often confuse core investment building blocks like stocks and bonds with the "envelopes" in which we usually hold those building blocks, such as tax-sheltered 401(k)s and IRAs (and even 529 savings plans for college). If we consider stocks and bonds as buckets in which we can organize our savings, then 401(k)s and IRAs are really the shelves in which we can place those buckets of stocks and bonds. In the final part of this book, we will discuss safeguards you should consider to protect your financial plans.

At the end of all of this, I hope you will know enough about financial planning to know what you know—and recognize what you don't. And most of all, I hope you will know enough about the ins and outs of creating a financial plan to actually go out and start one.

Paul J. Lim
July, 2006

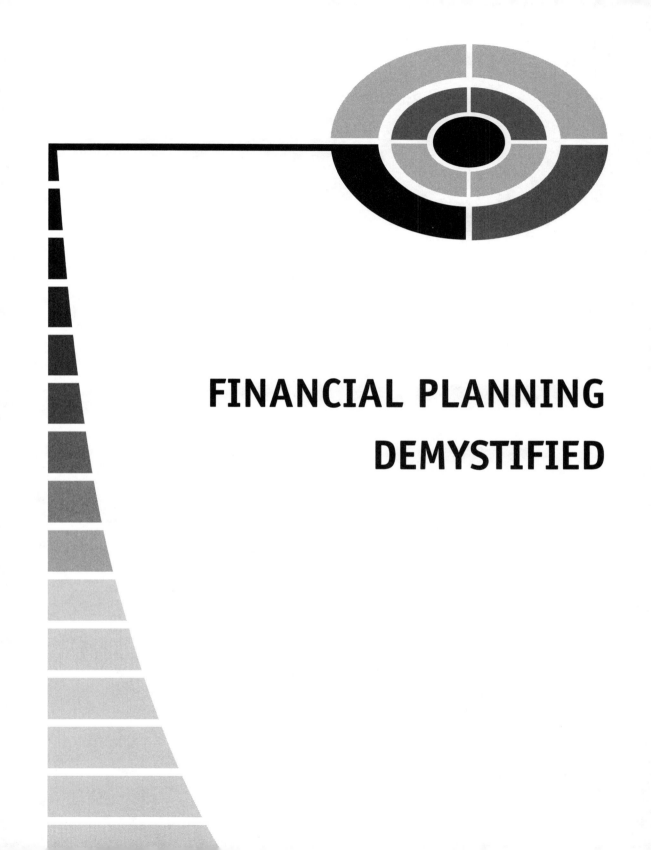

FINANCIAL PLANNING
DEMYSTIFIED

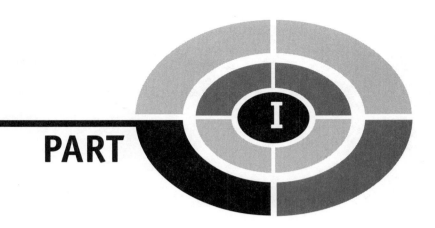

PART

I

Your Assets and Liabilities

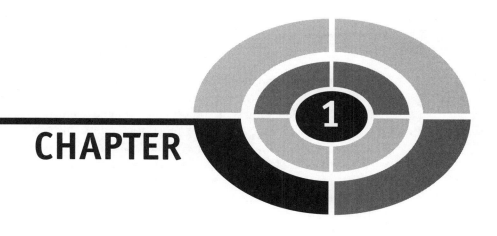

CHAPTER 1

Creating a Savings Plan

Why Save for the Future?

Call it the law of big numbers. All of the things that are truly important in life and that cost money—such as getting married, buying a home, having kids, educating those children, taking care of your parents in their golden years, and eventually retiring comfortably in your own old age—have become enormously expensive as of late.

A typical home might cost $300,000 or more. Taking care of your parents during a long (and hopefully happy) retirement can easily cost tens if not hundreds of thousands of dollars. And as for children, while priceless, they could end up costing you far more than you could ever imagine, once you factor in the price of diapers, food, health care, day care, clothing, toys, and education. Since the average U.S. household earns only around $50,000 a year, it's hard to imagine how any of us can afford the American Dream.

Yet somehow, we manage. And that's where financial planning comes in.

Taking the time to create a long-term financial plan is all about being realistic. It's about understanding that some money-related matters are completely out of your hands. For instance, even the most price-conscious consumers can't control how much health care, education, rent, and groceries will cost. Nor can we control what the federal, state, and local governments charge us every year in taxes. Yet when it comes to financial planning, there are some issues that are decidedly within your control, such as how much you spend, how much you save, and how you manage your nest egg. These are the pillars of a sound and sensible financial plan that we all need to concentrate on (and that we discuss at length in this book).

The fact is that modern life costs much more than most families earn in any given year. So by definition, your financial plan has to be a long-term endeavor. You simply can't get it done in a couple of years. There are no shortcuts or magic bullets when it comes to generating a lifetime of income. It's sort of like dieting. Every now and then, a new fad diet will come along that captures our attention. But 9 times out of 10, those diets wind up disappointing us—and our waistlines are the worse for it. Well the same goes for financial planning gimmicks and shortcuts, and it's our bank accounts that are worse off.

Time Is a Financial Plan's Best Friend

The good news is that time is our friend. You've all probably heard the phrase "time is money." Well it's true. There is a fundamental relationship between time and money that all of us who are constructing a financial plan need to understand. Academics will tell you that the time value of money is a very simple concept: Money that you have in hand today is worth far more to you than money that you might earn in the future because today's money can earn its own money along the way. What this means is that money saved today—and put to work in investment vehicles—is a far more valuable asset than its current value lets on. In other words, even if you only have a small amount of savings today, that money—so long as you don't frivolously spend it—can actually turn into rather large sums of money in the future. How large can those sums grow? It all depends on time. The more time you have to work with, the easier it will be to convert small buckets of money today into large amounts of money in the future.

In fact, the success of your financial plan will depend not only on how good a job you do saving and planning for the future but on when you get started. Sooner is always better. For example, say you were to start saving when you turned 25 years old. How much do you think you would have to set aside annually for the next 40 years, to create a nest egg worth $1 million at retirement? $15,000 a year?

Figure 1-1. Amount You'd Accumulate by Investing $10,000

Interest Rate	10 Years	30 Years	40 Years
5%	$132,100	$697,600	$1,268,400
7%	$147,800	$1,010,700	$2,136,100
10%	$175,300	$1,809,400	$4,868,500

$20,000 a year? No, the answer is just $5,000 a year, assuming you earn 7 percent annually on your money between the time you're 25 and when you turn 65. Think about it: To amass $1 million, all you would really need to save is $200,000 of your own money over the course of a lifetime (that's $5,000 times 40 years) so long as you have four full decades for that money to earn interest of its own. See Figure 1-1 for another example.

Now, say you procrastinated and waited until you were 35 to begin saving. Guess how much money you'd have to set aside annually, starting at that age, to accumulate $1 million at retirement? The answer is double the annual amount you would have needed to save if you started at 25. In other words, to amass $1 million, a 35-year-old would need to set aside $10,000 a year for the next 30 years. That means a 35-year old really needs to gather $300,000 in total savings over the course of a working career to hit the $1 million mark by retirement. Again, that's assuming that this person earns 7 percent a year on the money. This means procrastinating does come at a price. In our example, waiting 10 years will end up costing you $100,000 in extra savings to reach the same goal.

The situation is even worse for those who really drag their feet before starting a financial plan. For instance, say you waited until you were 45 to start saving in earnest. With only a 20-year time horizon until retirement, you'd have to save $23,000 annually, starting in your mid-40s, to reach the magical million-dollar mark. Not only is saving $23,000 a year a Herculean, if not impossible task— as it is around half the average annual income of households in the United States— you'd have to save that much every year for 20 years. That works out to a grand total of $460,000 in personal savings. So for those of you who think that there's little harm in waiting to start your financial plan, remember: A 45-year-old who gets a late start saving will have to set aside more than twice as much money as a 25-year-old simply to reach the same financial goal.

This brings us to lesson one of financial planning: You have to be patient. Small amounts of money, saved in drips and drabs, and properly organized, will turn into large amounts of money in the future to cover the staggering costs of modern life. See Figure 1-2. You have to take this at faith. So don't get hung up on the truly big numbers that frighten so many savers. Don't worry that sending your kid to college may end up costing you and your spouse $100,000—maybe $200,000 if you have more than one child. Be grateful that if you start saving for

Figure 1-2.   Amount You'd Accumulate by Investing $100 a Week

Interest Rate	10 Years	30 Years	40 Years
5%	$67,400	$361,200	$662,300
7%	$75,100	$528,120	$1,134,720
10%	$89,130	$986,040	$2,762,630

college bills the day your child is born, you will have an 18-year time horizon to work with. And if you have 18 years to work with, all you would need to save is $2,750 each year, from the time your child is born until he or she turns 18, to amass $100,000 (again, assuming you earn 7 percent a year on your money). That's doable, right?

The Power of Compound Interest

Why is time such a powerful force on our financial plans? It has to do with a concept related to the time value of money, which is the *power of compound interest*.

You've probably heard the axiom made famous by Benjamin Franklin: "A penny saved is a penny earned." Ol' Ben had it right. Well sort of. It's probably more accurate to say that "a penny saved is another penny that your original penny can earn."

Compound interest refers to the fact that if you begin to save and invest early on, the first batch of money you put to work will soon earn interest. And if you *reinvest* those proceeds back into the original investment—in other words, if you leave the money in the account, rather than spend it today—your interest will start earning interest of its own in a short while. Then, if you wait long enough, the interest that your interest generated will soon begin to earn interest of its own, and so on. What makes compound interest such a powerful force is that eventually your money literally works for you (instead of you working for your money) and helps you reach your long-term financial goals.

For instance, say you were to invest $1,000 in the first year of your financial plan. That money, if it were to earn 7 percent a year, would generate $70 of interest. Simple math would mean that over three years, you'd end up with $210 in interest. However, the rules of investment math aren't as simple, which turns out to be good news for long-term financial plans.

Let's say you wanted compound interest to work for you. So instead of pocketing that original $70 a year in interest income, you reinvested the money back into your portfolio. In this case, compound interest would help you earn $225, not $210. How? Remember, after Year 1, your account would have earned

$70 of interest. If you simply reinvested that interest into your account, your balance at the start of Year 2 would technically be $1,070. And 7 percent of $1,070 is $74.90. So in the second year of your savings regimen, you actually have earned more than the $70 in interest that you gained in Year 1, even though your account is growing at the exact 7 percent interest rate.

Now, if you were to reinvest that $74.90 back into your account, you'd have $1,144.90 to start Year 3. If you were to earn 7 percent interest again, that $1,144.90 would generate $80.14 of interest income in Year 3. Throw that back into your account, and you'd have $1,225.04 at the end of this three-year period. In other words, instead of earning $210 of interest over three years (based on simple math), the laws of compound interest have allowed you to earn $225.04 in interest.

You can use Figure 1-3 to find out how much your money will grow over time based on the laws of compound interest. Here's how to use the chart. Say you want to know how big your nest egg would become if you earned 8 percent a year on your money for the next 18 years. Well, go to the column that shows "8%." Then trace down that column to the row that says "18 years." The figure there is 3.996019. This is the compound interest factor that you will enjoy, based on your time horizon and your earnings rate.

Now, take whatever amount of savings you have today and multiply it by this figure. For instance, say you have $25,000 saved up. In 18 years, that money would grow to $99,900 if it were to earn 8 percent annual interest during this time. We arrive at this amount by multiplying your $25,000 times the factor 3.996019. If you had 28 years to work with instead of just 18 and you had an 8 percent annual earnings rate, your original $25,000 would grow to nearly $215,680. This amount is based on the compound interest factor of 8.627106 that you will see for "8%" and "28 years." This is quite telling. This means that if you had another decade to work with on top of your original 18 years, you could grow your nest egg by more than twice as much. That's the power of compound interest.

The Biggest Threat to Your Financial Plan

If time is your financial plan's best friend, what's its biggest enemy? As it turns out, it's inertia. According to Newton's first law of motion, bodies in motion tend to stay in motion, while bodies at rest tend to stay at rest. Well, the financial planning corollary is that families who don't start planning for the future early tend never to get going.

You've probably heard this statistic: On average, Americans spend more time planning a vacation trip or researching a new car purchase than they do planning for their financial futures. Sadly, it's true. The typical family will probably spend

Figure 1-3.   Compound Interest Factors (Growth of $1)

					Interest Rates					
Years	1%	2%	3%	4%	5%	6%	7%	8%	9%	10%
1	1.010000	1.020000	1.030000	1.040000	1.050000	1.060000	1.070000	1.080000	1.090000	1.100000
2	1.020100	1.040400	1.060900	1.081600	1.102500	1.123600	1.144900	1.166400	1.188100	1.210000
3	1.030301	1.061208	1.092727	1.124864	1.157625	1.191016	1.225043	1.259712	1.295029	1.331000
4	1.040604	1.082432	1.125509	1.169859	1.215506	1.262477	1.310796	1.360489	1.411582	1.464100
5	1.051010	1.104081	1.159274	1.216653	1.276282	1.338226	1.402552	1.469328	1.538624	1.610510
6	1.061520	1.126162	1.194052	1.265319	1.340096	1.418519	1.500730	1.586874	1.677100	1.771561
7	1.072135	1.148686	1.229874	1.315932	1.407100	1.503630	1.605781	1.713824	1.828039	1.948717
8	1.082857	1.171659	1.266770	1.368569	1.477455	1.593848	1.718186	1.850930	1.992563	2.143589
9	1.093685	1.195093	1.304773	1.423312	1.551328	1.689479	1.838459	1.999005	2.171893	2.357948
10	1.104622	1.218994	1.343916	1.480244	1.628895	1.790848	1.967151	2.158925	2.367364	2.593742
11	1.115668	1.243374	1.384234	1.539454	1.710339	1.898299	2.104852	2.331639	2.580426	2.853117
12	1.126825	1.268242	1.425761	1.601032	1.795856	2.012196	2.252192	2.518170	2.812665	3.138428
13	1.138093	1.293607	1.468534	1.665074	1.885649	2.132928	2.409845	2.719624	3.065805	3.452271
14	1.149474	1.319479	1.512590	1.731676	1.979932	2.260904	2.578534	2.937194	3.341727	3.797498
15	1.160969	1.345868	1.557967	1.800944	2.078928	2.396558	2.759032	3.172169	3.642482	4.177248
16	1.172579	1.372786	1.604706	1.872981	2.182875	2.540352	2.952164	3.425943	3.970306	4.594970
17	1.184304	1.400241	1.652848	1.947900	2.292018	2.692773	3.158815	3.700018	4.327633	5.054470
18	1.196147	1.428246	1.702433	2.025817	2.406619	2.854339	3.379932	3.996019	4.717120	5.559917
19	1.208109	1.456811	1.753506	2.106849	2.526950	3.025600	3.616528	4.315701	5.141661	6.115909
20	1.220190	1.485947	1.806111	2.191123	2.653298	3.207135	3.869684	4.660957	5.604411	6.727500
21	1.232392	1.515666	1.860295	2.278768	2.785963	3.399564	4.140562	5.033834	6.108808	7.400250
22	1.244716	1.545980	1.916103	2.369919	2.925261	3.603537	4.430402	5.436540	6.658600	8.140275
23	1.257163	1.576899	1.973587	2.464761	3.071524	3.819750	4.740530	5.871464	7.257874	8.954302
24	1.269735	1.608437	2.032784	2.563304	3.225100	4.048935	5.072367	6.341181	7.911083	9.849733
25	1.282432	1.640606	2.093778	2.665836	3.386355	4.291871	5.427433	6.848475	8.623081	10.834706
26	1.295256	1.673418	2.156591	2.772470	3.555673	4.549383	5.807353	7.396353	9.399158	11.918177
27	1.308209	1.706886	2.221289	2.883369	3.733456	4.822346	6.213868	7.988061	10.245082	13.109994
28	1.321291	1.741024	2.287928	2.998703	3.920129	5.111687	6.648838	8.627106	11.167140	14.420994
29	1.334504	1.775845	2.356566	3.118651	4.116136	5.418388	7.114257	9.317275	12.172182	15.863093
30	1.347849	1.811362	2.427262	3.243398	4.321942	5.743491	7.612255	10.062657	13.267678	17.449402

less than 24 hours in any single year researching exactly how much they'll need to reach a specific goal—be it college savings or retirement. In fact, according to a study by the Employee Benefit Research Institute (EBRI) in 2006, only 42 percent of workers (and their spouses) have actually sat down to figure out how much money they'll need to save for their golden years. That means the vast majority of us are simply flying by the seat of our pants.

This would explain some of the findings of other studies on American savings patterns. Indeed, research shows that more than two in five households aren't saving any money currently—for any purpose. And while a majority of families have set aside some money for retirement, 53 percent of those families have less than $25,000 saved, according to the EBRI. Around two-thirds of U.S. workers have less than $50,000 saved up (see Figure 1-4). And more than three-quarters

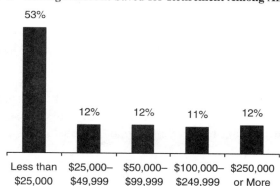

Figure 1-4.   **Average Amount Saved for Retirement Among All Workers**

Source: Employee Benefit Research Institute

have less than $100,000 amassed. Yet, academic research shows that if a retiree wants to safely generate $40,000 to $50,000 of annual retirement income over the course of his or her golden years, without fear of running out of money, that person would need to start with a nest egg closer to $1 million.

It's not just about retirement, though. Studies have shown that less than half of American households have put together a plan to achieve any of their financial goals. For example, only around a third of all parents of high school aged children say they have begun to save money for their kids' college educations. Is it any wonder, then, that Americans are growing increasingly anxious about their financial futures? Around 7 in 10 parents say they are worried about their ability to pay for their children's college bills. And nearly 4 in 10 parents are so concerned that they don't think they'll be able to send their kids to college.

The good news is that those households who sit down and create a financial plan are much more confident about their ability to achieve their long-term financial goals. That's because once you sit down and crunch the numbers, you will find that with time—and the help of compound interest—it's possible to get to where you want to go through a slow-and-steady savings regimen and investing strategy.

Start an Emergency Fund

All financial plans should start with a safety net known as an emergency fund. That's because the surest way to upset a long-term financial plan is to run headfirst into an unexpected emergency. What if you lose your job, for example? What if your child gets sick? What if you get sick and can't work full-time? Typically, emergencies such as these ruin a financial plan by forcing households to stop saving. Often, families faced with unexpected financial burdens are forced to go into debt to cover unexpected bills, which is a financial sinkhole that may take years to climb out of.

Unfortunately, most households fail to prepare for the unexpected. Indeed, a third of American households literally live paycheck to paycheck. And more than two out of five households have less than $1,000 in cash savings available to them at any given moment to meet emergency expenses. Yet $1,000 isn't going to cut it.

Most financial planners will recommend that families set aside at least three months' worth of expenses in an ultra-safe and ultra-liquid cash account. But some believe that families should play it safer and set aside at least four months' worth or more of their basic expenses. Why? For starters, it typically takes three to four months for an unemployed American to find a new job, according to recent surveys. So if the emergency you run into is losing your job, you may need a slightly bigger rainy day fund to get you over the hump. Now, if you're the sole breadwinner in the family, which means your spouse and children depend on your paycheck, you might want to play it even safer and set aside four to six months' worth of expenses. Unfortunately, only 3 out of 10 households have even three months' worth of expenses saved up.

Keep in mind that emergencies don't even have to be serious to set back your financial plan. A water heater that explodes or a roof that leaks or a car that breaks down all constitute minor emergencies that may require families with no rainy day fund to dip into valuable savings or slip into debt.

Some of you might consider your investment accounts to be your emergency fund. But keep in mind that if you rely on your investment portfolio to meet emergencies, you may be forced to sell out of winning stocks and stock funds at inopportune times. Selling winning stocks to meet emergency bills may also trigger capital gains taxes.

How Big Should Your Rainy Day Fund Be?

Contrary to popular belief, the size of your emergency fund is dependent on your monthly expenses, not on your monthly income. That's because one of the most common emergencies that arises is being laid off. And if you find yourself out of work, you'll want to know that you have at least enough money to get you by for the next few months.

To calculate your monthly expenses, factor in all your routine expenses including your mortgage payments, condo fees, car payments, insurance premiums (for life, health, home, and autos), utilities, food, and transportation. And don't forget monthly or quarterly tax bills that you owe.

Automate Your Savings

If it's true that inertia is a big threat to your financial plan—and it is—then why not let inertia work for you? Just as bodies in motion are likely to stay in motion according to the laws of physics, savings plans, once started, are likely to continue to keep going as long as you keep everything on autopilot. Indeed, academic research has shown that automated employer-sponsored retirement plans—such as 401(k) accounts that automatically enroll workers and automatically increase their savings rates over time—are far more successful in getting workers to save substantial sums than other means. So why not put other aspects of your savings plan on autopilot as well?

Fortunately, the financial services industry is racing to create automated programs for savers and investors. Indeed, just as you can instruct a 401(k) plan to deduct a certain percentage of your paycheck every month for investment, many mutual companies have established automated investing plans that will allow you to send $100 or $200 a month into a mutual fund that will in turn invest the money for you. Similar automated savings plans exist for individual retirement accounts, 529 college savings accounts, and basic money market accounts. See Figure 1-5.

Figure 1-5. Automated Savings Plans

Fund Company	Minimum Investment*
Vanguard	$3,000
American Funds	$50
Fidelity	$100
American Century	$2,500
Janus	$500
Dodge & Cox	$50
Putnam	$25
T. Rowe Price	$50

*Minimum investment required to start an automated savings plans.

Reduce Your Spending

It stands to reason that if money earned today is more valuable than the same amount of money earned down the road, then you should immediately save and invest as much of today's money as possible. That's if you want to take full advantage of the power of compound interest. But the only way to invest more money immediately is to save more money.

Culturally, that's been a difficult task for many American families. Indeed, in this increasingly materially oriented society, a new "must-have" item hits the market every day—whether it's a plasma screen television or a stainless steel refrigerator or an iPod. No wonder the average household carries credit card balances of more than $7,000—a figure that's expected to climb to more than $8,000 by 2008, according to The Nilson Report. See Figure 1-6.

But remember, the key to any financial plan is to start small and do the little things that will make a big difference in your finances down the road. For starters, whatever your goal is in terms of saving money, add $25 a week. In other words, if you think you can save $100 a week, or $5,200 a year, think about saving $125 a week instead, for an annual goal of $6,500.

Why? According to surveys, nearly three-quarters of Americans admit that they could easily set aside an additional $20 a week, over and above what they currently save routinely from their paychecks. Amazingly, even the vast majority of so-called nonsavers—those workers who aren't setting aside anything currently

Figure 1-6.   Outstanding Credit Card Balances per Household

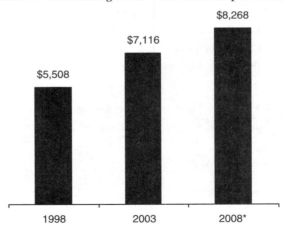

* Estimate.

Source: The Nilson Report

Figure 1-7.   Amount You'd Accumulate by Investing $25 a Week

Interest Rate	10 Years	30 Years	40 Years
5%	$16,850	$90,300	$165,580
7%	$18,775	$132,000	$283,700
10%	$22,280	$246,510	$690,650

for the future—admit that they could save $20 a week without much pain. If saving $20 a week is no problem, why not push yourself a little and strive for $25 a week?

If you think $25 a week is insignificant, you're dead wrong. Look at Figure 1-7 to see what $25 a week, invested for 10 years or more, could turn into based on various rates of interest. For example, if you're a 30-something and started setting aside an additional $25 a week every year for the next 30 years, you could parlay that modest sum into $132,000 of extra money by the time you retire (this is assuming you earn 7 percent a year on that money throughout that time period). If you're a 20-something and had a 40-year time horizon, you could see that money grow to more than a quarter of a million dollars by the time you leave the workforce.

There's another easy strategy to get you to spend less and save more. And that's to freeze your plastic. Obviously, in today's day and age, you need your credit cards to make basic purchases. Indeed, it's next to impossible to book a rental car or a hotel room these days without a credit card. And it would be hard to make online purchases without plastic. But to the extent that you can use cash for other basic purposes—such as groceries, buying clothes, dining out—try it.

Here's why. Research has shown that consumers are likely to spend more when they use plastic rather than cash. For instance, a while back, two professors at the Massachusetts Institute of Technology set up a fascinating experiment. They decided to see how much people would be willing to bid for a pair of Boston Celtics tickets. So they set up two separate auctions. In the first sale, only cash bidders were allowed to participate. In the second, credit card payments were accepted. Now, one would assume that because these were auctions for the same items—two identical pairs of Boston Celtic tickets—that the highest bids from both auctions would be somewhat similar. But as it turns out, the credit card bidders were willing to spend around twice as much for the same tickets as cash-only bidders.

It just goes to show that when people use their credit cards, they tend not to think of it as their money, but rather some abstract source of wealth. But when they use cash, it becomes a much more sober transaction. Similar studies have shown that households that use plastic to make fast-food purchases tend to spend more, per meal, than cash-only buyers. So if you're trying to squeeze out that additional $25 a week in savings, a good place to start is by not using your credit cards for basic transactions.

Pay Down Credit Card Debt

In most cases, it makes sense to pay off your credit card balances before you embark on a major savings program. Why? As we'll discuss at greater length in the next chapter, credit card debt is a highly deleterious form of borrowing. Unlike mortgages or student loans, you won't receive any tax deductions for interest payments you make on your credit card balances. And unlike margin loans on a brokerage account, you're not borrowing to invest when you use your credit cards. You are borrowing to spend.

Moreover, credit card interest rates are typically higher than most other forms of borrowing. That's because credit cards are an *unsecured* form of debt. With a home mortgage, for instance, the lender can take possession of your home if you default on your loan obligation. So the lender is protected. But if you were to default on your credit card obligations, the lender would not have similar safeguards, since this form of debt is not secured with an asset. Therefore, credit card issuers charge higher rates than other lenders because of the greater risks they face when extending these types of loans. See Figure 1-8 for rate comparisons.

In the spring of 2006, the average credit card was charging 16 percent interest. However, many card holders were being charged significantly higher interest rates because many credit card companies impose so-called penalty rates on card holders who miss even a single payment. Indeed, it is becoming increasingly common for credit card issuers to jack up the basic interest rates charged to card holders who are late with payments not only on that particular card but on any of their loan obligations. In other words, if for any reason you're late paying your American Express bill, your Visa card issuer might increase your interest rate from 16 percent to 29 percent.

These sky-high rates will almost certainly damage most financial plans. That's because consumer debt will work against you in a far greater degree than your investment portfolio will work for you. For example, when you put your savings to work in the stock market, you can expect to earn around 10 percent a year on average over long periods of time (we'll get into stocks at greater length in Chapter 3). But what good is it to earn 10 percent on a portfolio of $10,000 if you have credit card balances of $10,000 charging you 21 percent interest? The fact is, when you have credit card balances, you are shifting your financial plan into reverse, not drive. And no matter how smart you are at picking stocks, it will be next to impossible to consistently produce investment gains that beat annual credit card interest rates.

Think of paying off your card balances as the equivalent of being a shrewd investor. Every dollar you pay off on a credit card charging 21 percent interest is the equivalent of investing $1 in the stock market and earning 21 percent on

Figure 1-8.   **Average Credit Card Interest Rates**

Month	Prime	Fixed	Variable
May 04	4.00%	12.64%	11.58%
Jun 04	4.00%	12.69%	11.61%
Jul 04	4.25%	12.79%	11.73%
Aug 04	4.50%	12.85%	11.89%
Sep 04	4.75%	12.88%	12.11%
Oct 04	4.75%	13.00%	12.19%
Nov 04	5.00%	13.04%	12.37%
Dec 04	5.25%	13.09%	12.49%
Jan 05	5.25%	13.22%	12.67%
Feb 05	5.50%	13.25%	12.84%
Mar 05	5.75%	13.32%	13.08%
Apr 05	5.75%	13.39%	13.17%
May 05	6.00%	13.48%	13.45%
Jun 05	6.00%	13.59%	13.61%
Jul 05	6.25%	13.64%	13.84%
Aug 05	6.50%	13.76%	14.24%
Sep 05	6.75%	13.80%	14.49%
Oct 05	6.75%	13.87%	14.64%
Nov 05	7.00%	13.91%	14.89%
Dec 05	7.25%	13.93%	15.20%
Jan 06	7.50%	14.08%	15.53%
Feb 06	7.50%	14.11%	15.75%
Mar 06	7.75%	14.15%	15.81%
Apr 06	7.75%	14.19%	15.99%
May 06	8.00%	14.23%	16.02%

Source: CardData

your money. That's an amazing rate of return. Is there any safe, guaranteed way for you to invest money in stocks and earn 21 percent a year? Is there any safe, guaranteed way for you to invest money in real estate and come out 21 percent ahead? No. So you can easily turn this albatross into a gift horse by paying off your cards first.

Create a Budget

To save money for the long term, you have to live well within your means. But to figure out what level of spending qualifies as "within your means," you first have to take a full accounting of what you earn. And the best way to do that is to sit down with pen and paper and figure out your real monthly income.

Most of us only factor in our take-home pay when determining how much income we earn every month. But increasingly, workers are also generating additional income on the side, through other means including freelance work, home-based small businesses, and even eBay-based sales. Another source of monthly income to consider is the interest income you might receive from your bond or stock holdings.

After you figure out how much you really bring in each month, it's time to calculate your current spending.

There are two factors that make it difficult to figure out exactly how much you spend in any given month. The first is that some bills fluctuate. While your phone service, for example, may be billed as a flat rate every month, your gas and electric charges may fluctuate depending on use. Your gasoline costs may fluctuate as well, depending on how much you drive in a given month and how expensive gas prices are that month. Moreover, if you have adjustable-rate loans outstanding, the amount of money you owe every month on these obligations may change slightly as time progresses. For instance, if interest rates are rising, you may end up paying more each month on your adjustable-rate credit cards and adjustable-rate home mortgages (or ARMs) than you did at the start of the year.

The other difficulty in calculating exactly how much you spend each month is that a number of the small purchases you make—for instance, that $4 cup of coffee at Starbucks or that $5 magazine you buy at the airport or that $6 hotdog at the ballpark—often go unnoticed. Indeed, the things that upset many spending plans aren't the big-ticket items (such as vacations or cars) but rather the little things in life (like clothes and drinks and five-dollar items here and there that you buy at the grocery or convenience store).

To get a true gauge of what you're spending, then, you'll need to track your spending over several months. Indeed, financial planners will often recommend that consumers track their spending patterns for at least three months.

Here's a suggestion: Keep a pen and a small pad of paper with you wherever you go for the next three months. (If you're a tech-oriented person, you can do this on your electronic PDA.) Whenever you spend money, write it down—whether it's the weekly grocery bill, monthly car loan payments, or even a stick of chewing gum you buy at the corner convenience store. If you buy lunch at work, be especially mindful to track all your food expenses. Don't leave anything out. If you get hit with a quarterly tax bill, for instance, include it. If you go to the theater, include that.

As you're going along, make sure you categorize all of your spending in one of the line items, as shown in Figure 1-9. Now after three months of doing this, tally up all your line items. In other words, if your electric bill was $120 in Month 1, $200 in Month 2, and $70 in Month 3, add them up into a single figure; in this case, it's $390. Then divide all your three-month tallies by 3, to arrive at an

Figure 1-9.   Determining Your Income and Expenses

Money In

Monthly Salary	_____
Other Sources of Work Income	_____
Government-Related Income	_____
Investment Income	_____
Inheritance/Estate-Related Income	_____
Total Monthly Income	_____

Money Out

Mortgage Payment and/or Rent	_____
Electricity	_____
Heat/Heating Oil	_____
Water and Other Utilities	_____
Car Loan/Car Repair/Car Maintenance	_____
Car Insurance	_____
Home Owners' Insurance	_____
Life Insurance	_____
Health Insurance	_____
Home Repair/Maintenance	_____
Home Improvement	_____
Gasoline Costs	_____
Food/Groceries	_____
Food/Dining Out	_____
Other Transportation Costs	_____
Clothing	_____
Coffee	_____
Phone	_____
Cellular Phone(s)	_____
Cable	_____
Internet Service Provider	_____
Other Cable/Internet Subscriptions	_____

Figure 1-9.   Continued

Newspaper/Magazine Subscriptions	_____
Movies	_____
Other Entertainment	_____
Haircuts and Personal Care	_____
Out-of-Pocket Health/Dental Costs	_____
Set Asides for Taxes (property, income, etc.)	_____
Incidentals	_____
Total Monthly Expenses	_____
Total Monthly Income − Total Monthly Expenses	_____

average monthly expense for each category of spending. Finally, add up all your monthly average totals to come up with a single figure for your average monthly expenditures.

How Much Should You Save?

Even if you find that your average spending is lower than your average after-tax income, don't think that you're out of the woods. Academic research has shown that workers should really be saving at least 15 percent of their incomes every year. But to be really safe, a good target to shoot for is a savings rate of 20 percent to 25 percent of your annual income (this includes savings both inside and outside your employer-sponsored retirement accounts).

Why so much? Researchers at T. Rowe Price, the mutual fund company and asset manager, recently studied the success of workers' retirement plans based on various rates of saving. Twenty-somethings who have 40 years until retirement and save 20 percent of their current pretax salaries are likely to replace all of their current income when they retire. But those same 20-somethings who put away only 5 percent of their current salaries are likely to generate less than half of their current income when they retire. So your savings rate really matters.

The financial services firm Charles Schwab has done similar research on what households need to save for the long term. What Schwab researchers found harkens back to our initial point about the time value of money. If you're in your 20s and are just getting started, Schwab recommends setting aside 10 percent to 15 percent of your salary each year. If you're in your 30s, a savings rate of 15 percent to 25 percent would be more appropriate, according to the firm. And if

Figure 1-10.   Savings Targets by Ages

Age When You Start Saving	Percent of Your Salary You Need to Save
20s	10%–15%
30s	15%–25%
Early 40s	25%–35%
45	37%
46	41%
47	44%
48	48%
49	53%
50+	58% or more

Source: Schwab Center for Investment Research

you're in your early 40s and are just now starting to save, then you need to set aside as much as 25 percent to 35 percent of your income each year.

And what if you haven't started and you're 45 years old—or older? Then it becomes real tough. A 48-year-old who hasn't started saving at all probably needs to stuff nearly half of his or her income into a savings plan immediately. Obviously, it will be difficult—if not impossible—to save this amount of money. But this is yet another argument for why it's important to save early and take advantage of the time value of money. See Figure 1-10.

Quiz for Chapter 1

1. According to the "time value of money," the more time you have to save and invest ...

    a. the more money you must save.

    b. the less money you need to save.

    c. the more difficult it is to create a successful financial plan.

2. Which of the following statements best describes "compound interest"?

    a. A special type of interest rate that savers enjoy in certain types of accounts.

    b. The type of high interest rates that credit card companies impose.

    c. A condition where interest on your principal, if left alone, will begin to earn interest of its own. And if that interest is reinvested, it too will earn its own interest, thereby growing your account faster.

3. Based on the time value of money and the laws of compound interest, how much money would you need to set aside annually to amass $100,000 in 18 years, assuming a 7 percent interest rate?

    a. $5,500

    b. $2,750

    c. $3,500

4. Which should you do first—start an emergency fund or pay down your credit cards?

    a. Start your emergency fund.

    b. Pay down your credit card balances.

    c. The answer depends on the interest rates that your credit card companies impose.

5. Which should you do first—pay down credit card debt with an interest rate of 16 percent or invest in the stock market?

    a. Invest in the market, because you can easily earn a higher return than the interest rate on your credit card.

    b. Pay down the card balance first, because it's one of the worst kinds of debt you can carry.

    c. Split the difference—pay down half your card debt and invest the other half.

6. What's the best way to start an emergency savings fund?
    a. Maximize your 401(k) contributions.
    b. Invest in a mutual fund.
    c. Automate your savings through monthly contributions to a liquid savings vehicle such as a money market mutual fund.

7. How big should your emergency savings fund be?
    a. Enough to cover at least three months of your take-home pay.
    b. Enough to cover one month of expenses.
    c. Enough to cover at least three months of expenses.

8. How many Americans have a financial plan?
    a. Less than half
    b. 65
    c. 90 percent or more

9. How much money has the typical U.S. household set aside for retirement?
    a. Less than $100,000
    b. More than $300,000
    c. About $500,000

10. How much of your income should you plan to save annually?
    a. 5 percent
    b. 10 to 15 percent
    c. 15 percent or more

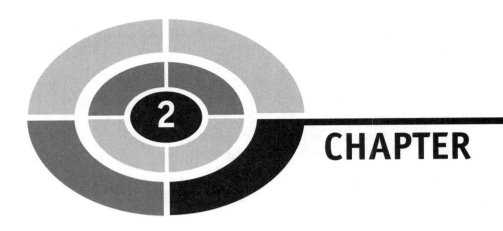

CHAPTER 2

Borrowing and Credit

Why We Borrow?

There is a tendency to believe that all forms of borrowing are bad. That's probably because of the horror stories you hear about the accumulation of debt among American households. Indeed, total consumer debt outstanding soared nearly 20 percent to $2.2 trillion between 2001 and 2006, according to the Federal Reserve (see Figure 2-1). And this was during a period when families generally enjoyed rising incomes and net worth, thanks in large part to the residential real estate boom at the start of this decade. Worse still, many Americans are in debt through the worst form of borrowing: high-interest credit card balances (see Figure 2-2).

Every three years, the Federal Reserve conducts an in-depth survey of the state of household finances. In its most recent study, looking at data collected from 2004, it determined that three out of four households used credit cards to manage their finances. And among those families, nearly 60 percent maintained credit card balances (i.e., they didn't pay off their balances in full at the end of each month). Given that the average credit card interest rate is now roughly 16 percent—and many cards charge as much as 29 percent or even higher—this is certainly grounds for concern. Indeed, a separate study conducted at around the

Figure 2-1. Total Consumer Debt Outstanding in Billions

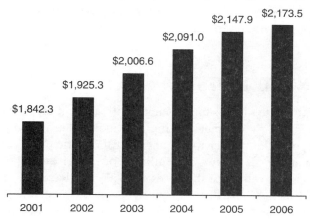

Source: Federal Reserve

Figure 2-2. Outstanding Credit Card Balances Per Household

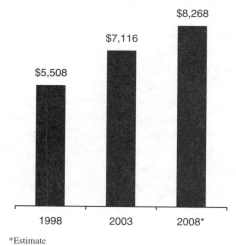

*Estimate

Source: The Nilson Group

same time by the research firm The Nilson Group found that the average family carried card balances of more than $7,000 in 2003. And that figure is expected to climb to nearly $8,300 by 2008.

Yet despite these concerns, there are instances where borrowing isn't simply necessary, it's productive. Think about the times we live in. It can easily cost $50,000 to send your son or daughter to college. And that's just to a public university. A new car might cost at least $25,000. And that's just for a compact model. For many households, it would be next to impossible to undertake these big-ticket transactions without borrowing some money for some period of time. In some cases, it would be foolhardy to try. The fact is that borrowing serves a number of purposes within a financial plan—some good and some bad.

BORROWING TO INVEST

We often think of borrowing as the financial equivalent of digging ourselves a big hole. Yet there are many instances within a financial plan where you can borrow money in a responsible manner to get ahead of the game. You've probably done it yourself. For instance, every year, millions of Americans take out mortgages to purchase homes or refinance the loans they already have. At the end of 2005, there was more than $1.2 trillion in mortgage debt outstanding in the United States. The act of borrowing money to buy a huge asset like a house offers a perfect illustration of how you can use debt to invest.

Consider a typical scenario: Say you purchased a home for $500,000 and put 10 percent down. That means you sunk $50,000 of your own money into the investment at the start. Now, say that within a year, you turned around and sold that property for 30 percent more, or $650,000. This works out to a capital gain of $150,000. While the original cost of the home was half a million dollars, you really only had to pony up $50,000 of your own hard-earned cash to generate that profit of $150,000. Where else can you triple your money in this fashion? Certainly not by investing in stocks or bonds or cash.

To be sure, one could argue that you actually spent more than $50,000 of your own money in this scenario, because within that first year of owning the home, you made mortgage payments on a monthly basis. True. For the sake of argument, let's say that your monthly mortgage cost was $2,500. But remember, had you not purchased that home with a mortgage, you still would have needed a place to live. So the vast majority of that $2,500 mortgage requirement could be chalked up to the imputed rent that you would have had to pay had you not purchased the house. Assuming you could have rented an equivalent property for, say, $2,000, a reasonable estimate of your "extra" housing costs might be $6,000 (that's $500 in additional housing costs per month). This means you really engineered that $150,000 profit with only $56,000 in cash. That's an enormous profit that you could never have pulled off without the mortgage loan.

In investing, we call this *leverage*. This is a fancy term describing the use of other people's money—in this case, the mortgage lender's capital—to boost the potential gains in your investment.

Had you not borrowed, there's no way you could have come close to achieving this type of return. For example, let's say that instead of putting $50,000 down on a $500,000 home, you chose to buy a much smaller piece of real estate, in

a much more affordable community, for $100,000. And let's say somehow, you were able to pay cash for the entire amount. Assuming you earned the same percentage gain as in the first example—30 percent—you would have sold your home for $130,000. That means you profited $30,000 off of a $100,000 commitment. Compare that to the earlier example, where you profited $150,000 off a $56,000 base.

There are other ways you can use debt to leverage your returns. For example, within an investment brokerage account, you could buy stocks on margin—by borrowing money on a short-term basis from your broker and then using those proceeds to invest in the market. Let's say you decided to use $20,000 of your own money to purchase shares of a particular stock. And let's say you borrowed another $10,000, for a grand total of $30,000. Now, assume that this investment climbs to, say, $50,000 over time, for a capital appreciation of $20,000 (which works out to a 66 percent gain). Had you only invested your original $20,000, your gain would have been only $13,333.

Be warned, however. When it comes to borrowing for investment purposes, you have to be extremely careful. That's because while leverage works for you when the price of your asset rises, leverage will work against you should prices fall. The risk is that you could end up losing way more than you can afford. A big reason why leverage works so well in the home mortgage market is that by definition, mortgages are long-term loans. And over extended periods of time—for example, 30 years, which is the typical duration of a mortgage—the odds are great that home prices will appreciate significantly.

Borrowing So You Can Invest Elsewhere

In many cases, households may have ample funds to pay for certain items. For example, say your leaky roof needs to be replaced and it costs $30,000. You may have more than enough saved in various stock funds and retirement accounts to pay for the repair. But should you tap into those funding sources instead of borrowing the money?

In some cases, the answer is no. For instance, what if you could take out a home-equity loan to make the fixes on your roof at an interest rate of, say, 6 percent? Historically, the stock market has returned more than 10 percent a year. So why would you take money out of an asset that's growing 10 percent annually when a lender is offering you an alternative funding source that will only cost you 6 percent? Moreover, if you sell stocks and other investments to pay for basic goods and services, there's a good chance that you will also have to pay capital gains taxes (if you sell a winning stock) on top of transaction fees.

The question—to borrow or not to borrow—is a whole lot more complicated than many financial planners make it out to be. When debating whether it makes sense to borrow, you have to ask yourself: What is the best interest rate I can get on the loan? And what's the *opportunity cost* of not borrowing and instead taking money out of my other accounts?

If, based on your credit profile and current market interest rates, the cheapest loan you can get is at 10 percent, then it's probably not worth the risk of borrowing. After all, stocks are only *likely* to earn 10 percent a year. There are no guarantees. There are plenty of occasions when stocks fall short of this average. And if your stocks return only 6 percent during a stretch when you're borrowing at 10 percent, you lose at both ends. If your choice is between cashing in a stock investment versus borrowing from a credit card charging 19 percent interest, then it absolutely makes no sense to borrow. That's because there's no guarantee you can earn 19 percent in the market consistently over long periods of time.

On the other hand, if you can qualify for, say, a home-equity loan charging only 5 percent, then borrowing may be the right decision. It all depends. If the opportunity cost of using your own money is significantly greater than the borrowing costs associated with a loan, then debt may serve a very useful purpose.

BORROWING TO SPEND

The problem is, when it comes to borrowing, many households aren't doing it to invest or to allow their other investments to grow. Rather, they borrow to spend. It's no coincidence that the greatest period of consumer spending coincided with the advent of easy borrowing through credit cards.

Today, the average household maintains around a dozen separate credit cards. And as noted in the previous chapter, research has shown that consumers who have access to credit cards tend to spend more, per transaction, than their peers who use only cash. It's also true that households with credit cards are also more likely to initiate more transactions than those who don't use cards. In fact, the average household in 2003 made 163 different purchases that year on plastic (this does not count the other transactions they made using cash or checks). By 2008, The Nilson Report predicts that households will make 213 separate credit card transactions a year, which is one purchase every 1.7 days, totaling nearly $20,000. See Figures 2-3 and 2-4.

Prioritizing Your Debt

Before you consider borrowing as part of your financial plan, it's wise to go through a series of questions to determine the utility and the consequences of

Figure 2-3.   Average Number of Credit Cards Transactions per Household per Year

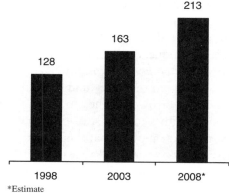

Source: The Nilson Report

Figure 2-4.   Average Annual Purchases on Credit Cards per Household

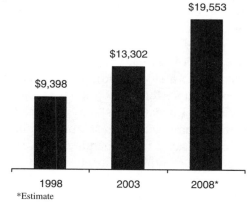

Source: The Nilson Report

adding to your debt. Every family's financial plan is slightly different. Whether borrowing makes sense for you will depend largely on why you're borrowing, at what terms you're borrowing, and whether you're dealing with a *benign* form of debt or a *malignant* form of debt. You should ask yourself the following questions:

QUESTION NO. 1: DO YOU REALLY NEED THE MONEY?

Since all forms of borrowing cost you some interest, it's important to be certain that you absolutely need to borrow. This is especially true for purchases made on credit cards. To be sure, there are certain transactions that are simply unavoidable. For instance, if your water heater breaks or your car is stolen, you will need to replace those items, and you may need to borrow in the short term to do so. But discretionary borrowing is a different matter.

You'll recall that we've introduced two important financial planning concepts already: *opportunity costs* and *compound interest*. When you borrow money to spend (rather than to invest), both of these fundamental financial concepts kick in. For example, let's say you borrowed money to go on vacation. And say it took two years to repay the loan, with a total cost of principal and interest of $5,000. Technically, it actually cost you more. That's because you haven't factored in your opportunity costs yet. Ask yourself: What could I have done with $5,000 instead? The opportunity cost, in this case, could have been the chance to invest that amount and earn *positive interest*, rather than to borrow and get hit with *negative interest*.

But remember, you're also dealing with the laws of compound interest. In the previous chapter, we discussed how small amounts of money, saved judiciously over time, could grow into big sums simply by letting the time value of money work for you. However, when you borrow money, compound interest works against you in a couple of ways.

First, by borrowing instead of saving, you not only lose your opportunity cost (for instance, an investment in a stock fund), you lose the potential compound earnings of that lost opportunity. Moreover, you have to account for the fact that your debt is compounding in a negative fashion. And the longer it takes you to pay back the loan, the more compound interest works against you. If you were to run up credit card balances of, say, $5,000 charging the average rate of 16 percent, and you made only minimum monthly payments on that card, it could take you around a quarter century to pay back the loan in full. That's a lot of time for compound interest to be working against you.

QUESTION NO. 2: HOW HIGH IS THE INTEREST RATE?

Borrowing is akin to investing—but in reverse. The higher the rate of interest charged on your loan, the harder it is to justify borrowing in the first place. See Figure 2-5 for sample rates of return.

If you're borrowing to invest in a home, for instance, you should ask yourself: Will this loan help my financial plan grow even faster than the debt itself is charging? In a low mortgage interest rate environment, the answer is often yes, since home values have risen around 6 percent annually since 1975 (in a number of major metropolitan areas, home prices have climbed significantly faster). The answer gets tougher when interest rates are high, as they were in the early 1980s.

Figure 2-5.   Rates of Positive and Negative Returns*

Small-Capitalization Stocks	+12.6%
Large-Capitalization Stocks	+10.4%
Long-Term Corporate Bonds	+5.9%
Long-Term Government Bonds	+5.5%
Intermediate-Term Gov't Bonds	+5.3%
30-Day Treasury Bills	+3.7%
Average 30-year Fixed-Rate Mortgage	−5.7%
Stafford Student Loans	−6.8%
Average 4-year Car Loan	−7.0%
Home-Equity Line of Credit	−7.6%
Home-Equity Loan	−7.8%
Average Credit Card Interest Rate	−16.0%

*Data as of July 2006.

Sources: Ibbotson Associates, Bankrate.com, Cardweb.com

And the answer is further complicated by where you live. The housing market, as we will discuss later, is extremely localized—meaning that expectations for home-price appreciation will vary depending on the city. After all, properties in land-strapped areas like Manhattan are more likely to appreciate over the long term than in spacious regions like Boise, Idaho.

As a general rule of thumb, you should be looking for loans that charge a rate of interest roughly in line with what long-term corporate bonds are yielding. The reason we compare loan rates and bond yields is that bonds are actually a form of credit that investors extend to corporations (we will discuss bonds in depth in a later chapter). In other words, they are comparable financial agreements. The only difference is, when you buy a corporate bond, you're the lender. And when you're taking out a private-sector loan, you're the borrower.

QUESTION NO. 3: IS IT GOOD DEBT OR BAD DEBT?

In addition to favorable and unfavorable interest rates, there are good and bad forms of debt. *Good debt* has certain attributes. For starters, good forms of debt are typically used to invest in some worthwhile asset. Sometimes, that asset represents an actual financial investment, such as a home or some other form of real estate. In other cases, you're purchasing an asset that doesn't really gain in value over time, but still provides a necessary service, such as a car.

In still other cases, that asset is much harder to quantify but is still considered worthwhile. A perfect example of this would be a student loan. There are student loans of various types, ranging from federal Stafford student loans, government-sponsored Perkins low-interest student loans, and so-called PLUS loans that parents can take out on behalf of their children. When you take out a loan for school, it's difficult to gauge with any statistical certainty whether that loan provided much leverage to the student's future earnings. After all, who knows how much difference a particular college degree made for a specific student? But in general, society does place value on college education—whether it translates into higher earnings or not—so this is a form of debt that most households are more than willing to take on.

Another form of debt that is generally considered benign would be home-equity loans whose proceeds are used for home improvements. Typically, a home-equity loan for a borrower in good standing would be only slightly higher than what long-term mortgages are charging (though it depends on how big a loan you take out, how much equity you have in the home, and your credit profile). Moreover, the fact that these loans can generally be used to improve the value of your biggest asset—your home—makes them worthwhile in many instances.

All of the forms of debt we've discussed here—with the possible exception of car loans—have another attribute in common: the interest rates they charge tend to be favorable relative to other forms of borrowing (again, for borrowers in good standing). These rates tend to be roughly in line with bank prime lending rates, which make them relatively competitive.

Moreover, all of the above forms of debt, again with the exception of car loans, have yet another thing in common. They offer some borrowers a tax break. And this is a major consideration when prioritizing debt.

For example, interest on home mortgages on first or second homes is tax deductible, provided the total value of your mortgages does not exceed $1 million. Interest payments on home-equity loans are also deductible, though there may be restrictions if your loan value exceeds $100,000. And student loan interest is at least partially deductible for single taxpayers earning $65,000 or less or married taxpayers earning under $135,000 (that was in tax year 2006).

Bad debt, on the other hand, such as revolving credit card borrowing, offers no such tax breaks. Moreover, the credit card companies often charge among the highest interest rates in the marketplace. Indeed, in the summer of 2006, many credit cards were charging twice the prime lending rate.

QUESTION NO. 4: CAN YOU AFFORD THE DEBT PAYMENTS?

Corporations rely on several different financial statements to gauge their health. One is their *balance sheet*, which measures all their assets and all their liabilities. But there's also something called the *statement of cash flow*. This measures how much money flows in and out of the corporation at any given period of time. This can be a useful tool, since even companies whose assets far exceed liabilities can run into a financial crisis if more money is being paid by the firm every month than is coming in via revenues.

When households borrow money, they often consider only how that additional debt will impact their personal balance sheets. But they also need to consider how debt affects their cash flows.

The fact is, as Americans have fallen deeper into debt, the share of their disposable income required to make routine monthly debt payments has grown. In the early 1980s, for example, only around 10.5 cents of every $1 that Americans enjoyed in disposable income (simply defined as after-tax money) went to paying off debt, according to the Federal Reserve. By 2006, that figure grew to 14 cents of every $1. See Figure 2-6.

At first blush, a jump of around 4 percentage points doesn't sound alarming. But you have to keep in mind that a good percentage of household disposable income is already spoken for. For example, studies have shown that Americans spend between 30 and 40 percent of their disposable income on housing. Another 10 percent goes to the cost of food. And let's assume that another 10 percent goes to utilities and entertainment. If 14 percent of the remainder goes to covering your monthly debt payments, that leaves you with just 26 percent to spend.

But wait: In the previous chapter, we discussed how families really need to shoot for a savings rate of 20 percent of their income. If that's the case, you would only be left with 6 percent of your disposable income once you settle your debts. Assuming you owe more than the average household, your debt payments may eat up an even bigger percentage of your income. And that might leave you with nothing left at the end of the month. So before you take on any more debt, you have to sit down and calculate what that debt will do to your cash flow situation.

Figure 2-6.   Debt Payment as a Percentage of Disposable Income

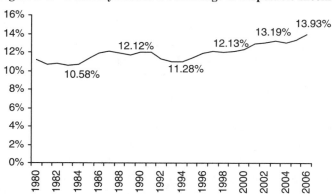

Source: Federal Reserve

What's Your Credit Score?

Whether it makes sense to borrow or not may well depend on the interest rate you can obtain on a loan. And how much interest you're likely to be charged is often dependent on your credit score. What's a credit score?

A credit *score* is not to be confused with your credit *report*. A credit report is a dossier maintained by the three major credit bureaus—Equifax, TransUnion, and Experian—that documents all your past borrowing and repayment activities. When new loans or lines of credit are obtained, for example, those three credit bureaus will record this fact in your files. When you are late with a monthly car loan payment, that information will be logged as well into your permanent record.

A *credit score,* on the other hand, is a numeric value assigned to each borrower that is based on information found in those credit reports. Credit scores are assigned to help lenders assess what type of risk you pose. Think of it as your own personal bond rating. Just as bond-rating agencies slap grades on corporate debt so fixed-income investors can assess the credit-worthiness of various securities, the credit-scoring system slaps a score on individuals to help banks and other lenders assess your ability and propensity to repay your debts.

While there are number of different proprietary credit-scoring systems used in the lending markets, typically, when people talk about credit scoring, they are referring to a system run by a California company called Fair Isaac. Fair Isaac's so-called FICO scores, which are three-digit numbers that range from 300 to 850, are used by roughly three-quarters of all leading U.S. banks and around 90 percent of credit card issuers. Every time you sign up for a credit card, car loan, or a home mortgage, the prospective lender will likely punch up your credit score. And based largely on that three-digit figure, the lender will determine whether it is willing to extend you credit—and at what interest rate it is willing to lend you the money.

The higher your score, the better off you are. For instance, within the range of 300 to 850, scores of 700 or higher are generally considered to be good. Scores above 750 would classify you as an outstanding credit risk. The good news is that around two in five consumers score 750 or higher, according to Fair Isaac (see Figure 2-7). In fact, a majority of Americans score 700 or higher, which may seem somewhat surprising, given the debt levels of the typical American consumer. But FICO scores aren't just about how much you owe. They also consider how good a job you've done repaying your existing debts (we'll get into the specific components of your FICO score in a moment).

If scores above 700 classify you as being highly credit worthy, scores below 600 would classify you as a big risk. Fortunately, only around 15 percent of the population scores below 600. And only 7 percent score below 550, which

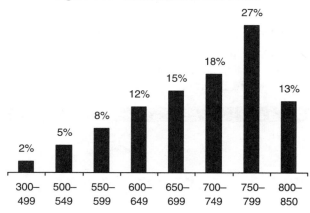

Figure 2-7. Distribution of Fico Scores

Source: Fair Isaac

often puts a borrower on the bubble when it comes to being able to obtain a mainstream loan.

Which FICO Score...

Since FICO scores are based on information found in your credit reports, and since there are three different credit bureaus that put together these files, you actually have three separate FICO scores.

For example, the FICO score generated off your Equifax credit file is known as your *Beacon score*. The score based on your Experian file is called the *Experian/Fair Isaac Risk Model*. And your TransUnion FICO is called your *EMPIRICA score*. The problem is that you never know which FICO your lender is using to judge your credit-worthiness. So you should make sure you know all three scores.

What makes the FICO scoring system frustrating to many consumers is that often, these three scores will differ—and by a noticeable margin. Indeed, a study of credit scores by the Consumer Federation of America revealed that one out of every three borrower's scores varied by as much as 50 points. Why the disparity? Chances are that the three credit bureaus have slightly different information in their files. Some of it could be caused by delays in logging your recent activity. But some of it is also due to errors. Studies have shown that the vast majority of credit reports contain some inaccuracies and nearly one-third show serious mistakes.

So it's important for consumers to periodically check all three of their credit reports, along with all three FICO scores. By law, every consumer is eligible to receive one free credit report from each of the three major credit bureaus every year. Moreover, you can purchase your specific FICO scores for a small fee from Fair Isaac (www.myfico.com), Experian (www.experian.com), TransUnion (www.transunion.com), and Equifax (www.equifax.com).

Why is Your Credit Score Important?

What you score will go a long way toward determining how much interest you will be charged on your loans. In fact, it's often the sole determinant in being able to obtain credit and in obtaining credit on favorable terms.

For example, in July 2006, a person who scored 760 or higher could have obtained a 30-year fixed-rate mortgage charging 6.50 percent. By comparison, if that same person scored just 100 points less—660—chances are his lender would have charged him 7.12 percent interest on the exact same loan. If your FICO was even lower—say, 620—your best rate would have been 8.09 percent.

Is that a big difference? Absolutely. For instance, assuming you took out a $216,000 loan, that 30-year fixed-rate mortgage at 6.5 percent would require monthly payments of $1,366. At 7.12 percent, you'd be looking at mortgage payments of $1,454. And at 8.09 percent, your monthly bill would jump to $1,599. That means the difference between scoring 760 and 620 would cost you $233 in additional mortgage expenses every month. On a 30-year mortgage, that works out to nearly $84,000 in additional borrowing costs over the life of the loan. See Figure 2-8.

Figure 2-8.   How Fico Scores Affect Your Mortgage*

Credit Score	Interest Rate	Mortgage Payment
760–850	6.50%	$1,366
700–759	6.72%	$1,397
680–699	6.90%	$1,423
660–679	7.12%	$1,454
640–659	7.55%	$1,517
620–639	8.09%	$1,599

*Assumes a 30-year fixed-rate mortgage for $216,000 (July 2006).

Source: Fair Isaac

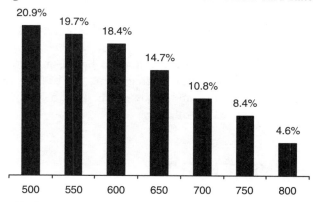

Figure 2-9.   How Fico Score Affects Your Credit Card Rates

Source: Providian, Cardata

But remember, it's not just $84,000. It's what that $84,000 could have earned in opportunity costs had you been allowed to invest the money and earn positive interest along the way. So improving your score can make a huge difference in your future borrowing costs and your financial plan. Indeed, improving your FICO is often a more effective tool for improving your finances than becoming a better investor.

FICO scores don't just affect home mortgages. Everything from car loans to credit card rates will also be affected by your score. For example, an average score of 650 might have gotten you a credit card interest rate of around 15 percent in 2006. But if you scored over 700, that could have dropped your card rate to around 11 percent. See Figure 2-9.

What's more, FICO scores don't just affect borrowing rates anymore. These days, prospective employers may use FICO scores in the hiring process on the theory that a credit-worthy job applicant would make a responsible worker. Insurance companies will often use FICO scores to help set your auto and home-owners' insurance premiums. This is based on studies that show that lower-scoring consumers tend to file more claims. And some phone companies and utilities may require large deposits if your score is too low.

How is Your Credit Score Calculated?

Contrary to popular belief, FICO scores have nothing to do with your assets, income, or net worth. Instead, the system focuses entirely on the liability side of your ledger—in other words, your debt. This means that two consumers can have the identical FICO score based on identical debt levels even though one is an executive earning $300,000 annually and the other is a laborer making $30,000 a year.

Although the actual FICO scores are generated based on a complicated algorithm, you can attribute the makeup of your score to five basic components. They include your payment history, the amount owed, the length of your credit history, new credit sought, and your credit mix.

#1: YOUR PAYMENT HISTORY

Do you pay your bills on time? Have you been paying all your bills on time throughout the course of your borrowing history? Your track record of paying debts on schedule makes up the largest part of your FICO score: 35 percent. See Figure 2-10.

One reason why the majority of Americans score so well on their FICOs, despite their debt, is that they do a decent job making at least their monthly minimum payments. According to Fair Isaac, less than half of all consumers have ever been 30 days or more late on their payments. And less than 30 percent have ever been 60 days or more overdue. (Be warned however: In recent years, credit card companies have shortened the duration of their grace periods—the time between the end of a billing cycle and the date that the payment is due. The average grace period is currently around 20 days, down from 30 days in 1990. So it is technically easier to be "late" with your payment than it used to be.)

In addition to late payments, this component of your FICO score will consider how many accounts are past due, how much of your debt is past due, how long it's been since you were last tardy on an obligation, and any "adverse public records" on your files, such as bankruptcies, liens, and garnishments of your

Figure 2-10. What Goes Into Your Fico Score

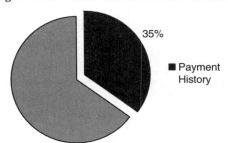

wages. Fortunately, only one in five consumers has ever had a loan or a revolving credit account closed by a lender due to missed payments.

#2: YOUR TOTAL DEBT LEVEL

The second biggest component of your score, accounting for 30 percent of your FICO, is the total amount of debt you have outstanding. This includes money owed on credit cards, car loans, student loans, and other obligations. See Figure 2-11.

FICO will consider where your debt resides. For example, if you owe $50,000 in total, and all of it is held in the form of high-interest credit card accounts, you may be viewed as a poorer risk than someone with $50,000 in debt spread out among student loans and secured car loans.

The good news: Most consumers do a fairly good job keeping their balances in check. While the average household carries a credit card balance of around $7,000, a small percent of borrowers with huge balances skew that figure. Indeed, around two in five card holders sport balances of less than $1,000, according to Fair Isaac. And around half carry balances of less than $5,000.

Ironically, having a tiny amount of debt outstanding is often viewed as beneficial to having no debt at all. The reasoning is that some debt provides lenders with a track record of your payment behavior. If you've never carried any balances in your credit history, for example, lenders wouldn't know how you're likely to behave once you do amass card and loan balances.

Now, a common practice among disciplined savers is to cancel credit cards that they've just paid off or that they haven't used for a while. This can actually be a mistake. That's because in addition to your total debt, FICO will consider the ratio of your debt to your total credit limit. Every time you cancel an existing account, you reduce the total amount of credit available to you. For example, say you owe $5,000 in on one credit card, but enjoy a total credit limit among all your

Figure 2-11. What Goes Into Your Fico Score

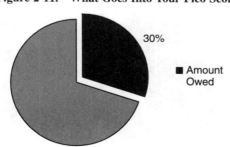

cards of $60,000. If you were to cancel a different card that had a zero balance, you would still owe $5,000 on that other account. But at the same time, your total credit limit might shrink to $50,000.

According to FICO, the typical borrower has access to $19,000 on his or her credit cards, and uses less than 30 percent of that credit limit. However, one in seven borrowers is using up to 80 percent of his or her credit limit.

#3: THE LENGTH OF YOUR CREDIT HISTORY

Because lenders are keenly interested in your track record in meeting your obligations, another big component of your FICO score is the length of your credit history. This accounts for 15 percent of your score. See Figure 2-12.

The longer you've managed debt—and managed it well—the less risk you're likely to pose to a potential lender. At least that's what lenders think. For example, a bank might be faced with two customers with pristine credit histories, including tiny balances and no late payments. But if one of those customers has maintained that good track record for 25 years while the other has done it for only 5 years, then the customer with the longer track record is likely to merit a higher score.

In determining your credit history, FICO will consider both the age of your oldest account as well as the average age of your entire credit and loan portfolio. According to Fair Isaac, the average consumer's oldest account is 14 years old, and a quarter of all borrowers have credit histories that extend back more than 20 years.

Because the length of your credit history is so important, this is another reason not to close out old credit card accounts, even if you don't use them. This is because canceling out old accounts could inadvertently lower your score by shortening your credit history. For instance, let's say you held three credit cards. The oldest account was opened 15 years ago, while the other two accounts were started 5 years ago. In this case, your average credit history would be 8.33 years.

Figure 2-12.   What Goes Into Your Fico Score

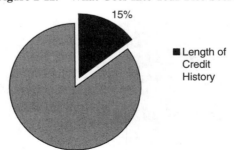

15%

■ Length of
Credit
History

Figure 2-13. What Goes Into Your Fico Score

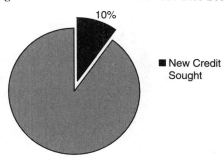

10%

■ New Credit
Sought

If you were to cancel your oldest account, you would not only lose the credit limit on that card, you would reduce the average age of your portfolio considerably. In this case, it would drop from more than eight years to only five.

#4: NEW DEBT SOUGHT

Are you taking out new loans? Are you applying for more credit? Lenders typically don't want to see this, since consumers who are seeking out new loans are often in financial trouble. This is why 10 percent of your FICO score is based on how many new accounts you've opened recently (or sought to open). This portion of your FICO score will also consider how long it's been since you last opened a new account. See Figure 2-13.

Every time you apply for credit—whether it's for a credit card or a home mortgage—lenders will put in a request for your credit score. And whenever this occurs, it will be recorded in your credit report as an "inquiry." The more inquiries you have, the worse off you're likely to be.

However, sometimes, consumers apply for new loans not because they are in dire financial need, but because they are simply shopping for lower interest rates on credit cards, for example. Or, they may be in the market to purchase a new home, and they may be mortgage shopping. If you are simply shopping for rates—instead of frantically seeking debt—make sure you do so within a fairly narrow window of time. For example, if you seek requests for mortgage rates from four different lenders in less than a two-week period of time, the credit scoring system will likely view this as a single inquiry.

#5: YOUR CREDIT MIX

The final 10 percent of your score is based on the mix of credit and loans you have outstanding. As we discussed earlier, there is a hierarchy of good and bad debt.

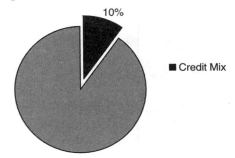
Figure 2-14.   What Goes Into Your Fico Score

10%

■ Credit Mix

Good debt is secured by an asset and serves an investment function. Bad debt, on the other hand, is unsecured and is used primarily for spending. Credit cards are a classic example of bad debt. So having a disproportionate number of your accounts as credit cards—as opposed to more benign forms of debt like mortgages and student loans—could be detrimental to your score. See Figure 2-14.

According to Fair Isaac, the average consumer has a total of 13 accounts on his or her files (this includes credit cards, department store cards, gas station charge accounts, auto loans, student loans, and mortgages). And on average, nine of these accounts are credit cards. If you have 13 accounts and all 13 are credit cards, chances are you'll probably score lower in this portion of your FICO.

A DIFFERENT CREDIT SCORE

In 2006, the three major credit bureaus—Experian, TransUnion, and Equifax—announced the launch of a competing credit-scoring system to FICO. This system, called the *Vantage Score*, also ranks consumers based on a three-digit figure, but the scores run from 501 to 990. In an attempt to simplify matters, the Vantage Score system links its numeric scores to traditional letter grades such as those found in a report card. So for instance, anyone who scores 901 to 990 under this system would merit an "A" on their credit report card. Those who score 801 to 900 would get a "B." Scores between 701 and 800 are graded "C." A Vantage Score of 601 to 700 is the equivalent of a "D." And those consumers who score 510 to 600 in this new system would get an "F."

Quiz for Chapter 2

1. As a rule, you should never borrow money for any reason. Doing so will only hurt your financial plan.
    a. True
    b. False

2. All debt is a form of "negative investing"?
    a. True
    b. False

3. What percent of U.S. households maintain credit card balances?
    a. 90 %
    b. 60 %
    c. 20%

4. When it comes to your credit card debt, the laws of compound interest...
    a. Will help you, since your repayments will earn interest, making it easier for you to wipe out the debt.
    b. Will hurt you, since your debt will be growing at a faster-than-expected rate.
    c. The laws of compound interest do not apply to credit cards.

5. Which of the following would be considered a form of "good debt"?
    a. A low balance (less than $100) on a credit card.
    b. A low-interest $20,000 student loan that is tax deductible
    c. A $200,000 home mortgage
    d. All of the above

6. Why are home mortgages and student loans often considered good debt?
    a. As a borrower, you will not be seriously penalized for late payments.
    b. As a borrower, you are given long terms to pay off the debt.
    c. As a borrower, you may be eligible for tax breaks.

7. Credit score is another term for the credit reports issued by the three major credit bureaus (Equifax, Experian, and TransUnion).
    a. True
    b. False

8. Why is knowing your credit score so important?
    a. It helps determine whether you will be approved for a loan
    b. It helps determine what interest rate you will be charged on a loan

    c. In some cases, it will affect your ability to gain employment

    d. All of the above

9. Which of the following will not affect your credit score?
    a. Your debt to income ratio
    b. Your past track record of paying your monthly bills on time
    c. How many credit cards you have
    d. Debts owed to the government

10. As a general rule, you should always cancel credit card accounts that you don't need.
    a. True
    b. False

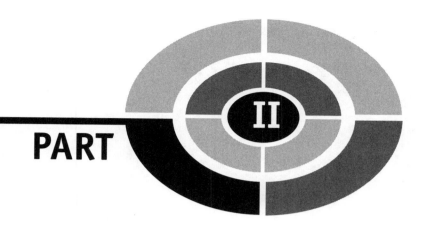

Your Investments

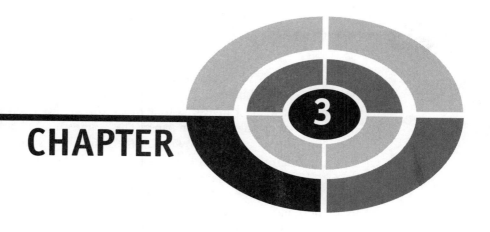

CHAPTER 3

Corporate Stocks

What Is a Stock?

"Taking stock, paying dividends, blue-chip ideas." The language of stocks has permeated our everyday vernacular. But what exactly is a stock? What does it mean to be a stockholder? And why do stocks play such a critical role in our long-term financial plans?

Stocks are issued by corporations to denote shares of ownership. So whenever you invest in the stock of a publicly traded company, you are literally buying part of that business. Stockholders are *business owners*—it's as simple as that.

How much of that business you own will depend on how many shares of that company you purchase and on the total number of shares of stock that exist in that company. Every company carves out units of ownership in a slightly different fashion. Chances are that if you hold shares of a large "blue-chip company," you're likely to own only a tiny fraction of even a single percent of that firm, as giant multinationals are often valued in the tens of billions of dollars. On the other hand, if you own shares of a relatively new start-up, your stake in that firm could be surprisingly substantial. It all depends.

Ironically, though investing in stocks translates into the literal ownership of a business, most stockholders don't think of themselves as partners in the firm. In fact, many of today's investors treat stock ownership as an abstract financial arrangement conducted entirely on paper. This is unfortunate because as a result of this attitude, many of us have grown extremely impatient with our stock holdings, which can be detrimental to a long-term financial plan. Jack Bogle, founder of the mutual fund giant Vanguard Group and a champion of disciplined, gimmick-free investing, likes to point out that the average stock investor today hangs on to his or her shares for less than one year, on average. That's hardly the way a long-term business owner should behave. After all, if Bill Gates gave up on Microsoft in its infancy, when it wasn't the cash cow that it grew into in the 1990s, then he probably wouldn't be where he is today, that is, the world's richest man. Indeed, a generation ago investors typically held stocks for five years or longer, and sometimes even for decades.

Compounding this sense of distance between investors and the companies they own is the fact that most have never had direct interactions with the companies in which they invest. This too is a shame. To be sure, many investors have used the products and services produced by the companies they invest in. This is, after all, the core of the investing philosophy made famous by former Fidelity Magellan fund manager Peter Lynch: "Invest in what you know." But for most of us, what we know about our companies is limited. If you own shares of McDonald's, chances are, you've eaten a Big Mac at some point in your life. Or if you own shares of Coca-Cola, you've probably taken a swig of soda. Yet most of us have never visited the factory floors of the companies we invest in. Most of us have never conversed with the managers who lead the companies we own. And most stockholders have never attended an annual shareholders' meeting—even though every publicly traded company is legally obligated to hold such a gathering.

As a result of all these factors, most stockholders act as if they are renters, not owners. In fact, it is becoming increasingly common for investors to jump into and out of stocks in a short window of time. In the late 1990s, this mentality became so prevalent that it garnered its own name: *day trading.* But day trading—or *swing trading,* which is a milder, though still aggressive (and highly dangerous) form of jumping into and out of stocks every few days or weeks—proved to be a dangerous investing tactic that destroyed a lot of those traders' ability to retire young and retire well. It's a lesson we should all take to heart.

Day trading or swing trading or even *market timing*—an umbrella term referring to tactics that try to game the stock market, based on the false assumption that you might know something that other investors don't—are antithetical to establishing a sound long-term financial plan. By definition, *a financial plan is a long-term strategy* that attempts to achieve a long-term goal. Financial plans are marathons—not sprints.

Always keep in mind that the whole point of investing in stocks is to buy a small stake in a company in order to take part in the growth of that firm over time. This is why investors spend so much time fretting about stock selection. The point is to carefully investigate hundreds of different companies and buy shares of those select few that you think will be able to grow profits significantly and consistently over a long period of time. Your hope is that this growth in corporate earnings will eventually be reflected in the company's stock price. That way, as the stock price increases, so will the value of your portfolio.

Although a company's stock price doesn't have to go up just because its earnings are growing, over the long run, this is typically what happens. Indeed, the long-term earnings growth rate for large, blue-chip U.S. companies is around 7 percent to 10 percent. And historically that's about what stocks have delivered in investment gains.

Why We Buy Stocks

There is a simple reason why stocks get the lion's share of our attention. Over the long run (I'm talking 10 or 20 years or even longer) stocks are the only mainstream investment proven to be able to consistently outrun the deleterious effects of inflation. And inflation—the slow and steady loss of your money's purchasing power over time—is enemy number one of your financial plan. Figure 3-1 shows the effects of inflation on today's dollar over time.

Consider that inflation has run at an average annual rate of 3 percent going back to 1926 (according to Ibbotson Associates, a financial research firm). In some decades, inflation has run much higher. This is a huge headwind to any financial plan. It means that if your money were to earn, say, 7 percent a year on average, which is decent by historical standards, you'd really only be advancing

Figure 3-1. Effects of Inflation on the Real Purchasing Power of Your Financial Assets (based on a 3 percent annual rate of inflation)

Today's Dollars	10 years	20 years	30 years
$50,000	$36,900	$27,200	$20,000
$100,000	$73,700	$54,400	$40,100
$200,000	$147,500	$108,800	$80,200
$300,000	$221,200	$163,100	$120,300
$400,000	$295,000	$217,500	$160,400
$500,000	$368,700	$271,900	$200,500

Figure 3-2.   Historical Rates of Return for Various Assets Between 1926 and 2005.

Investment	Average Annual Return
Small-Company Stocks	12.6%
Large-Company Stocks	10.4%
Long-Term Corporate Bonds	5.9%
Long-Term Government Bonds	5.5%
Intermediate-Term Government Bonds	5.3%
U.S. Treasury Bills (Cash)	3.7%

Source: Ibbotson Associates

4 percent in real terms, after you account for the fact that inflation is diminishing the true value of your savings and investments every year.

Yet most asset classes can't come close to generating 4 percent in real terms over long stretches of time—except for stocks. See Figure 3-2.

Take cash. Over the past 80 years, an investment in cash has earned roughly 3.7 percent a year on average, according to Ibbotson. That's based on the performance of Treasury bills dating back to 1926 (we'll talk about the different forms of cash in a later chapter). In other words, if you were to put all your money in cash for the next several decades, chances are your nest egg would only be worth slightly more than it is today. True, cash provides an ultra safe parking place for your money. But it's not a growth vehicle. And growth is exactly what your long-term financial plan craves, since you want your money to work for you (and not the other way around).

Let's assume, for instance, that you had $100,000 saved toward your retirement. And say you wanted to retire in 20 years. At a real rate of return of just 0.7 percent (which is the 3.7 percent rate of return of cash minus the 3.0 percent rate of growth for inflation), your $100,000 would turn into less than $115,000 two decades from now had you invested entirely in cash. If you think $115,000 will be enough to fund a comfortable retirement, you're kidding yourself. And should you happen to retire during a period of hyperinflation—such as the 1970s, when inflation ran at an annual rate of 7.4 percent, or the 1980s, when inflation jumped 5.1 percent a year on average—the true purchasing power of your money could actually diminish, even though your assets are technically appreciating on paper. See Figure 3-3.

By comparison, stocks—or equities as they're sometimes called—have delivered average annual returns of 10.4 percent over the long run. Small-company stocks, which are shares of tiny (and often risky) up-and-coming firms, have done even better, posting annual gains of 12.6 percent. These types of returns can make a huge difference in the long-term trajectory of your money. For instance, let's

Figure 3-3. Historical Rates of Return for Various Assets Versus Inflation (in Percent)

Investment	1920s*	1930s	1940s	1950s	1960s	1970s	1980s	1990s	2000s†
Large-Corporate Stocks	19.2	−0.1	9.2	19.4	7.8	5.9	17.5	18.2	−1.1
Small-Corporate Stocks	−4.5	1.4	20.7	16.9	15.5	11.5	15.8	15.1	12.8
Long-Term Corporate Bonds	5.2	6.9	2.7	1.0	1.7	6.2	13.0	8.4	9.9
Long-Term Corporate Bonds	5.0	4.9	3.2	−0.1	1.4	5.5	12.6	8.8	9.9
Long-Term Government Bonds	4.2	4.6	1.8	1.3	3.5	7.0	11.9	7.2	6.4
U.S. Treasury Bills	3.7	0.6	0.4	1.9	3.9	6.3	8.9	4.9	2.7
Inflation	−1.1	−2.0	5.4	2.2	2.5	7.4	5.1	2.9	2.6

*1920s figures reflect 1926–1929.
†2000s figures reflect 2000–2005.

Source: Ibbotson Associates

go back to the previous example. A $100,000 investment that earns 7.4 percent a year over the next 20 years (that's the 10.4 percent rate of return for equities minus 3 percent for inflation) would turn into nearly $420,000. If you invested that sum in small-capitalization stocks, earning 9.6 percent a year (again, that's 12.6 percent minus the 3 percent rate of inflation), you'd have more than $625,000 saved up after two decades. Now we're talking about real money.

Of course, inflation isn't the only reason why a financial plan needs to have a heavy dose of equities. The fact is that low-risk and low-return investments like bonds and cash—on their own—just won't cut it when it comes to growing a nest egg.

At the start of this decade, for example, many checking accounts were paying out less than 2 percent in interest. Yet at 2 percent, guess how many years it would take to double your money? Thirty-five. Bonds have historically generated a bit more than cash. In fact, the average annual gain for long-term government bonds has been 5.5 percent, dating back to the turn of the last century. Long-term corporate bonds have generated slightly more—5.9 percent a year. Let's be generous and round that up to 6 percent. If you were to put all your money into bonds and were lucky enough to earn the average historical rate of 6 percent, it would still take you 12 years to double your portfolio.

Now, if you were to invest that money in stocks and earned the historical average rate of growth of 10.4 percent a year you'd be able to double your money in only eight years. That's the reason we invest in stocks.

STOCK ALLOCATIONS BOOST RETURNS

Academic research clearly shows that the single biggest determinant of your returns over time is your *asset allocation strategy*. This is a fancy way of describing your mix of stocks and bonds (and also cash). For instance, a person who holds 60 percent of his or her money in equities and 40 percent in bonds is said to have a 60–40 asset-allocation mix. To be sure, over short periods of time, the specific stocks and fixed-income securities you select for your portfolio will help determine how much your investments return over a brief period of time. But if you are a well-diversified investor, over the long run, how much of your total portfolio is held in stocks (not which stocks you choose) will be the biggest determinant of your overall performance.

Researchers at the Vanguard Group, the nation's leading low-cost mutual fund company, recently studied various asset allocation strategies over the past four decades and came to an obvious—but nonetheless important—conclusion. As it turns out, the greater the percentage of stocks you hold in your portfolio (versus bonds), the bigger the returns you will enjoy in your long-term financial plan.

For example, Vanguard looked at stock and bond market performance between 1960 and 2003. The firm's researchers discovered that investors who put 100 percent of their money into bonds during this stretch would have earned 7.3 percent a year. By historical standards, this is quite good, as the average bond investment has really only generated total returns of less than 6 percent since 1926. But had investors added even incremental amounts of stocks to their financial diets during this time frame, they would have boosted their annual returns significantly, bringing them that much closer to achieving their long-term financial goals.

Indeed, a 100 percent bond allocation generated 7.3 percent annually. But had you allocated a mere 20 percent of your portfolio to stocks (leaving the remaining 80 percent in bonds), you would have boosted your returns to 8.1 percent a year. While the difference between 7.3 percent a year and 8.1 percent doesn't sound that big (in fact, to many, it might seem insignificant), it's a huge difference when you plug in real numbers. For instance, let's assume that you were investing $100,000. Had you invested that amount at the start of 1960 and earned 7.3 percent a year, you'd have amassed $2.22 million by the end of 2003. But had you earned 8.1 percent on that money during this same period of time, constantly reinvesting money along the way, your nest egg would have grown to $3.08 million over those 44 years. The difference, in this case, turned out to be around $860,000 over the course of an investing lifetime. And in this case, you would not have added that much risk. Indeed, during this stretch, both portfolios—the 100 percent bond portfolio as well as the 20 percent-stock and 80 percent bond portfolio—lost money in only five calendar years between 1960 and 2003.

Now, had you gone to a "balanced" asset-allocation strategy, which is generally regarded as a 60 percent stock and 40 percent bond allocation, you would have earned considerably more. This type of portfolio has historically generated average

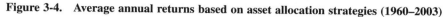

Figure 3-4.   Average annual returns based on asset allocation strategies (1960–2003)

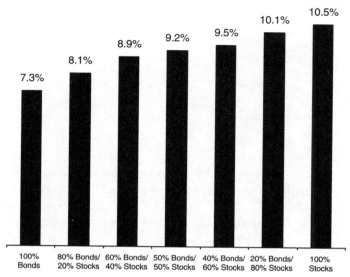

Source: Vanguard Group

annual returns of 9.5 percent, according to Vanguard. Going back to our earlier example, a $100,000 portfolio that earned 9.5 percent a year between 1960 and 2003 would have grown to $5.422 million by the end of this time period. In other words, by taking a generally balanced approach between stocks and bonds, you would have earned more than double the money you would have generated from an all-bond mix during this 44-year stretch. Finally, the most aggressive portfolio during this time period—an all-stock mix—would have gained 10.5 percent a year, according to Vanguard. By taking your portfolio to such extremes, you would clearly be adding a huge amount of risk to your financial plan. Indeed, an all-stock portfolio would have severely boosted your odds of losing money in any single calendar year. However, the average return you would have earned by going 100 percent stocks would have been far greater than you could ever earn in bonds. See Figure 3-4.

STOCKS AND THE POWER OF COMPOUND INTEREST

Because stocks have delivered around twice the annual gains of bonds and about three times the gains of cash accounts over the long term, the argument for investing in stocks is already clear. But over the long term stocks have an even bigger edge.

Figure 3-5.   Rates of Return Needed to Reach Goals

Number of Years	2X*	3X*	5X*	10X*
3 Years	26.0%	44.2%	80.0%	115.4%
5 Years	14.9	24.6	38.0	58.5
7 Years	10.4	17.0	25.8	38.9
10 Years	7.2	11.6	17.5	25.9
25 Years	2.8	4.5	6.6	9.6

*2X, 3X etc. means earnings double, triple, etc. your original investment.

This goes back to the concept of *compound interest,* where money earning interest will eventually earn interest of its own, which will eventually earn interest of its own, and so on. Should you be able to earn 10.4 percent a year in stocks, which is around two times the 5.5 percent returns generated by long-term government bonds, over time, you will earn even *more* than twice as much in stocks than in bonds.

Consider the following: At 10.4 percent a year, a $100,000 investment in stocks will grow to nearly $270,000 over a decade's time. That means your profit would be $170,000 (that's $270,000 minus your original principal investment of $100,000). That same $100,000, earning 5.5 percent a year in bonds, would become $170,000. In this case, your real gain would be $70,000 ($170,000 minus the original $100,000). This means that over 10 years, your gains in stocks would be 2.4 times as big as your profits in bonds—not just twice as big.

Over 40 years, the spread widens substantially. Let's go back to our example. A $100,000 investment in equities—over four decades based on the average annual gains for stocks since 1926—would grow to $5.23 million, for a profit of $5.13 million. But at just 5.5 percent a year, your bond investment would grow to $850,000, for a profit of $750,000. This means that over four decades, your stock money is likely to grow nearly *seven* times your bond investments.

Figure 3-5 shows the average annual returns you would need to grow your money by various factors. For example, if you had 25 years to reach your goals, you could turn $1 into $3 by earning 4.5 percent a year on your money.

How We Own Stocks

Unlike certain financial products, such as bank certificates of deposit, stocks can't be purchased through just any financial services firm. Stocks are listed by publicly traded companies on stock exchanges. In the United States, the most prominent exchanges are the New York Stock Exchange, the American Stock Exchange, and the Nasdaq.

While the stock market has certainly become democratized in recent decades—thanks in large part to mutual funds and 401(k) retirement accounts, which utilize equity investments—small investors still cannot go to those exchanges on their own. They need the help of a third party. Often times, this means investing through a brokerage or a mutual fund company.

DIRECT STOCK OWNERSHIP

For most of the twentieth century, the way investors bought and sold stocks was through traditional full-service brokerage houses. And back then, you had to bring a decent amount of wealth to the table to enjoy the services of the industry's best brokers. But today, stocks can be purchased and held through a variety of means.

For starters, you can still buy equities by opening an account through a traditional brokerage firm like Merrill Lynch or Morgan Stanley. Like a real estate broker, a stock brokerage firm acts as a middle man between buyers and sellers. If you want to purchase shares of IBM, for example, the brokerage firm will match you up with a current IBM shareholder who wants to sell shares at a given price. Sometimes, if there isn't a willing seller of a stock, the brokerage might have to go through what's known as a *market maker.* These are institutions that facilitate free flowing trade of specific stocks. A market maker for IBM shares on a given exchange, for instance, stands ready to purchase shares of the stock when other investors don't want to buy from would-be sellers. Conversely, when no one wants to sell a specific stock, market makers, or specialists (as they're referred to on the New York Stock Exchange), stand ready to sell shares from their own inventory to satisfy would-be buyers.

Although transaction costs are often higher through a full-service brokerage than through other means, traditional brokerages provide investors with personalized advice to help them make buy, sell, and hold decisions when it comes to their equities.

Another option is to go through an online brokerage such as Charles Schwab, E*Trade, or TD Ameritrade, where you may receive some written advice concerning stock investments. But by and large, you make the decision when to buy or sell, and which stocks to buy or sell, on your own. You can place trades on your holdings either through an automated phone system or online. While the lack of highly personalized service may put you at somewhat of a disadvantage, the lower costs that online brokers charge makes it easier for smaller investors to participate in the market. Indeed, many online brokerages charge only around $10 or $15 per transaction.

Moreover, among online brokers, there is now a new breed of financial services firms that allow small investors to trade fractional shares of a single stock. For example, if you had only $5,000 to invest but wanted to create a diversified mix of, say, 100 different stocks, a regular brokerage account may be cost prohibitive. That's because some stocks trade for $400 a share. The "A" class shares of Berkshire Hathaway, the investment firm that Warren Buffett runs, sell for more than $100,000 each. But some brokerages like Share-builder (www.sharebuilder.com) will let you buy fractional shares of certain stocks, allowing small investors to instantly diversify their holdings without breaking the bank. Some of these brokerages, like FolioFn (www.foliofn.com) also make it easier for individuals to purchase fully diversified baskets of securities for small amounts of money.

Of course, there is one way stock investors can buy shares of a company without going through a third-party brokerage firm. It's called a *dividend reinvestment plan*, or DRIP for short. DRIP programs are run by some, though not all, publicly traded corporations in an effort to reward loyal shareholders with an easy way to keep investing in the firm. DRIP programs are carrots of sorts to convince investors to bet on the firm. To participate in a DRIP, all you need is to own one share of that company's stock. Once you do, the company will allow you to reinvest the dividend income you receive from that firm back into more shares of the company stock on a routine and automated basis. Moreover, many DRIP programs will allow existing shareholders to purchase additional shares of the company stock without paying any of the transaction fees that are typically associated with brokerage transactions.

INDIRECT STOCK OWNERSHIP

A number of *indirect* stock ownership options are available in addition to these *direct* stock investments. For instance, you can purchase a diversified basket of stocks through a stock mutual fund (we will discuss mutual funds at length later in the book). A stock fund literally pools money from thousands of small investors and then purchases and manages those equities on their behalf as if the fund was a single, large investor. The downside to this strategy is that you never have full control over which stocks the fund's manager will purchase and which he or she will sell. Yet there are general advantages to indirect stock ownership through a fund.

For instance, a fund will allow small investors to gain access to the market at a low price—often, for as little as an up-front investment of $2,000 or less. A fund will provide those same investors with instant diversification. Academic studies have shown that an investor probably needs to hold 50 to 100 stocks to be properly diversified. Well, the average stock mutual fund holds around 175 different stocks, according to the fund tracking firm Morningstar.

In addition to mutual funds, there are other forms of indirect stock ownership, which we will discuss in the coming chapters. They include exchange-traded funds, or ETFs. These are preconstructed portfolios of stocks that are like mutual funds, in that you can own a cross section of different stocks in one fell swoop for little money up front. However, unlike a fund, which can only be bought or sold once a day, ETFs, can be bought or sold throughout the day like an individual stock. Just as with mutual funds, exchange-traded funds might give you exposure to hundreds of different shares, but they do not give investors any say in which stocks are held.

Stocks can also be held in mutual funds and mutual fund-like accounts within employer-sponsored retirement accounts, such as 401(k)s, 403(b)s, and 457s. In fact, a majority of American households that own stocks today (half of all American households) own those equities through mutual funds within their 401(k) accounts and other retirement accounts. Indeed, a common way that individuals own mutual funds is through an individual retirement account set up through a brokerage like Schwab or a fund company like Fidelity or Vanguard.

How Stocks Pay

You'll often hear investors discuss how much they've made in the stock market. In the late 1990s, for instance, investors used to crow about how they doubled their money in a short period of time. But how do you literally make money in equities?

Stocks reward investors in one of two ways. For starters, shares of fast-growing companies appreciate in price over time. And when stock prices climb, each share of the stock you own increases. For instance, let's say you purchased shares of Company X at $10 a share and put them away in a drawer. Two years later, you open up that drawer and discover that the stock is now trading at $12.50 a share. That is a gain of 25 percent over that two-year stretch. Now, say you owned 100 shares of the stock. That means your initial investment of $1,000 (that's 100 shares times $10 a share) has grown to $1,250 (100 times $12.50), for a profit of $250. Based on your original cash investment of $1,000, that $250 profit represents a 25 percent gain. This is called capital appreciation.

In addition, some, though not all, stocks offer investors a carrot of sorts for buying their shares. They do this by throwing off *dividend income* to shareholders. Dividends are paid in part to return a portion of the company's profits back to shareholders. When publicly traded companies earn profits, they have several choices as to what to do with the money. They can (a) invest the proceeds back into the firm (for instance, they can buy a new factory or expand a particular division); (b) they can buy back their own stock (the idea is that companies that repurchase stock that is outstanding shrink the pool of ownership to a smaller group of people, so that each person left owning shares of the stock owns a slightly greater percentage of the firm); or (c) they can kick back the money in cash payments to shareholders.

Combined, the capital appreciation of a stock in a certain window of time plus the dividend payment issued by the company (if there is a dividend) equals a stock's *total return*. So for instance, say you own a stock that has gone up in price by 9 percent in a given year. And assume for a moment that the stock paid out 2 percent in dividends that year. This means that your total return on that investment for that 12-month period of time was 11 percent.

Historically, stocks used to derive as much as 40 percent of their total returns in the form of dividend income. This is a big reason why older investors continue to favor stocks that pay fat yields. But in the 1990s, the trend reversed. During the high-tech boom of that decade, many companies purposefully did not pay dividends to investors on the theory that the money would be better served if it were reinvested back into those firms to help them grow quickly so that their stock price would inflate rapidly. Sure enough, as technology stocks started to boom, many investors began to ignore dividend income and dividend payouts started to fall out of favor.

By 2006, the stock market, as measured by Standard & Poor's 500 Index of blue-chip stocks, was paying a yield of only around 2 percent. In other words, while stocks were returning around 8 to 10 percent a year, dividend yields were adding another 2 percent or so on average to the mix—translating into total returns of 10 to 12 percent. This means that instead of accounting for the historical two-fifths of stocks' total returns, dividends recently contributed only around one-fifth.

But the trend again is reversing because more and more companies—including technology companies—are starting to either issue dividends or increase the dividends that they already pay out. This is probably a result of recent changes in the federal law that have driven down the maximum tax rate on qualified dividend income from as high as 38.6 percent to just 15 percent.

Indeed, in 2002, only 350 of the 500 stocks that comprise the S&P 500 Index paid any dividends. But by 2006, that figure had climbed back to nearly 400 (that's still shy of the market's peak in 1980, when 469 of the 500 companies in the S&P 500 were issuing dividend payments to shareholders). Even if you think a 2 percent yield is paltry, remember the power of compound interest. Though small, dividends that are reinvested into stock will generate growth and dividends of their own, boosting your portfolios real gains.

Consider this: Between 1995 and 2004, the stocks in the S&P 500 rose 164 percent, on average, in terms of pure capital appreciation. That's a pretty good return. But if you factored in the dividend payments made by S&P 500 companies during this stretch (and remember, this was a period marked by declining dividends), the total return for the S&P 500 was 212 percent. In other words, even in a period of diminishing dividends, the small payouts still amounted to a sizeable difference in performance. So ask yourself: Am I willing to walk away from those extra gains?

Think of it this way: If you had $100,000 at the start of this 10-year window, by the end, that money would have grown into $264,000. That's if you simply focused on capital appreciation. But if you included dividends during this stretch, you would have amassed $312,000, for a $48,000 increase.

Dividends are a literal manifestation of profit sharing. Moreover, some stocks, especially shares of overlooked companies pay dividends to investors as an incentive for those investors to keep holding the stock. Think of it as a payment for waiting while the company grows its earnings and sees that profit growth reflected in its stock price. Moreover, those dividends will come in handy in years when the stock price falls. Remember, a stock that falls 1 percent in price but that pays out 2 percent in dividend income has generated a *positive* total return of 1 percent despite its drop in value.

Stock Investing Risks

Okay. Okay. We get it: stocks are great. But if equity investing is so fruitful, why not just invest every last cent you have in stocks and forget about bonds and cash and real estate and commodities? The answer is simple. Stocks are probably the best *long-term* investment vehicle around. But not all of our financial needs are long term in nature. Some of the financial goals we have are short term. For instance, what if we want to pay for a vacation next year? What if we want to save for a down payment on a house two years from now? What if we want to pay for our children's college tuition bill three years from now?

While it's true that stocks have historically beaten other asset classes over long periods of time, in the short term, stocks are much more volatile than bonds and cash. Stocks are much more likely to lose money in a short period of time than bonds—and they're much more likely to lose a greater amount of money in that short window of time. This goes back to a fundamental relationship that all savers and investors need to be aware of: The more reward an investment delivers, the more risk it puts your money at.

This means that even though stocks might be the best long-term place to put our long-term financial assets over time, equities are often the worst place to park short-term money. Because with stocks—unlike with bonds or cash—there is no guarantee that you will recoup your investment at any given point in time.

If you need to be convinced of this, just look back to the bear market years of 2000 through 2002. Between the stock market's peak March 2000 and its trough on October 2002, the S&P 500 lost around half of its value. That means if you bought $100 worth of stocks in March 2000, chances are, you were left with $50 by October 2002. Had you invested in technology stocks, you probably lost around 75 percent of your money, from peak to trough. That's about how much the Nasdaq composite index (a benchmark of stocks comprised heavily of technology-oriented shares) fell during the bear market. And had you invested in certain individual stocks, you might have lost all your money, as some companies went under in that bear market. Remember, owning stock is owning a business. And sometimes, businesses go bankrupt or fold altogether.

All stock investors need to be mindful of several different types of risks that come with owning stocks. Again, there is a fundamental relationship between risk and reward. The greater the risk, the greater your potential for reward. Think of a lottery. A lottery gives you a tiny chance of winning which means there is a tremendous risk of losing your original investment (the dollar to buy the lottery ticket). However, on the slim chance you do win, you will probably win a huge amount relative to the cost of the original lottery ticket. Similarly, the lower the risk of an investment, the smaller your potential reward. Think of a bank account. A bank savings account offers federally insured guarantees that you will get your money back even if something bad happens at the bank. But in exchange, savings accounts pay a paltry interest rate. So let's discuss the risks associated with stock investing.

RISK 1: MARKET RISK

The first, and perhaps most obvious, risk with investing in stocks is that the equity market is cyclical. There will be years when stocks are going gangbusters. Then there will be years when stocks tank. The recent bear market that began in 2000 is evidence of this fact. But that bear market—though one of the worst in historical terms—was par for the course. In fact, since 1950, there have been 11 major *corrections* (defined as a loss in stock prices of 10 percent or more) or *bear markets* (defined as a drop in the broad equity market of 20 percent or more). And on average, these short-term market sell-offs have erased around 33 percent of the value of stocks in the short run. See Figure 3-6.

Figure 3-6.   Major Corrections in the Stock Market (S&P 500 index)

Date of Market Peak	Date of Market Trough	Losses
March 24, 2000	October 9, 2002	−49%
July 17, 1998	August 31, 1998	−19%
July 16, 1990	October 11, 1990	−20%
August 25, 1987	December 24, 1987	−34%
November 28, 1980	August 12, 1982	−27%
September 21, 1976	March 6, 1978	− 20%
January 11, 1973	October 3, 1974	−48%
November 29, 1968	May 26, 1970	−36%
February 9, 1966	October 7, 1966	−22%
December 12, 1961	June 26, 1962	−28%
August 2, 1956	October 22, 1957	−22%
Average Market Decline Since World War II		**−32%**

Source: The Leuthold Group

It's important to consider not only the extent of the potential losses you can suffer in the stock market during a bear market, but also the amount of time it could potentially take to recoup those losses after the bear. Historically, it has taken stocks about two years to climb out of the hole they dig for themselves during bear markets, according to a study by The Leuthold Group, an investment advisory service. But that's just the average. In some cases, it can take much more time. For example, it took the stock market nearly four years to fully recover from the bear market of 1973–1974, which is considered the third worst market meltdown this century—just behind the Great Depression and the recent bear market that started in 2000.

Speaking of the bear market of 2000, that downturn officially ended in October 2002. But by June 2006—nearly four years after the sell-off—stocks were still a far cry from being back. The S&P 500, for example, peaked in 2000 at a level of more than 1527. By June 2006, well after a new bull market had begun, the S&P was still only at 1200.

The Nasdaq composite index offers an even clearer illustration. At its peak in March 2000, the Nasdaq traded as high as 5048. But as of the summer of 2006, the Nasdaq was still only at 2100—and that was after a tremendous recovery.

It just goes to show how frightening market risk can be. This should remind you that you should really only invest your "long-term money" in equities. Given the historical track record, only money that you won't need to tap for 5 to 10 years or longer should be invested in stocks, since it may take that much time for equities to recoup short-term losses they suffer in bear markets along the way.

Frequency of Stock Losses

Here's a quick fact to keep in mind. Going back to 1900, the stock market has tended to experience a 10 percent drop every one and a half years; a 20 percent drop every two and a half years; a 30 percent drop every four and a half years; and a 40 percent loss every nine years, according to InvesTech Research.

Ways to Minimize Market Risk

Of course, there are several ways for investors to reduce the impact of this so-called market risk. One way that is to diversify what types of assets you own. For example, you don't have to put all your money in stocks. You can keep your long-term money in stocks, while putting your intermediate-term money (funds you will need to spend in three to five years) in bonds, and parking your short-term money (funds you will need to tap in less than three years) in cash. This way, the risk of a bear market will only impact a portion of your total financial portfolio.

Moreover, investors can minimize the risk of a bear market in stocks by diversifying the stock markets they invest in. Remember, in this age of globalization, it's not just the U.S. stock market. Each developed and developing nation has its own stock market, which is accessible to small investors in the United States thanks to mutual funds and exchange-traded funds. So, if you invest only a portion of your long-term money in U.S. stocks, while putting the remainder into a diversified mix of European, Asian, and Latin American equities, you may be able to reduce the impact of a severe bear market here in the United States. Be forewarned: You cannot totally eliminate market risks by diversifying abroad, because the global markets have recently become highly correlated with one another (in other words, what happens in the United States often impacts Europe and Asia) thanks to globalization. Still, you can reduce some of your risks.

Another possible solution to market risk is time. Going back to my earlier point, stocks, while risky in the short term, are a good bet over long periods of time. And if you have enough time to wait it out, the positive returns that stocks consistently generate over time will eventually swamp the short-term market corrections that stocks suffer. In other words, if you have enough patience, bull markets will come in and restore the market values that were destroyed by bear markets. And rest assured, bull markets eventually follow bear markets just as sure as day follows night.

Your Odds of Losing Money in the Stock Market

T. Rowe Price, the mutual fund giant, studied market activity between 1926 and 2002, and came up with some interesting findings. If you have only one year to invest money, there is a whopping 27 percent chance that you will lose money in stocks over any 12-month period of time. However, if you have three years to invest, the odds of losing money in the broad market drops to 14 percent. If you have five years (which I would consider the minimum amount of time needed to invest in stocks), there's only a 10 percent chance of losing money in equities. And over a decade's time, the odds of losing money in stocks are only 4 percent. So remember, if you do plan on investing in stocks for the long term, make sure your long term is at least five years, but better still 10 years or longer.

Finally, there's one other way investors can minimize market risks in their financial plans. That's to diversify *when* they choose to invest in stocks. In the financial markets, this is called *dollar cost averaging*. This term refers to a basic strategy that many of us already employ in our 401(k) retirement accounts. If you participate in an employer-sponsored retirement plan (and we will discuss these plans in depth later on in the book), you are essentially instructing your employer to direct a small percentage of each paycheck every week or month into your 401(k) account. This money is then invested in your choice of stock funds or bond funds. This means that at regular intervals spread out over time, you are investing a small chunk of your money into the stock market rather than investing a single lump sum. By doing so, you are ensuring that you won't be investing all your money into the stock market at the worst possible time.

Well, you can practice the same approach when it comes to the rest of your stock investments. Instead of investing tens of thousands of dollars in a lump sum on a single day, divide the money into smaller segments and put it to work in the market at routine intervals—perhaps every month or every quarter. Now, if you're looking to maximize your gains, dollar cost averaging won't get you there. That's because the whole point of this exercise is to divvy up your money and

invest it throughout the year, so that your "cost basis"—the amount you pay for your stock—is spread out and averaged out over time. In a rising market, dollar cost averaging will prevent you from squeezing every last penny in stock market appreciation, since you won't be putting all your money to work immediately in the rising market. However, when stock prices are falling, dollar cost averaging will ensure that you never buy into the market at its peak—just before a bear market.

RISK 2: STOCK-SPECIFIC RISK

In addition to bear markets, stock investors must worry about the fact that even though the market might be doing fine, their individual stocks could drop in value. Individual stocks can lose money even during a roaring bull market for any number of reasons. For instance, the company could be nearing bankruptcy, it might be losing market share to a rival, or its products or services might be obsolete. A worst-case scenario is a situation like Enron, the energy giant that was heralded among the country's biggest corporations. That is, until the energy giant fell into bankruptcy—a historic meltdown caused by corporate malfeasance in the form of accounting fraud. In Enron's case, this corporate wrongdoing cost investors not just millions, but tens of billions of dollars of paper wealth.

It's important for all investors to recognize that investing in an individual stock is never a slam dunk. To be sure, over the long run, equities are a good bet. But that's over several years, if not decades. And that's spread out over the entire stock market.

Here's a classic illustration of the vagaries of stock-specific risks. Say you invested in General Motors stock in 1993. At the time, GM was the world's largest automaker, as well as being a symbol of the industrial strength of the United States. It sure seemed like a safe bet. For the sake of argument, let's assume you purchased 1,000 shares of GM for $27.22 a share (that was the split adjusted closing price for the stock on December 31, 1993). By the end of December 2005, GM had lost market share to foreign rivals and had run into difficulties simply selling its basic cars. As a result, the stock tumbled to $19.01 a share. That means your original investment of $27,220 had fallen to just $19,010, representing a loss of 30 percent.

Now, assume that instead of investing in GM you bought shares of Toyota Motors on December 31, 1993. Back then, shares of the Japanese automaker were trading for $28.98 a piece. So, 1,000 shares of Toyota would have cost you $28,980. Because the two companies compete in the same industry and often compete in the same markets, you would think that their results would be somewhat similar. Yet by December 31, 2005, Toyota's shares had ballooned to

$104.62 a piece. In other words, your original investment of $28,980 would have grown to $104,620, for a whopping gain of 261 percent. That's a stunning difference that illustrates the stock-specific risk of guessing wrong and stock-specific reward of guessing right in the stock market.

Ways to Minimize Stock-Specific Risk

The simplest way to reduce stock-specific risk is to *diversify* your holdings among dozens if not hundreds of different stocks. Just to play it safe, you may want to invest in at least 50 different stocks. While financial planners used to say that investors needed to own, say, a couple dozen different stocks to be properly diversified, the stock market has become more volatile in recent years than in decades past. As a result, investors now probably need closer to 50 different stocks to sufficiently diversify away stock-specific risk. At least that's what current academic research would indicate. You may need even more if your 50 stocks are concentrated in any single sector of the economy or industry. For instance, if 10 of your 50 stocks are technology shares, you may be disproportionately hurt in a bear market in technology stocks.

The good news is that if you own a stock mutual fund, you're probably already there. According to Morningstar, the average stock fund owns 175 different shares of stock. Some funds own well in excess of 1,000 different stocks at any single moment in time. An exchange-traded fund will similarly provide you with instant diversification.

RISK 3: THE RISK OF NOT BEING IN THE MARKET

Wasn't it Franklin Roosevelt who once said, "The only thing we have to fear is fear itself?" He might as well have been talking about the stock market. That's because when it comes to investing in equities, one of the biggest risks of all is the risk of not being in the stock market—and therefore falling short of reaching your financial goals.

For instance, remember when I discussed the historical rates of return for equities, and argued how important it was to capture the 10.4 percent annual gains that stocks have delivered? Well, that's all fine and well. But if you pull your money out of the stock market from time to time out of fear of market losses, chances are you'll do more harm to your financial plan than good. Why? For starters, it's next to impossible to time the market with any precision. Therefore, you may end up exiting the market on the best day for stocks, only to return to stocks on their worst day. The fact is, no matter how good you may be at selecting stocks your ability to forecast precise market movements is limited.

Figure 3-7.   Risk of Not Being in the Market

Time Period	S&P 500 Annualized Returns
1/92 to 12/01	12.9%
1/92 to 12/01 minus best month	12.2%
1/92 to 12/01 minus best 2 months	11.4%
1/92 to 12/01 minus best 3 months	10.5%
1/92 to 12/01 minus best 6 months	8.0%

Sources: Crandall, Pierce & Co., Jack Brennan, *Straight Talk on Investing*, John Wiley, Hoboken, N.J., 2002.

Miss-timing the market can be costly. The University of Michigan ran an interesting study a while back that asked the question: What would happen to your stock market returns if you were out of the market on some of the best days for equities. As it turns out, a lot could happen. The University of Michigan studied the S&P 500 during the period between August 1982 and August 1987. During that window, stocks were enjoying a major bull market, posting average annual gains of more than 26 percent.

But according to the university's researchers, if you had missed out on just 20 of the best days in the stock market during this stretch, your returns would have fallen to 13.1 percent. If you missed out on the 40 best days during this period, you'd have only generated returns of 4.3 percent. Similar research conducted in the 1990s bull market would seem to confirm these findings. See Figure 3-7.

Different Types of Stocks

COMMON STOCKS VERSUS PREFERRED STOCKS

When people refer to stocks, they are typically referring to *common shares,* which are the most basic unit of corporate ownership. When investors purchase common shares of a publicly traded company, they are buying a unit of ownership that gives them basic rights. Common stockholders can vote on the leadership of the corporation, through elections of boards of directors. Those directors, in turn, have a say in who serves in the management of the firm. And the managers, in turn, have a say in how the company is run, how its earnings are invested, and how some profits are distributed to shareholders in the form of dividends or share repurchases. In a sense, when you own common stock, you are like a citizen of the United States with the power of the vote. Like the citizen of a republic, you don't have direct say in how the corporation is run. But you do get to vote on who the leaders of the corporation are. And the board, like the Electoral College, in turn gets to vote on who the actual decision makers of the firm will be.

Yet common stockholders are disadvantaged in one big way. If the company you invest in goes bankrupt, or worse, a line will form to recoup money from the firm. Among the players in this line will be the banks that lend money to the corporation, bond holders who also lend money to the firm, vendors and suppliers who are owed money by the company, and stockholders of that firm. Unfortunately, common stockholders of the bankrupt company are pretty much last in this line to recoup losses. In front of this line will be secured creditors and bondholders, as well as owners of so-called preferred stock.

Preferred shares, like common stock, also represent a unit of ownership unit of a corporation. But preferred stockholders don't normally get traditional voting rights in the firm. So why would anyone choose to invest in preferred stock rather than common stock?

Well, preferred stock typically throws off larger dividend payments than common shares. And those dividends can be counted on no matter what types of troubles the firm may be in. Indeed, during economic downturns, some firms will cap or reduce the amount of dividends they pay to common shareholders in an effort to shore up their finances. But typically, those firms will continue to pay dividends to preferred stockholders, which makes preferred stock much more dependable when it comes to income. This is not to say that preferred stock is the best vehicle for long-term investors. While high-net-worth and income-oriented investors favor the higher yields offered by these stocks, preferred shares don't necessarily deliver the same type of price gains as common shares.

LARGE CAPS VERSUS SMALL CAPS

While we often discuss the stock market as if it were a monolithic entity, it's not. There are various types of common stocks to invest in. And one of the most basic distinctions that investors make is on the basis of market capitalization.

Market capitalization simply refers to the value that the stock market places on a given firm. A stock that trades at $10 a share, for example, and has 1 million shares outstanding is said to have a market cap of $10 million. A stock that trades at $100 a share with 10 million shares outstanding would have a value of $1 billion.

In general, stocks that are valued at $10 billion or more are considered large-capitalization stocks, *large caps* for short. Stocks with market caps of between $1 billion and $10 billion are often referred to as *mid-cap stocks.* Publicly traded companies valued at $1 billion or less are often referred to as *small caps* or

Figure 3-8.   Breaking Down the Stock Universe

	Capitalization Range	Best Fit Index
Mega Cap	$25 billion or Higher	Dow Jones Industrial Average
Large Cap	$10 billion or Higher	S&P 500 Index, Russell 1000 Index
Mid Cap	$1 billion to $10 billion	S&P 400 Index
Small Cap	$300 million to $1 billion	S&P 600 Index or Russell 2000 Small Cap Index
Micro Cap	$300 million or lower	Wilshire Micro Cap Index

small-company stocks. And truly tiny firms with market caps of $300 million or less are often considered *micro caps*. See Figure 3-8.

Within this mix, the most important distinction is probably between large-cap and small-cap stocks. Large-caps, which are often referred to informally as "blue chips," are typically industry leaders. These are the Microsofts and General Electrics of the world that not only dominate their businesses in the United States but often have a major global presence.

Because these firms are already large in size and stature, they typically can't grow as fast as smaller firms. Blame it on the law of large numbers. A large-cap company that sees its earnings grow $10 million off a $100 million base is only growing 10 percent. But a small firm that grows its earnings $10 million off a $10 million base has just doubled its profits, for a 100 percent gain. But on the other hand, large-cap stocks are much more stable, due to their size, than small-cap stocks. This means that in an economic downturn, large stocks will tend to hold up better, as large companies rely on global sales, not just domestic sales. And large companies, because of their market dominance, can often dictate prices to consumers. This means that large firms may not experience a huge downturn in sales during recessions.

Small-cap and micro-cap stocks, on the other hand, are shares of young companies that still have tremendous room to grow. This means small stocks don't appeal to stability-minded investors. Rather, small stocks appeal to risk takers who want to hitch their wagons to companies that they believe are about to enjoy meteoric growth. In other words, small-company investors are typically on the hunt to find the next Microsoft or Yahoo or Google.

The downside to investing in small caps is that in exchange for the greater growth potential, small stocks expose investors to far greater short-term volatility. Sometimes, that volatility works to an investor's advantage. For instance, small stocks tend to outperform the broad stock market when investors are feeling good about the economy and the economy is expanding rapidly. This tends to happen just as the economy is emerging from recession and is about to enter into a new period of economic expansion. But when the economy begins to cool, investors tend to do better in large stocks, since large-cap shares offer investors greater

Figure 3-9.   Annual Returns: Small Versus Large Stocks

Year	Small Stocks*	Large Stocks
2005	4.55%	**4.91%**[†]
2004	**18.33%**	10.88%
2003	**47.25%**	28.67%
2002	**−20.48%**	−22.10%
2001	**2.49%**	−11.89%
2000	**−3.02%**	−9.10%
1999	**21.26%**	21.04%
1998	−2.55%	**28.58%**
1997	22.36%	**33.36%**
1996	16.49%	**22.96%**
1995	28.45%	**37.53%**

*Small stock performance reflects the Russell 2000 Index of small stocks.
[†]Large stock performance reflects the S&P 500 Index of large stocks.

Source: Morningstar

consistency and stability of earnings growth. This, in turn, tends to translate into more consistent (though not as spectacular) stock market performance. See Figure 3-9.

Because large stocks tend to represent the majority of the nation's total stock market capitalization, investors are typically told to use large stocks to make up the foundation of their equity holdings. In fact, large stocks should represent the majority of your stock exposure. But because of the added growth that small stocks can deliver to a long-term financial plan, small-cap shares should be represented among your holdings. And because it's difficult to predict with any certainty when large stocks or small stocks will officially take over market leadership, it's wise to hold some representation of large-cap and small-cap equities at all times. See Figure 3-10.

Figure 3-10.   Periods of Small-Stock Leadership

Years	Length in years	Excess Annualized Returns*
1932–1937	4.8	16.0%
1940–1945	6.0	13.9%
1963–1968	6.0	10.8%
1975–1983	8.5	14.5%
1991–1994	3.3	11.3%
1999–2004	5.0	11.7%

*Reflects additional annualized total returns small stocks delivered over large stocks during these periods.

Source: Prudential Equity Group

GROWTH VERSUS VALUE

Another distinction investors need to be aware of is between *growth-oriented* and *value-oriented stocks*. Growth and value speak to two different styles of investing, which tend to run in rather unpredictable cycles.

Growth stocks, as their name implies, are shares of fast-growing companies that are already firing on all cylinders. A classic example of growth stocks were technology shares in the late 1990s. Back then, investors favored growth stocks over value since growth-oriented companies were expanding very quickly as a result of the booming 1990's economy. The prototypical growth company back then was Cisco Systems, a tech firm that enjoyed rapidly expanding earnings and that was also expanding quickly through acquisitions.

At their core, growth stocks are shares of firms whose earnings are literally growing faster than the market as a whole. You'll recall that historically, the corporate earnings growth rate for companies in the S&P 500 has been about 7 percent to 10 percent a year. Therefore, a simple definition of growth stocks is shares of firms whose profits are growing faster than that. Indeed, according to the mutual fund tracker Morningstar, the average stock in a growth-oriented mutual fund enjoyed annual profit growth of 29 percent a year for the three years ending April 30, 2006.

This doesn't mean that value stocks are necessarily slow growers or unprofitable firms. Value stocks are defined as shares of companies that are typically undervalued by investors or that are overlooked. Often times, a value-oriented stock will be neglected by investors simply because it isn't growing as fast as growth-oriented shares. Sometimes, value stocks are neglected because they are in boring industries, such as consumer staples or basic materials (many value stocks are also found in traditional "smokestack" industries such as utilities). But there are occasions when a value stock is beaten down for good reason. For instance, companies may slip into "value" status due to a short-term business problem. See Figure 3-11.

Why would an investor purposefully choose to bet on a stock that isn't popular? There are several reasons. For starters, a value stock that is beaten down by investors is probably trading at a deep discount to the stock market as a whole. And some investors are like bargain-basement shoppers—they don't mind buying a stock that's been dented or dinged so long as the price is slashed as well. The idea behind value stock investing is the hope that shortly after you purchase the shares, the company will find a way to right itself and begin to grow more rapidly, at which point the stock price will increase. Value stocks are also popular because they tend to pay out greater dividends than growth stocks. While a growth-oriented company may use its profits to expand the business, value companies often convince shareholders to be loyal by throwing off more dividend income.

Figure 3-11.   Traditional Growth & Value Sectors of the Economy

---

Classic Value Sectors

Financial Services
Industrials
Consumer Staples
Energy
Basic Materials
Utilities

Classic Growth Sectors

Technology
Health Care
Consumer Cyclicals
Telecommunications

There's one other reason why safety-minded investors tend to favor value shares. Because these stocks are already beaten down to some extent, they often fall less during a stock market slide, as they have less room to drop. Growth stocks, on the other hand, because they are high flyers, tend to lose more ground during corrections and bear markets.

Since it's impossible to predict with any certainty when a new bear market or correction may take place—and because growth and value stocks often take turns leading the market—it's often wise to invest in a balanced mix of growth and value. If you own a diversified stock fund that represents the entire S&P 500, you probably already have decent diversification between the two types of equities. See Figure 3-12.

DOMESTIC STOCKS VERSUS FOREIGN SHARES

The last major distinction in the equity markets is between domestic and foreign stocks. Up until recently, most American investors pretty much stayed within the U.S. borders when it came to stocks. Yet with the increasingly global economy, there is less distinction these days between foreign and U.S. equities. Indeed, many large-cap companies are "multinationals," meaning that they do business not only in the United States but also in Europe, Asia, and Latin America.

Take a quintessential American company like Wal-Mart. The nation's biggest retail chain, founded in Bentonville, Arkansas, operates more than 1,500 of its 5,000 stores overseas. Citigroup, the nation's largest bank and financial services

Figure 3-12. Value Versus Growth Stocks

Year	Value Stocks*	Growth Stocks[†]
2005	**8.71%**	1.14%
2004	**15.03%**	6.97%
2003	**30.36%**	27.08%
2002	**−16.59%**	−28.10%
2001	**−8.18%**	−16.12%
2000	**−0.51%**	−19.14%
1999	4.88%	**37.38%**
1998	18.91%	**38.16%**
1997	31.87%	**34.73%**
1996	20.54%	**25.43%**

*Reflects performance of S&P 500/Citigroup Value Index.
[†]Reflects performance of S&P 500/Citigroup Growth Index.

firm, technically does business in more than 100 countries. And as for Coca-Cola, it sells its sodas and nonalcoholic beverages in more than 200 different nations. In fact, Coke derives nearly three-quarters of its sales from outside of North America.

Given that we already invest abroad when we invest in major U.S.-based multinationals, why limit your stock choices to shares of firms domiciled only in the United States? The fact is that American companies comprise only around half of the world's total stock market valuation. This means that by considering only domestic stocks, you are limiting your choices to half of the world's stock choices. Indeed, why just consider Ford and G.M.? Why not also consider Toyota and Hyundai? Why consider only Pfizer and Merck when there's GlaxoSmithKline and Novartis out there as well? Why consider just Motorola when Samsung and Nokia also exist?

In addition to the fact that foreign stocks increase your choices, there are a couple more reasons to think globally. For starters, even though foreign stocks and U.S. equities enjoy greater correlation as a result of the global economy, international investments serve to diversify our portfolios. To be sure, the economies of North America, South America, Europe, and Asia do move more in synch today than they did a generation ago. But academic research shows that a small, but substantial, investment abroad can still help diversify your holdings during rocky times in the U.S. markets. Researchers from Standard & Poor's have concluded, for instance, that a 25 percent stake in overseas equities is sufficient to offer some degree of ballast for your U.S. holdings.

Another reason to invest abroad is that sometimes foreign stocks simply outperform U.S. equities. This was certainly the case shortly after the bear market of 2000 in American stocks. In the five-year period between June 2001 and June 2006,

Figure 3-13.   Foreign Versus Domestic Stocks

Year	U.S. Stocks*	Foreign Stocks‡
2005	6.93%	**17.50%** [†]
2004	12.27%	**17.87%**
2003	31.75%	**40.07%**
2002	−19.84%	**−11.84%**
2001	**−8.60%**	−14.84%
2000	**2.66%**	−14.77%
1999	26.95%	**49.32%**
1998	**15.42%**	7.45%
1997	**23.99%**	4.42%
1996	**19.06%**	14.78%

*Reflects average performance of U.S. stock funds.
[†]Reflects average performance of International stock funds.

Source: Morningstar Inc.

for example, the average U.S. stock fund delivered total returns of around 5.5 percent annually, according to Morningstar. But during this same stretch, the typical foreign stock fund surged more than 14.4 percent a year. That's a huge difference. But just as with growth and value stocks as well as large- and small-cap equities, U.S. and foreign shares take turns leading the market. And it's often difficult to tell which market will lead and which will follow. So it makes sense to invest in both types of equities at all times. See Figure 3-13.

ACCESS TO FOREIGN MARKETS

While it's not often easy to access foreign stock exchanges directly, there are plenty of ways for U.S. investors to gain exposure to foreign stocks. For starters, the easiest way to invest abroad is through a foreign stock mutual fund. According to the mutual fund research firm Morningstar, there are around 2,600 different funds that invest exclusively or primarily abroad. These funds are the simplest path to overseas stocks as they are professionally managed (so you don't have to select the foreign stocks themselves), diversified, and open to small investors. These funds are particularly useful in providing small investors safe access to the so-called emerging markets, which are shares of companies based in developing nations like Russia and Mexico and South Korea. If you're looking for a list of foreign stock funds to choose from, visit Morningstar's Web site, www.morningstar.com.

In addition to mutual funds, there are so-called exchange-traded funds that provide investors either to broad access overseas or to baskets of stocks in specific nations, such as China, Brazil, France, and the United Kingdom. To find a list of these types of ETFs, go to www.ishares.com. (We will discuss ETFs at greater length in Chapter 9.)

Finally, investors can also invest directly in foreign companies, through what's known as an *American Depository Receipt*, or *ADR*. An ADR is a security that represents a share of a foreign company. While the actual shares of that foreign stock are held by a bank in the United States, the receipts for those shares trade on the major U.S. stock exchanges, like the NYSE, the Nasdaq, or the American Stock Exchange. Investors can then buy and sell ADRs as if they were U.S. stocks.

Quiz for Chapter 3

1. Money put to work in the stock market should be considered...
    a. an investment.

    b. savings.

    c. a risky bet.

2. A short-term 10 percent drop in the stock market is considered extremely rare.
    a. True

    b. False

3. How much can you expect to earn in the stock market over long periods of time?
    a. You can earn an annual rate of 7 percent to 10 percent.

    b. You can earn an annual rate of 12 percent to 15 percent.

    c. You cannot safely expect to earn any consistent returns from equities.

4. The returns on stocks tend to outpace those of other investments because...
    a. stocks are typically held for longer periods of time.

    b. stocks earn money both through capital appreciation and dividend yields.

    c. stock returns are correlated with long-term corporate profit growth.

5. The best strategy to achieve gains in the stock market while minimizing risk is to ...
    a. concentrate your bets only in those types of equities that you feel have the best risk-reward characteristics.

    b. invest no more than half your money in the equity markets.

    c. diversify the types of stocks you own.

6. What is an asset-allocation strategy?
    a. It is the mix of various types of stocks you hold in your investment portfolio.

    b. It is the mix of various types of assets you hold in your investment portfolio.

    c. It is your mix of different investment accounts inside your financial plan.

7. Why is dollar cost averaging an effective investment strategy?
    a. It maximizes your returns in a rising market.
    b. It prevents your portfolio from losing money in a falling market.
    c. It ensures that you will never buy stocks at the worst possible moment.

8. Blue-chip stocks have historically...
    a. returned more than risky small-company stocks.
    b. returned less than risky small-company stocks.
    c. returned about the same as risky small-company stocks.

9. If you are investing for a short-term goal like sending your child to college in two years, that money should be invested in...
    a. a diversified basket of blue-chip stocks.
    b. a diversified collection of large- and small-cap stocks, growth and value stocks, as well as foreign and domestic shares.
    c. a mix of cash and short-term bonds.

10. It's always better to invest in value-oriented stocks.
    a. True, because they tend to pay out high dividends.
    b. True, because they typically trade at deep discounts to growth stocks.
    c. False.

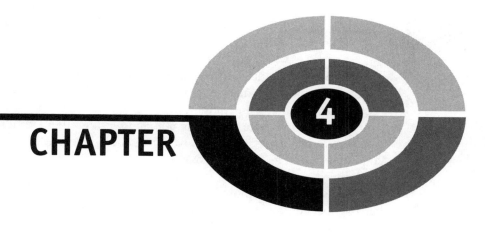

CHAPTER 4

Corporate Bonds

What Are Corporate Bonds?

When a corporation issues stock, it is divvying up part of the company to bring new investors into the fold. In effect, it is raising cash by selling off parts of the company to outsiders. Now, when that same corporation issues bonds, it is also attempting to raise cash. But instead of selling part of the company, the firm is trying to raise capital by selling loans in the capital markets.

This means that when investors purchase corporate bonds, they are playing the role of de facto banker to the company. That's because they are literally buying an I.O.U. from the company they are lending money to. And that I.O.U. comes with certain promises and terms.

To be sure, corporations also borrow money from actual banks, typically for short-term purposes. Often times, however, corporations will find it advantageous to borrow in the bond market because they can tailor their debt securities to suit their particular time horizon. This explains why there are tens of thousands of individual corporate bonds that investors can choose from on the open market, making the bond market an even bigger market, in terms of the number of securities available, than equities.

It's important to note that being a bond investor is quite different than being a stock investor. Stock investors are part owners who are counting on long-term consistent earnings growth from the companies they own stock in. As such, stock investors tend to think in terms of best-case scenarios. For instance, a stock investor will want to know whether the company in which he or she owns stock has the chance to evolve into the next Microsoft or Google.

However, as a bond investor, you are literally playing the role of a bank. And just as a bank does not care if the company it loans money to grows 20 percent or 30 percent in a given year—so long as it grows fast enough to pay back the original loan with interest—bond investors don't care that much about the limitless possibilities of the issuing company. Instead, bond investors tend to worry about worst-case scenarios. The things that bond investors care about include whether the company whose bonds they just purchased stays in business long enough to return their original investment on the agreed upon date; whether the company will be able to keep paying them the interest due on the loan; and whether there is a possibility that the firm might default on its loan.

As a result, it is critical that bond investors understand two things: the financial health of the company they are buying the bonds of, and the precise terms of the loans they are purchasing.

Bonds are contractual agreements that spell out exactly how the bond buyer can expect to make money. For instance, bonds come with a *fixed maturity date*, which is sort of like an expiration date. Before corporations issue bonds, they establish a date certain (possibly 3 years or 5 years or even 30 years in the future) at which point they promise to pay the original loan back in full to the bondholder. This means bond investors should only buy those securities that mature in time to meet their own financial needs. For instance, if you need the proceeds of your bond investment back in 10 years to pay for your children's college bills, then you should make sure that you do not buy bonds that are longer than 10 years in maturity.

Bond Maturity

Although bonds come with a specific maturity date, some bonds may be *called* prior to maturity by the issuer. So it's important to know, before you purchase a bond, whether the security is *callable* or *noncallable*. Some companies issue callable bonds to give themselves some financial flexibility to refinance their debt.

The period before a callable bond can be redeemed by the issuer is referred to as the *deferment period*. During a bond's deferment period, the bond investor enjoys *call protection*. But after the deferment period ends, all bets are off. Now, to compensate the investor for recalling the bond early, some corporate securities come with what's known as *call premium*. In other words, when some corporate issuers redeem their bonds prematurely, they agree to pay the investor a slight premium above par to compensate them for their troubles.

Of course, the reason investors purchase bonds isn't simply to get their original principal investment back in full. They also expect to get paid for doing the bond issuer a favor by purchasing their debt. So in exchange for the loan, corporations agree to pay investors a predetermined fixed amount of interest along the way. This is why bonds are sometimes referred to as *fixed-income securities*.

The interest payments that bond issuers promise to deliver is expressed as the *coupon rate* on the bond. For example, say you buy ten $1,000 bonds each with a coupon rate of 5 percent. So long as you hold these bonds to maturity, you know they will pay you $500 a year (that's $50 annually per bond times 10 bonds).

"Coupon Cutting"

Why is a bond's interest rate referred to as its coupon yield? Up until the digital age, bonds literally came with coupons or certificates attached to them. That way, the bondholder would detach one coupon when it was time to receive an interest payment. He or she would then send this coupon to the corporate issuer. Obviously, there are more efficient ways for bondholders to get paid these days. So coupons are out, though the reference is still a part of bond lore.

How Bonds Pay

Before we get too far ahead of ourselves, we should probably discuss how bond-holders make their money. Most of us think of bonds as income instruments.

That is to say, bonds pay investors annual interest (actually, to be precise, most bonds make semiannual interest payments). But bonds, like stocks, make investors money in two ways. First, there's the interest rate component. That's the coupon rate we've discussed. That's the simple part.

But bonds, once issued by a corporation, trade on a secondary market, just like stocks do. Throughout the course of their contract existing bonds are bought and sold like equities on an exchange everyday. As a result, bonds, like stocks, come with a price. And that price will fluctuate throughout each trading day, as demand by other investors for the corporate debt ebbs and flows.

For instance, while a corporation may issue a bond with a face value, or *par value,* of $1,000, that same bond may trade at a premium or discount to par value a few days later. Why would someone pay $1,100 for a bond that on paper is only worth $1,000? Well, what if that existing bond is paying a coupon rate of, say, 7 percent at the same time that market interest rates have fallen to around 5 percent? When market interest rates fall, the price of older existing bonds with higher rates will rise. And this extra interest may be well worth it for some investors to pay a premium for a bond.

Conversely, a bond investor may decide to sell his or her $1,000 bond for only $800 or $900 if market rates rise. Again, that's because if market rates were to rise, demand for existing bonds sporting lower rates will fall, taking their price down with it. This brings us to a fundamental relationship that all bond investors need to memorize: Bond prices move in the opposite direction of market interest rates. It's sort of like a teeter-totter. When rates rise, bond prices fall. When rates fall, bond prices rise.

There's another reason why a bond may be trading at a discount to its par value. If there are financial troubles at the issuing company—for instance, if there are growing concerns that a bond issuer might be on the verge of defaulting on its interest payments to bondholders—an existing bond investor may choose to cut his or her losses by selling the securities on the open market to another investor below face value.

For long-term "buy and hold" bond investors, whether a bond is trading at a discount or premium to par doesn't really matter. That is because bond investors can simply choose not to trade their bonds on the secondary market. Instead, they might choose to simply hold the bond to maturity, at which point the corporation agrees to pay back the initial principal investment in full.

However, not all investors hold their bonds to maturity. A bond mutual fund manager, for example, may decide to trade his or her securities when the market for them is optimal. An individual investor who purchased individual bonds as part of her long-term financial plan may decide to sell those bonds in the open market, rather than holding them to maturity, if there are changes to her financial circumstances. For example, what if your child or parent needs medical care

that might require you to cash in some of your bonds? What if you find yourself unexpectedly unemployed and you need to sell some of your assets to raise income until you find new work?

The fact that bond prices can fluctuate means that bonds must be measured in two ways. The total return for a bond, then, represents its interest rate plus or minus any change in the underlying bond's price.

Why Bonds?

In the previous chapter, we discussed how stocks are the best investment for the long term. But even if you are a long-term investor, not all of your investment needs are long term in nature.

Even if you're in your 20s and 30s—with an extremely long time horizon before needing to worry about retirement—you still have short- and intermediate-term needs to consider. You may be setting aside extra money to go toward a down payment on a house two years down the road. You could be saving some extra cash to pay for a dream wedding or vacation three years later. You might be thinking of going to graduate school a few years after that. What if you're in your late 50s and are within five years of retirement? Even if you've always considered yourself a long-term investor, your time horizon shrinks as you approach a major financial need, such as generating retirement income.

In situations like this, it does not make sound financial sense to be fully invested in stocks—in other words, to put every last cent you own in the equity markets. Doing so could be disastrous, since stocks need long periods of time for their potential rewards to overcome their short-term risks.

You'll recall that in the previous chapter, we discussed the odds of losing money in equities. In any one-year period, stocks have lost money 27 percent of the time. Even in any five-year period, stocks still manage to lose ground 10 percent of the time. So you have to wonder: Am I willing to accept 1-in-10 odds of losing my savings by investing all of it in the equity markets?

Luckily, investors have other options, such as bonds. But it's important to keep in mind the role bonds play in your financial plan. Because bonds are loans that you extend to a corporation in exchange for a fixed rate of interest, bonds give investors something that stocks don't—some degree of certainty that you will recoup your money and earn a steady stream of interest. This makes bonds an ideal place to park your *intermediate-term money*—money that you won't need to tap for another three to five years, if not longer.

But bonds are not necessarily a great place for your short-term money. That's because bonds are not 100 percent guaranteed. A corporate bond issuer could

CHAPTER 4   Corporate Bonds

easily go bankrupt between the time you purchase its bonds and the time your bonds come due. And when market interest rates rise, the price on older bonds that are paying out lower interest rates will likely fall in the open market. And this, too, could lead to losses.

Still, those losses aren't going to be anywhere near as severe as what investors can expect in the equity markets. Between 1996 and 2005, for instance, the Lehman Brothers Aggregate Bond Index, the broadest measure of the fixed-income market, lost value only once—in 1999. Moreover, the index lost less than 1 percent of its value that year, which goes to show not only that bonds lose money less frequently than do stocks but that the losses they suffer tend to be miniscule compared with stock market drops.

Bonds often get short shrift from investors, especially young savers, because it's hard to get rich quick in the fixed-income markets. Historically, bonds have paid investors around half the annual total returns of stocks.

THE GROWTH ARGUMENT

It's a fallacy to believe that stocks always outpace bonds in the short run. To be sure, fixed-income securities play a critical role in protecting your portfolio during market storms, as we will discuss in a moment. But the value of bonds goes well beyond simply losing less during downturns. There are times when bonds add some real juice to your portfolio. In fact, there have been a number of years when bonds have produced stocklike gains—even double-digit total returns.

For example, the period between June 2001 and June 2006 was marked by the end of a bear market for equities and the start of a new roaring bull market for stocks. Yet taken as a whole, blue-chip stocks pretty much went nowhere during this long stretch. The Dow Jones industrial average—an index composed of 30 of the largest stocks in the United States, which is often used to gauge the health of the overall equity market—advanced less than 1 percent annually during this window of time. Yet bonds surprisingly held up their end of the bargain. In fact, during this stretch, bonds were the real drivers of growth in the investment markets, as the Lehman Brothers Aggregate Bond Index delivered total returns of around 5 percent a year. See Figure 4-1.

In some years, bonds have really soared. In 1995, for example, bond investments produced total returns of more than 30 percent. And in 2000, bonds gained nearly 20 percent. But it's not just single years from time to time. There have been many extended periods of time—decades even—when bonds have not only provided investors with greater assurances of principal protection but also delivered significantly greater total returns. In the Great Depression years of the 1930s,

Figure 4-1.   Bonds Zig When Stocks Zag

Years	Stocks	Bonds
1929	−8.4%	+3.4%
1939	−24.9%	+4.7%
1931	−43.3%	−5.3%
1932	−8.2%	+16.8%
1933	+54.0%	−0.1%
1934	−1.4%	+10.0%
1935	+47.7%	+5.0%
1936	+33.9%	+7.5%
1939	−0.4%	+5.9%
1940	−9.8%	+6.1%
1941	−11.6%	+0.9%
1942	+20.3%	+3.2%
1943	+25.9%	+2.1%
1944	+19.8%	+2.8%
1945	+36.4%	+10.7%
1995	+37.5%	+30.1%
1996	+22.9%	−1.3%
1997	+33.2%	+13.9%
1998	+28.6%	+13.1%
1999	+21.1%	−8.7%
2000	−9.1%	+19.7%
2001	−12.0%	+4.3%
2002	−22.2%	+16.7%

Source: Edward Jones, Morningstar

for example, long-term corporate bonds managed to deliver sizeable gains of 6.9 percent a year. This took place during a decade when blue-chip stocks lost 0.1 percent a year on average, according to Ibbotson Associates.

In the recession-riddled years of the 1970s, long-term corporate bonds again beat large-capitalization stocks, this time by an annualized margin of 6.2 percent versus 5.9 percent. Stocks regained market leadership in the 1980s. But there was no shame in defeat that decade. That's because corporate fixed-income securities still managed to deliver impressive total returns of 13 percent a year in the 1980s. In most decades, that would have trounced stocks, but the bull market years of the 1980s propelled equities to average gains of nearly 18 percent that decade. See Figure 4-2.

Finally, bonds regained market leadership at the start of this decade, when one of the worst bear markets in history struck equities. Between 2000 and 2005, large-cap stocks lost around 1.1 percent a year. Yet during this stretch, corporate bonds managed to post stocklike returns of 9.9 percent.

Investment	1920s*	1930s	1940s	1950s	1960s	1970s	1980s	1990s	2000s†
Large-Company Stocks	19.2%	−0.1%	9.2%	19.4%	7.8%	5.9%	17.5%	18.2%	−1.1%
Long-Term Corporate Bonds	5.2	6.9‡	2.7	1.0	1.7	6.2	13.0	8.4	9.9

Figure 4-2.   Bonds versus Stocks

*1920s figures reflect 1926–1929.
†2000s figures reflect 2000–2005.

Source: Ibbotson Associates

The problem is that it's next to impossible to guess with any precision the specific years that bonds will trounce stocks. So if you're putting together a long-term financial plan, chances are you'll be better off owning a combination of stocks and bonds at all times.

There is a simple explanation why bonds sometimes outpace stocks. Bonds and stocks are competing assets. Every day, bonds and stocks fight to attract investor dollars. So in years when bonds are delivering sizeable gains, it's not surprising to find that investors are selling out of the stock market so that they can move more of their money into the fixed-income market. The fact that stocks and bonds take turns leading the market means that it's probably good to hold stocks and bonds at all times.

Stocks typically excel during periods when the economy is firing on all cylinders and corporate profits are soaring. Then, when the economy starts to cool, investors naturally turn their attention to bonds, since bonds will at least pay them a steady rate of return, whether or not the underlying company's profits are growing and whether or not the economy is expanding.

THE DIVERSIFICATION ARGUMENT

Even if you're not sure whether bonds will beat stocks in a particular decade, there are good reasons to own some bonds to go along with your equities. One of the chief reasons to own bonds is to *diversify* your equity portfolio.

Long-term financial plans crave diversification. That's because a diverse portfolio consisting of not only different types of stocks but also different asset classes ensures that there will never be an occasion where all your money will be caught in a perfect storm of a bear market. So to play it safe, long-term investors always want to have some money in bonds so that when stocks slip into a downturn, fixed-income securities will be there to keep at least some of their portfolio afloat.

Consider this real-world example. During the recent bear market that started in 2000, the S&P 500—an index composed of 500 different blue-chip equities—tumbled more than 17 percent in its worst three-month period of time. That was

Figure 4-3.   Asset Allocation: Worst-Case Scenarios

Asset Mix	Worst One-Year Performance
100% Stocks and 0% Bonds	−43.1%
80% Stocks and 20% Bonds	−34.9%
60% Stocks and 40% Bonds	−26.6%
50% Stocks and 50% Bonds	−22.5%
40% Stocks and 60% Bonds	−18.4%
20% Stocks and 80% Bonds	−10.1%

Source: Ibbotson, Vanguard

between July 2002 and September 2002. In other words, a $100,000 portfolio invested entirely in the S&P 500 would have shrunk to less than $83,000 in just 90 days. Now, say that you decided instead to put half of your money into bonds while keeping the other half in S&P 500 stocks. Had you chosen this course, your portfolio would have only lost 7 percent during that stretch between July 2002 and September 2002. So, instead of seeing your $100,000 shrink to $83,000, it would have fallen to just $93,000. That's the benefit of diversification.

As you can see in Figure 4-3, the more bonds you add to your portfolio (relative to stocks), the less money you are likely to lose during market downturns. Historically, the worst single-year loss for a diversified mix of stocks has been more than 43 percent. That was during the most recent bear market. But the worst loss for a portfolio that consisted of 50 percent stocks and 50 percent bonds was around half that.

THE BALLAST ARGUMENT

Many investors, in particular retirement investors, tend to fixate on the interest rates that bonds are paying out. This is understandable. For many retirees, these payouts will determine the lifestyle that they can lead in retirement. But bonds are much more than income generators.

All investors should consider having at least some portion of their money in bonds because of the ballast they provide an overall portfolio. During periods of extreme market volatility, bonds are often useful in keeping a diversified portfolio from gyrating too much. The fact is that one of the biggest threats to any financial plan is a short-term market scare. The more volatile financial markets are, the more likely investors are to flee those assets at the worst possible moment (just when they're about to recover and soar). This tends to happen in every asset class, whether we're talking about stocks or real estate or commodities. Yet selling your assets due to short-term fear will upset your long-term financial plan.

Figure 4-4. Bonds Reduce Volatility*

Asset Mix	Standard Deviation
100% Stocks	17.0%
80% Stocks and 20% Bonds	13.8%
60% Stocks and 30% Bonds and 10% Cash	10.6%
40% Stocks and 40% Bonds and 20% Cash	7.6%
20% Stocks and 50% Bonds and 30% Cash	5.2%

*Based on market performance between December 31, 1955 and December 31, 2003.

Source: T. Rowe Price

So to the extent that they can dampen market gyrations, bonds play a vital role in any financial plan. Take a look at Figure 4-4. One way investors can measure market volatility is by considering an investment's so-called standard deviation. *Standard deviation* is a statistical term that speaks to how volatile an investment is behaving relative to its long-term average performance.

For example, let's say you come across two different portfolios with average annual returns of 10 percent. For the sake of argument, let's say that one of those portfolios arrived at that 10 percent average by gaining 8 percent in the first year, 10 percent in the second, and 12 percent in the third. While there is a rather complex mathematical formula to calculate an investment's true standard deviation, we can roughly state that this portfolio's standard deviation is about 2 because it bounced 2 percentage points above and below its three-year average.

Now, on the other hand, say that the second portfolio you come across arrived at its average gains a different way. Let's say that it lost 20 percent in the Year 1, gained 10 percent in Year 2, and soared 40 percent in Year 3. This portfolio, like the first one, enjoyed a 10 percent average annual return. But because it bounced 30 percentage points above and below its long-term average, its standard deviation was closer to 30.

The higher an investment's standard deviation, the more it tends to gyrate over time. So to the extent that you can lower your portfolio standard deviation, the better off you're likely to be. As you can see from Figure 4-4, bonds will help you accomplish this goal. History shows that the more bonds you have in your portfolio (relative to stocks), the lower your portfolio's standard deviation is likely to be. This means the less volatile your portfolio will be.

This "bond effect" was particularly evident in the bear market of 2000, when many portfolios that were heavily weighted toward equities (and growth-oriented equities in particular) were battered. Meanwhile, well-diversified portfolios that had core weightings in bonds—which means anywhere from 20 to 50 percent— held up surprisingly well. Consider the performance of the hypothetical portfolios

Figure 4-5.   Performance of Various Portfolios in 2000 Bear Market (3/31/2000 to 9/30/2002)

Asset Allocation	Total Return	Growth of $100,000
100% Nasdaq Stocks	−74.4%	$25, 600
100% S&P 500 Stocks	−43.8%	$56, 240
60% Stocks/30% Bonds/10% Cash	−20.8%	$79, 165
47% Stocks/37% Bonds/16% Cash	−12.9%	$87, 136
25% Stocks/40% Bonds/35% Cash	+2.8%	$102, 838

Source: T. Rowe Price

shown in Figure 4-5 during that downturn. Pay close attention to those portfolios that had a decent smattering of fixed-income securities.

As you can see, those who put all their assets in stocks lost more than 40 percent of their wealth during this bear market stretch. And those who invested in the riskiest types of stocks—technology shares that make up a big portion of the Nasdaq composite index—lost even more: three-quarters of their money. Indeed, a $100,000 portfolio in Nasdaq stocks shrank to a little more than $25,000 in about two and a half years. But investors who socked away at least 30 percent of their money in bonds during this stretch ended up losing only around a fifth of their money during the worst bear market since the Great Depression. Those who put 40 percent of their money in bonds and only 25 percent in stocks—with the remainder being socked away in cash—actually ended up making money during this bloody period in the equity markets.

As we've discussed, being a bond investor is about considering worst-case scenarios. And in this case, bond investors need to ask themselves not only how much they can lose in the worst case, but what are the odds of losing money. The Vanguard Group actually crunched these numbers and came up with something very interesting. Between 1960 and 2003, a 100 percent stock portfolio lost money in 12 out of those 44 years. That means the odds of losing money in a single year, during this 44 year stretch, was 27 percent. But by adding a 50 percent stake to bonds, you could have dropped that percentage to just 18 percent. By moving to 60 percent bonds, you would have lowered the risk of losing money in any single year to less than 14 percent. And had you invested entirely in bonds, you would have suffered losses in only 5 out of the 44 years between 1960 and 2003. See Figure 4-6.

THE INCOME ARGUMENT

As we stated earlier, some investors will purposefully choose to buy and hold bonds to maturity. If that's the case, they don't care as much about the total returns that a bond generates, but rather just the interest income that they throw off.

Figure 4-6. **Percent of Losing Years Asset-Allocation Strategies (Based on stock and bond market performance between 1960 and 2003)**

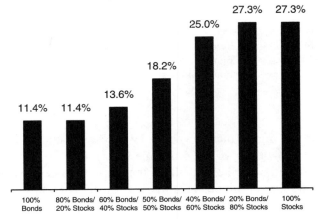

Source: Vanguard Group

Older investors who are concerned about generating retirement income are particularly likely to buy bonds primarily for the income stream they produce. Younger investors who are using bonds to fund a particular intermediate-term need—for instance, paying for graduate school three years down the road—might also consider using bonds in this way.

Bond Income

Why are bonds the preferable vehicle for generating income? Call it the law of small numbers. Say you chose to generate an income stream using only a cash account, like a bank certificate of deposit. Say that you can earn 3 percent on a CD. At that rate, how much would you need to put into that CD for it to generate a reasonable amount of income to live off? Well, 3 percent of $250,000 is $7,500. That's hardly an adequate amount to pay for annual living expenses. Indeed, to achieve that $40,000 of annual income, you'd have to have more than $1.3 million saved in CDs. Obviously, to generate an adequate income stream, you'll need to invest in assets that throw off much more income each year.

That's where bonds come in. Not only do bonds typically yield more than cash, they also tend to throw off more in interest income than stocks do in the form of dividend income. And unlike stocks, bonds don't put your principal investment at so much risk.

Different types of bonds will yield more or less, based on the amount of interest rate risk and credit risk they expose an investor to. Generally speaking, the longer the maturity of a bond, the higher the interest rate it will pay out. This is because longer-term bonds tie up an investor's money for lengthy periods of time, and there are always additional risks that are associated with locking down your assets for long periods of time.

Companies with poor credit quality must also pay out higher yields on their bonds, since investors who buy their debt are taking a risk by doing business with such a company. Moreover, corporate bonds tend to have to pay out more than government bonds, since they aren't backed by the full faith and credit of Uncle Sam.

Bond Risks

CREDIT RISK

Bonds expose investors to two basic types of risks. The first is called *credit risk*. This is the chance that your bond issuer will run into financial difficulties before your bond matures, forcing it to default on its promise to pay you a set amount of interest and repay your principal investment. Always keep in mind that even though a corporation may make promises to its bondholders, there are no guarantees that the company will be able to meet those promises in full. This is why it's so important for bond investors, like banks, to be confident in the long-term financial health of the firms they invest in.

Managing Credit Risk

While there is no way to totally eliminate credit risk when investing in corporate debt, there are some simple steps bond investors can take to reduce the effects of potential defaults in their portfolio. For starters, you can diversify your bond holdings by investing not just in one corporate bond, but in hundreds of fixed-income securities.

The fact is that the vast, vast majority of bonds make good on their promises to investors. Only a tiny fraction of the entire bond universe defaults in any given year. So by investing in dozens of different securities, you will reduce the impact that any single default could have on your portfolio. Think about it: If 1 out of 100 bonds in your portfolio fails to meet its obligation, the other 99 will be there to prop up your account.

Since bonds are often issued in $1,000 increments—and are often sold in large lots to institutional investors—it may be difficult for small investors to achieve

adequate diversification on their own. But don't worry: An easy way for individual investors to own hundreds of different bonds at once is through a professionally managed bond mutual fund. According to Morningstar, the average bond mutual fund invests in more than 400 different securities at once. Some funds own thousands of different bonds at one time.

Yet another way to manage credit risk is to stick with high-quality bonds. Within the corporate bond universe, there are two basic types of bonds. There are those issued by healthy, growing corporations with strong balance sheets. These are often referred to as *investment-grade bonds*. They tend to pay out modest yields, since they expose investors to only a modest degree of principal risk. Then there are those bonds issued by companies of questionable financial health. These are often referred to as *high-yield* or *junk bonds*. As the name implies, a bond issued by a financially questionable firm needs to pay a higher rate of interest to convince investors to take on credit risk.

CREDIT RATINGS

There's a simple way investors can judge the financial health of a company issuing a bond. They can turn to the bond ratings generated by the major bond rating agencies: Moody's, Standard & Poor's, and Fitch. Each of these firms maintains a slightly different rating system. See Figure 4-7.

But the ratings are somewhat similar. Anything rated BBB or higher (or in Moody's system, Baa or higher) is considered investment grade. And an AAA rating (for Moody's, it would be Aaa) is considered the gold standard for bond issuers. Meanwhile, debt graded BB (or for Moody's, Ba) or lower is regarded as junk.

But you still have to do your own homework. The fact is, sometimes, the bond rating agencies get it wrong. For example, bonds issued by the former energy giant

Figure 4-7. Bond Ratings

Credit Rating	Moody's	S&P	Fitch
Highest Quality	Aaa	AAA	AAA
High quality, but small degree of risk	Aa	AA	AA
Good quality, but susceptible to risk	A	A	A
Medium quality	Baa	BBB	BBB
Start of "junk" status	Ba	BB	BB
Speculative grade; major uncertainties	B	B	B
Poor quality; vulnerable to nonpayment	Caa	CCC	CCC
Highly vulnerable, likely to default	Ca	CC	CC
Lowest quality	C	C	C

Enron were classified as investment grade debt only days before the company filed for bankruptcy.

■■■

Those investors who want to minimize credit risk should probably focus on investment grade debt rated BBB or higher. To play it really safe, you may want to focus on bonds rated AA or better. That's because historically, less than 2 percent of bonds rated AA or higher by Standard & Poor's has defaulted. And less than one-tenth of 1 percent of bonds with the highest rating—AAA—have ever defaulted. By comparison, a significant percentage of junk bonds have defaulted, as Figure 4-8 shows.

INTEREST RATE RISK

Another major type of market risk that bond investors need to be mindful of is interest rate risk. As we discussed earlier, bond prices move in the opposite direction of market interest rates. Again, that's because the market craves yield. And if you purchase a bond with a coupon rate of 5 percent and then market interest rates rise to say, 6 percent, why would anyone want to buy your older, lower-yielding bonds over newer ones that are paying out more?

Figure 4-8.   Cumulative Default Rates Based on Bond Ratings

S&P Bond Rating	Default Rate*
Investment Grade	
AAA	0.67%
AA	1.30%
A	2.88%
BBB	9.77%
Junk Status	
BB, B	24.51%
CCC, CC, C	41.09%
D	60.70%

*Figure represents cumulative default rate in 15-year period following initial rating.

Source: Charles Schwab, Standard & Poor's

Figure 4-9. Bond Performance in 1994

Bond Type	Percent of Funds That Lost Money	Average Loss in 1994
Long-Term Government	96%	−8.6%
Long-Term Corporate	100%	−6.4%
Intermediate-Term Government	99%	−3.8%
Intermediate-Term Corporate	99%	−4.1%
Short-Term Government	72%	−1.2%
Short-Term Corporate	65%	−1.0%
Ultra-Short-Term Corporate	3%	+2.0%
High-Yield Bond	91%	−3.2%
Multisector Bond	100%	−4.9%
All Taxable Bonds	88%	−3.4%

Source: Morningstar

This means that if market interest rates climb after you purchase your bonds, the price of your older bonds will probably fall. And if prices on your existing bonds fall more than those bonds are yielding, you could see negative total returns from your fixed-income investments. In 1994, for example, the Federal Reserve jacked up interest rates aggressively in an effort to keep inflation at bay. As a result, bond prices took a major hit, and more than 88 percent of taxable bond funds posted negative total returns that year. See Figure 4-9.

Managing Interest Rate Risk

There is a simple way to sidestep this type of interest-rate risk: Just buy individual bonds—not bond funds—and hold them to maturity. The fact is that if you buy and hold your bonds to maturity, whether a bond loses 10 percent in price doesn't really matter. It's all just noise. At redemption, you can simply go back to the bond issuer and get your original par value back—in full. The problem is that this strategy takes patience, so investors who opt for this approach should be extremely confident of the companies they're investing in.

There's a second problem: This strategy doesn't work for bond *fund* investors. That's because unlike individual bonds, bond mutual funds do not come with a single maturity date. Bond mutual funds aren't a single security. They are professionally managed portfolios of fixed-income securities, all with different maturity dates. And often, those managers won't hold their bonds to maturity. Instead, they will trade some securities from time to time in the secondary market to take advantage of market interest rate trends. The bottom line: There is no date certain at which a bond *fund* will mature and kick back to investors their original principal investment.

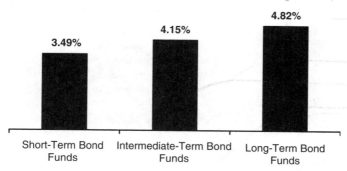

Figure 4-10.   Average Bond Mutual Fund Yields (April 2006)

However, bond fund investors do have options. They can stick with bond funds that specialize in short-term corporate debt or ultra-short-term securities. Let's define what a short-term bond is. *Short-term bonds* are fixed-income securities with maturity dates of around two years or less. And *ultra-short-term bonds* are a subset of the short-term universe that matures in around a year or so. By contrast, *intermediate-term bonds* tend to mature in 2 to 10 years. And *long-term bonds* typically mature in a decade or more.

Because short-term bonds tie up your money for shorter durations than long-term debt, they tend to pay investors lower interest rates. For example, take a look at Figure 4-10. It clearly shows that there is a distinct "yield curve" that starts off low, with short-term bonds, but rises as you get to the "long" end of the fixed-income market.

Even though short-term bonds pay a lower yield there is still an advantage to owning short-term bonds. These bond funds expose investors to less risk because they turn over much faster. Indeed, in periods of rising market interest rates, short-term bonds will come due much faster than long-term debt. So you'll recoup your money sooner as the bonds mature, and you can turn around and reinvest that money immediately in new, higher-yielding bonds. As a result, short-term bond funds are able to minimize some of the interest rate risk that's inherent in the bond market.

Another Type of Interest Rate Risk

Interest rates don't always rise. Sometimes, they fall. For most bond fund investors, falling rates is a good thing. That's because as market rates tumble,

Figure 4-11.   Hypothetical Bond Ladder

Total Amount to Invest: $50,000

$10,000	Bonds maturing in 1 Year
$10,000	Bonds maturing in 3 Years
$10,000	Bonds maturing in 5 Years
$10,000	Bonds maturing in 7 Years
$10,000	Bonds maturing in 10 Years
$50,000	Average Maturity: 5.2 Yrs.

the higher yields on their existing bonds will become more attractive to other investors. And their bond prices are likely to climb in the secondary market.

But investors who own individual bonds sometimes face a different type of interest rate risk when market rates fall. For example, if all your bonds are about to mature just as market rates are hitting a new low, you may be forced to reinvest that money back into new bonds at the worst possible moment—when fresh bonds are yielding virtually nothing. This type of *reinvestment risk* is particularly harmful to older investors, since they often rely on the interest that bonds throw off to generate a steady stream of retirement income.

Yet there's a way around this type of interest rate risk as well. It's called *laddering your bonds*. The term refers to a basic strategy employed by fixed-income investors to diversify their portfolios. But instead of diversifying the *types* of fixed-income securities they hold, this strategy calls for diversifying *when* your bonds mature. Think of it as the bond equivalent of dollar cost averaging. Here's how a ladder might work: Rather than putting all your money to work in bonds maturing in five years, split it up and buy bonds of different maturities, thereby averaging out your portfolio's overall maturity and duration. A typical ladder might look something like Figure 4-11.

In the example in Figure 4-11, you are holding bonds ranging from 1 year to 10 years in maturity. But the average maturity across the entire portfolio is roughly five years. Now, after a year of holding this portfolio, your one-year bond—the shortest-term security among your holdings—will come due. When you receive your original investment from that bond back from the issuer, simply reinvest the money back at the long-end of the curve: for example, in a new 10-year bond. This will allow you to take advantage of the higher rates that long-term bonds are likely to offer. But because of your ladder, your average maturity will still be close to five years. And by creating a bond ladder, you ensure that at no point in time will all of your bonds come due at the worst possible moment.

One Other Type of "Bond"

Technically, a *fixed immediate payout annuity* is not a corporate bond. It is actually an insurance contract. In exchange for a lump-sum investment, typically made to an insurer at retirement, the insurance company promises to pay you a set amount of interest for the rest of your life.

A fixed immediate payout annuity is not to be confused with a *variable annuity*, which we will discuss in a later chapter on mutual funds and other "basket" investments. While a variable annuity is a managed investment product—structured somewhat like a mutual fund—designed to help investors accumulate wealth, an immediate payout annuity is much more like a bond.

Of course, there are slight differences between these types of annuities and bonds. In an annuity, instead of lending money to a corporation, you are entering into a contractual agreement with an insurer. And unlike a bond, a payout annuity has no official maturity date. In fact, immediate annuity investors never receive their original investment back. That's handed over to the insurer for good. But in exchange, the insurer promises to pay the investor a fixed (or in a few cases, adjustable) rate of monthly income for the rest of his or her life.

An Annuity Advantage

Insurers that offer immediate payout annuities pool the money of thousands of annuity buyers. They also pool their life expectancies. The idea is, since some people will die sooner than expected, the money that they bring to the table can be used to benefit the surviving investors in the pool.

As a result, immediate payout annuities can often offer retired investors a better rate of income than retirees could safely generate on their own through bonds. For example, a conservative retiree might only be able to generate $5,000 in retirement income through a $100,000 portfolio of bonds. But that same person might be able to go to an insurer and get a fixed annuity paying around $7,500 a year for the rest of his or her life. The actual amount of income you can expect from an immediate payout annuity will depend on market interest rates, your age, your life expectancy, and how much money you decide to invest.

An immediate annuity investor will come out ahead if he or she lives longer than the average American (insurers will base the amount of interest they agree to pay you on mortality rates for American men and women). For example, say you bought a $100,000 immediate annuity that promises to pay you $7,500 a year for the rest of your life. If you bought the annuity at 65 and live until you're 95, you'd end up collecting $225,000 in total payouts (that's $7,500 times 30 years) even though you contributed just $100,000. But if you die sooner than expected, you may not receive sufficient income over your lifetime to justify the annuity. Think about it: If you bought this $100,000 income annuity at age 65 and died at 70, you'd have received only $37,500 in payouts over the course of your life. So there's a risk.

Placed within the context of a diversified retirement portfolio, a payout annuity will act much like a bond, because it offers a steady stream of income and ballast during market storms. In fact, there are times when an immediate payout annuity can actually be better for your portfolio than bonds. Baylor University finance professor William Reichenstein studied the performance and durability of various retirement portfolios between 1972 and 2000. He discovered something interesting: A 65-year-old retiree with a $1 million portfolio in 1972, invested in a mix of 40 percent stocks and 60 percent bonds, would have theoretically run out of money in 1995, at age 88. That's if he or she withdrew $45,000 a year from the account. Part of the reason for the failure of this portfolio is that stocks ran into a severe bear market in the early 1970s.

Now, had this person taken half of his or her portfolio and bought a fixed annuity instead, that person would still have had $136,000 left at age 95, based on numbers crunched by Reichenstein. Of course, there are no guarantees that payout annuities will similarly beat out bonds in the future. It all depends on market interest rates and market performance. And these types of payout annuities only work in the context of a retirement portfolio. That's because the older you are when you purchase the annuity, the higher the income you can expect (if you buy an annuity before you turn 65, it won't generate much income). But these types of annuities are still an option—and often a good one—for a long-term financial plan.

Quiz for Chapter 4

1. Why do companies issue bonds?
   a. To raise financing for projects or general purposes
   b. To lower their overall level of debt
   c. Because it's cheaper than issuing stock

2. Why are bonds also called "fixed-income securities"?
   a. Because the total returns they generate are fixed
   b. Because investors are paid a fixed amount over the life of the bond
   c. Because investors are promised a fixed rate of interest on the bond

3. Historically, bond market performance always trails stock market gains.
   a. True
   b. False

4. If bonds typically pay out lower rates of return than stocks, why do investors consider buying bonds?
   a. Bonds address inflation risks better than stocks.
   b. Bonds generate income and provide ballast for a broadly diversified portfolio.
   c. Bonds are cheaper to invest in than stocks.

5. One of the difficulties of investing in corporate bonds is that there are fewer fixed-income securities to choose from than individual stocks.
   a. True
   b. False

6. What is a bond's coupon rate?
   a. The discount an investor seeks when buying a bond from a troubled company
   b. The interest rate investors can expect to earn annually if they purchase a bond at face value and hold it to maturity
   c. The interest rate a company promises to pay investors if the bond is recalled early

7. The best time to buy a bond mutual fund is...
   a. when interest rates are rising.
   b. when interest rates are falling.
   c. It makes no difference.

8. You can never lose money in a corporate bond if you hold it to maturity.
   a. True
   b. False

9. An easy way to minimize credit risk is to...
   a. buy a diversified bond mutual fund.
   b. buy short-term bonds.
   c. avoid bonds altogether, and invest in equities.

10. An easy way to minimize interest rate risk is to...
    a. invest in a diversified bond mutual fund.
    b. invest in short-term bond funds.
    c. invest in long-term individual bonds.
    d. invest in individual bonds and hold them until maturity.

CHAPTER 5

Cash

What Is Cash?

Cash is probably the one asset class that most of us are intimately aware of. It is the currency through which we literally get paid. It is also the means through which we save money, buy goods and services, and invest in other assets such as stocks and bonds. Yet there are still a number of misconceptions about what cash is.

For instance, when we hear the word "cash," most of us picture tangible currency, whether it's paper money in our wallets or coins jangling in our pockets. But the term *cash* really refers to any ultra *liquid* asset. This means any investment vehicle with an extremely short maturity and that can be tapped fairly quickly to meet various short-term needs.

Any fixed-income instrument with a maturity of six months or less is often considered to be cash, or at least a *cash equivalent,* even though it may take some time to physically convert it into paper currency. Examples of cash accounts range from bank products like savings accounts and certificates of deposit; investing vehicles such as money market mutual funds; and government securities such as Treasury bills that mature in three or six months (we'll discuss T-bills in Chapter 6).

The interest rates that cash vehicles pay out are influenced by several forces, including the fixed-income market and the U.S. Federal Reserve Board. The Fed, as it is often called, is the nation's central bank. This governmental institution is charged with overseeing the nation's monetary policy. Among the Fed's jobs is to ensure that the domestic economy remains balanced and strong, and that prices in the economy remain stable (i.e., inflation remains under control).

Sometimes, the Fed will choose to lower short-term interest rates—in particular, a key rate known as the *federal funds rate,* which is what banks charge one another on overnight loans—in an effort to jump start economic growth. Lower rates have the effect of boosting economic activity, since cheap borrowing costs encourage companies to invest in new projects and expand. When the Fed lowers rates, or *loosens* monetary policy, cash accounts and cash equivalents are likely to fall in lock-step. This means in periods of Fed rate cuts, investors will likely see their cash investments lose their attractiveness. During the depths of such periods, you'll often hear the phrase: "cash is trash." That's because when interest rates are falling, it's often bullish for stocks and bonds and bearish for ultra-short-term securities.

Conversely, when the Fed chooses to raise short-term rates, cash accounts and cash equivalents are likely to boost their yields, which is great for cash investors. The Fed will often raise rates, or *tighten* monetary policy, in an effort to slow the economy in hopes of keeping inflation from overheating (inflation is thought to be a natural outgrowth of economic activity, so the Fed sometimes tries to slow inflation by moderating growth). Rising rates have the effect of slowing economic activity by making it more costly for companies to borrow money. During the heights of such periods, cash yields are likely to rise along with other short-term rates and you'll often hear the phrase: "cash is king."

Cash increases in value in another way during periods of Fed tightening. Typically, when cash yields and short-term rates go up, stock and bond investments tend to lag, especially if the Fed lifts rates so much that the underlying economy slips into recession. When stocks are in a bear market, cash, by its very definition, increases in real value. That's because when equity prices fall, the same amount of cash will be able to purchase more shares of a given stock. While investors don't necessarily value cash based on what a unit of currency can buy in stocks and bonds, they should. Keep in mind that stocks, bonds, and cash are in a perpetual competition for investor dollars. So to the extent that investors are souring on stocks and bonds, cash is likely to come out well. See Figure 5-1.

Figure 5-1.   Cash Returns through the Decades

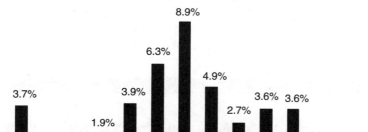

Source: Ibbotson Associates

Why Cash?

Cash has historically paid out much less than stocks and bonds. In fact, there have been several periods in history when cash actually trailed the annual rate of inflation. In other words, there are times when cash, in real terms (i.e., on an after-inflation basis) goes negative. This happened in the 1940s, the 1950s, and the 1970s. Moreover, cash and inflation were virtually tied in the beginning half of the 2000s. See Figure 5-2.

Figure 5-2.   Cash Versus Inflation

Investment	1920s	1930s	1940s	1950s	1960s	1970s	1980s	1990s	2000s
Cash	3.7	0.6	0.4	1.9	3.9	6.3	8.9	4.9	2.7
Inflation	−1.1	−2.0	5.4	2.2	2.5	7.4	5.1	2.9	2.6

Source: Ibbotson Associates

Cash in the 1970s

The 1970s offers an interesting example of the vagaries of investing in cash. Back then, cash accounts were actually yielding far more than their historical averages. In fact, had you invested in cash throughout that decade, you would have earned 6.3 percent on your money annually. That's more than double the historical rate of return for this asset class. And toward the end of the decade, you would have earned even more, as many cash accounts were paying double-digit returns. However, the attractiveness of cash is based on the real rate of inflation. During the 1970s, inflation ran at an annual rate of 7.4 percent. This means that even with the historically high rate of return for cash, you would have gone backward in real terms in this asset class.

So why does cash need to be a major component in anyone's long-term financial plan? The answer is simple: Every long-term investor has short-term needs in addition to long-term goals. And cash is really the only financial asset that is suitable to meet those short-term needs. That's because cash is the one investment in your portfolio that provides assurances that you won't suffer principal losses in your original investments.

To be sure, bonds provide stability and ballast for your portfolio. But in any single year bonds can still lose value, so long as their prices fall more than the bond itself is yielding. In 1994, for example, 96 percent of long-term government bond funds and 100 percent of long-term corporate bond funds lost value as the Fed was hiking rates that year. For any investor who needed to tap their accounts in 1994 to generate retirement income, buy a house, or pay for a child's college bills, such losses proved to be quite disruptive. Indeed, the worst thing that can happen to a financial plan is for your portfolio to lose money just as you need to spend it. Think about it: If you have, say, $100,000 saved up and need to tap $10,000 from your account, you're already withdrawing 10 percent of your savings. If in the same year, that account were to lose 10 percent of its value thanks to stock and bond market losses, all of a sudden, you'd be one-fifth poorer. This could be the difference between having enough money to get you through a particular period in your life and falling just short.

Cash is designed not to lose ground in any short period of time—in fact, some cash accounts, as we will discuss in a moment, are federally guaranteed. This underappreciated asset plays a vital role in any financial plan, and this is especially true when you're approaching periods when you'll need to tap a portion of your savings.

CASH FOR SAVINGS

Because cash is designed to *preserve* your money instead of growing it, cash is often considered a savings vehicle, and not an investment. This distinction between savings and investments is actually quite important for those who are creating a financial plan.

Money that is *invested* is by definition put at risk. The degree of risk that your money is subjected to will be determined by what you invest in. But regardless of whether you invest in stocks, bonds, commodities, or real estate, there will be a chance that you won't get exactly 100 percent of your principal investment back at the moment you want to redeem it. In exchange for accepting this risk, stock, bond, real estate, and commodity investments typically deliver returns that are likely to exceed the rate of inflation over long periods of time. Cash does not.

On the other hand, money you consider part of your savings (i.e., funds that you will need in two years or less) should never be exposed to risk. That money belongs in a savings vehicle that will emphasize capital preservation over capital appreciation. In fact, any money you will need to tap in 24 months or less (for instance, money set aside to cover pending college bills, this year's taxes, an upcoming vacation, or an emergency fund) should be held in some type of cash or cash equivalent account.

CASH FOR INVESTING

This doesn't mean cash can't play a role in your overall investment plan. For starters, there will be years in which cash will actually beat stocks in terms of real total returns. Indeed, investors who moved money into cash during the recent bear market—here, I'm talking about 2000, 2001, and 2002—wound up beating the returns of most blue-chip stocks during this stretch. To be sure, cash investors didn't get rich. But at a time when most investors saw their portfolios lose ground, cash investors kept their heads above water.

For instance, say you started out in 2000 with $10,000 in cash. By 2003, that money would have grown to $11,095. This is based on the 5.75 percent returns for money market mutual funds in 2000, their 3.63 percent gain in 2001, and the 1.25 percent gain in 2002. Had you invested that same initial amount entirely in stock mutual funds during this same period, that $10,000 would have shrunk to $7,520 by the start of 2003. See Figure 5-3. To be sure, the gains that cash produced during these years were nothing to write home about. But the meager gains cash produced during the bear market were still stellar in comparison to the huge losses suffered by equities between 2000 and 2002.

Keep in mind that cash is also the currency through which you buy other assets such as stocks and bonds. So it will always play some role in managing your portfolio. After all, money invested in stocks during the life of a financial plan will inevitably have to shift to cash as you get closer to needing those resources. Think of cash as the final step in a long journey of investing that begins with stocks, shifts to bonds as you get older, and then finally to cash.

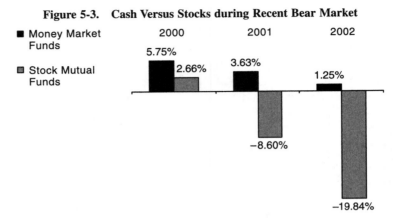

Figure 5-3.   **Cash Versus Stocks during Recent Bear Market**

- ■ Money Market Funds
- ▨ Stock Mutual Funds

Source: Morningstar Inc.

CASH TO PROTECT GAINS

One of the biggest mistakes an investor can make in his or her financial plan is to leave everything on autopilot—forever. For instance, investors who made a fortune on paper during the 1990s bull market, and who did not book some of those profits by selling winning stocks by the end of 1999, saw a good deal of those gains evaporate in the subsequent bear market that began in March 2000. The idea of investing is to buy low and sell high. But unless you sell at some point and *realize* your paper gains, everything is theoretical. See Figure 5-4.

This is where cash can play an important role. By selling stocks and moving the money temporarily into cash—while you decide what other assets you want to invest in—cash accounts serve to protect the gains you've already earned in the market.

CASH AS A SHORT-TERM PARKING PLACE

In addition to preserving your gains, cash can also play an important role during transitional points in a person's investment plan. The worst thing a long-term investor can do is to be so impatient about putting money to work in stocks that

Figure 5-4.   Cash Versus Stocks

Investment	1998	1999	2000	2001	2002	2003	2004	2005
Money Market Funds	4.9%	4.6%	5.8%	3.6%	1.3%	0.6%	0.8%	2.6%
S&P 500 Stocks	28.6%	21.0%	−9.1%	−11.9%	−22.1%	28.7%	10.9%	4.9%

Source: Morningstar Inc.

Figure 5-5. Average Cash Positions of Mutual Funds*

Type	Percentage of Assets in Cash
All Domestic Stock Funds	5.3%
All International Stock Funds	4.0%
All Taxable Bond Funds	12.4%
Large-Cap Growth Funds	2.9%
Large-Cap Value Funds	3.5%
Large-Cap Blend Funds	3.7%
Mid-Cap Growth Funds	2.9%
Mid-Cap Value Funds	4.7%
Mid-Cap Blend Funds	4.9%
Small-Cap Growth Funds	3.4%
Small-Cap Value Funds	4.7%
Small-Cap Blend Funds	4.4%
Technology Funds	3.6%
Natural Resources Funds	13.2%
Precious Metals Funds	6.5%

*Data as of April 30, 2006.

Source: Morningstar

he or she selects a poor security for his or her portfolio. By temporarily stashing some of your assets in cash, you can give yourself time to make wise decisions without putting your money at risk of short-term losses.

This is what professional mutual fund managers often do. While fund managers try to be "fully invested" at all times—meaning most of their assets are supposed to be in the stock or bond market—the reality is that most managers sit on some level of cash. In some cases, it's a modest sum, perhaps 1 percent to 5 percent. But when it becomes harder and harder to find good bargains in equities, some professional investors might put as much as 10 percent or even more of their portfolios in cash while they investigate their options. This is a prudent move that prevents an investor from forcing the action. See Figure 5-5.

To be sure, putting money into cash might slow the overall pace of your investment portfolio, as cash returns about a third as much as equities do over long periods of time. In the investment industry, this is referred to as a "cash drag." But for long-term financial planners, a slight cash drag might be better than making fool-hardy short-term decisions in your portfolio.

Dollar Cost Averaging with Cash

A common strategy in which an investor can use cash in conjunction with stocks is *dollar cost averaging.* As we discussed earlier, dollar cost averaging is a fancy way of describing an investment approach in which a person puts money to work gradually—in routine intervals, such as every month or every quarter—rather than making a single lump sum investment all at once. This is what we do when we invest in our 401(k) accounts at work, as small investments are made into our retirement accounts with every paycheck.

When you dollar cost average, you are literally diversifying when you invest your money to ensure that not all your money is in the market at the worst possible time. A dollar-cost-averaging strategy relies heavily on cash. That's because while you put your first chunk of money to work in stocks, the remainder of your assets are likely to be held in some type of cash account. Note that this strategy will create a cash drag on your portfolio, as the money that's held in cash will probably earn less than equities. But that slight drag on your portfolio is well worth it in many cases, since dollar cost averaging ensures that you will never be "all in" the market at the worst possible time.

CASH AS A PIGGY BANK TO INVEST IN OTHER ASSETS

In addition to being a good defensive parking place, cash can also help investors take advantage of opportunities in other assets. Think about it: If you held every last cent of your investment portfolio in stocks, bonds, and commodities, every time you came across a new investment idea, you'd have to sell shares of an existing holding. Then you'd have to wait for the cash proceeds, and only then could you use the money to invest in new ideas. By the time that takes place, the stock might not look as attractive to you as it once did.

Moreover, selling the existing holding will likely trigger capital gains taxes; that is, if you sell stocks that have appreciated in value over time. Although the federal government has recently lowered the maximum tax rate on capital gains to 15 percent, this is still 15 percent that you could lose off the top of your investment gains. By holding a small amount of your assets in cash at all times—again, say, 5 percent to 10 percent—you would have a funding source for new investment ideas that would not require you to sell existing holdings. This means that cash, though not an investment per se, can make all investors more nimble.

Risks of Cash

As we've discussed, there isn't any market risk associated with cash, since most cash accounts will virtually guarantee that at the very least you will get your

principal investment back at redemption. However, because cash returns are so modest relative to stocks and bonds, investors who put a sizeable portion of their portfolios in cash run the risk of missing out on opportunities in other assets. And this means that financial plans that rely too heavily on cash for long periods of time will run the risk of falling short of meeting long-term goals.

Moreover, because cash returns are not guaranteed to outpace the rate of inflation, all cash investments expose investors to inflation risk, as rising prices could easily eat away at the purchasing power of your cash reserves. Finally, depending on which type of cash account you utilize, you could be exposing yourself to some level of interest rate risk.

Indeed, if you invest in cash instruments that float with market interest rates, there are no guarantees that you will continue to be able to earn a particular rate of interest. For example, say you invested in a money market mutual fund when cash was yielding, say, 5 percent. If the Federal Reserve slashed short-term interest rates over the next several months, your 5 percent cash accounts might soon be yielding closer to 3 percent. And if the Fed keeps short-term interest rates low for several months thereafter, you might not see 5 percent yields for several years.

Of course, to protect yourself from this type of interest rate risk, you might decide to invest in a bank certificate of deposit, which is a form of cash that offers a fixed rate of return for a set period of time. For example, you might invest in a one-year CD that pays out 4.5 percent throughout that period (regardless of what happens to short-term market rates). But in this case, you would be subject to a different form of interest rate risk. That's the risk that at the precise moment that your one-year CD comes due and your bank gives you back your money, interest rates might be at an all-time low. So after earning 4.5 percent a year, you'd be forced to reinvest that cash at, say, 2 percent.

Since different types of cash accounts expose investors to different forms of risk, let's go over your choices for cash.

Different Cash Vehicles

BANK CDs

Bank certificates of deposit, or CDs, are among the most popular forms of cash. Part of this is because banks are federally regulated. As a result, bank CDs typically come with FDIC (Federal Deposit Insurance Corporation) protection. In other words, should your bank run into financial difficulties—which would be rare—up to $100,000 of your deposits would be guaranteed by the federal government.

CDs also provide investors with another guarantee: Unlike most other forms of cash, CDs promise to pay a fixed yield for a set period of time, no matter what happens to short-term interest rates. In this sense, bank CDs are more like bonds than they are savings accounts or money market accounts. Indeed, CDs come with specified maturity dates, typically ranging anywhere from one month to five years, at which point the bank will return your original investment. And the longer you agree to tie up your money, the higher the interest rate is likely to be. Moreover, banks are likely to offer slightly higher rates to savers willing to commit $25,000 or more at a time. If you commit $100,000 or more at one time, you could be eligible for a jumbo CD, which pays out even higher yields.

Like bonds, CDs expose investors to two types of interest rate risk. First, there's the risk that during the life of the CD, market interest rates will rise, making other cash vehicles more attractive. For example, a person who bought a three-year CD in June 2004 earning, say, 2 percent started out way ahead of other cash investors. That's because short-term interest rates in June 2004 were paying out only around 1 percent. But in the two years between June 2004 and June 2006, the Fed raised short-term rates 17 times, lifting cash rates to around 5 percent. Since money held in a CD is locked away until maturity—with some exceptions—a CD investor would not be able to easily shift into a higher-paying cash account to take advantage of rising rates. (Of course, on the flipside, the fact that CDs pay out a fixed rate of return means they could work to your advantage in periods of falling interest rates.)

The other interest rate risk that CDs expose you to is the possibility that, once the deposit matures, your money will be kicked back to you at the worst possible time—when market interest rates are at their lowest. This risk is referred to as *reinvestment risk,* since you might be forced to reinvest your original CD in a much lower-paying instrument.

CD Ladders

One way to manage the interest rate risks posed by CDs is to ladder them, much as you would do with bonds. In other words, if you wanted to invest $30,000 in cash, consider spreading the money out evenly over, say, a three-year stretch. For example, buy a $10,000 CD maturing in one year, a $10,000 CD maturing in two years, and another $10,000 CD maturing in three years. The idea is that if interest rates rise shortly after you make your investment, you can take the proceeds of the one-year CD when it comes due and reinvest the money in a new three-year CD. Remember, by the time you reinvest, that new three-year CD will reflect the higher interest rates commanded by the market.

But what if interest rates should fall? Well, if that's the case, the ladder works on your behalf as well. The fact that you've spread out your money over three CDs with varying maturities means that you will never have to reinvest *all* of your cash at the worst possible moment—again, when rates are near their lowest.

Because of their fixed maturities, CDs may be a good place to park cash that you know you'll need on a date certain. For example, if your daughter's college bill is due in one year and you want to protect that cash, you can take out a one-year CD that comes due slightly before your tuition check is due.

However, since your money is tied up in a CD for a set period of time, these accounts are not an ideal place to stash your emergency fund, since the whole point of setting up a rainy day fund is to be able to easily access money needed for unexpected purposes. You can pull your money out of a CD prior to maturity, much as you can withdraw money from a 401(k) prior to retirement. But doing so may lead to stiff penalties, depending on the bank. On average, expect to lose around three months' worth of interest income if you withdraw money prematurely from a one-year CD. If you break a two-year CD prematurely, expect to lose up to six months' worth of income.

SAVINGS ACCOUNTS

Another traditional savings vehicle is a basic savings account at a bank. A generation ago, the most common form of cash savings for small investors might have been an old-fashioned *passbook savings account,* where the bank literally gives customers a statement book that lists all their transactions. But in today's electronic world of banking, you're more likely to utilize a so-called *statement savings account*—which is fine, since these accounts (which send out monthly statements listing your transactions) are likely to pay out slightly more than passbook accounts.

The advantage to a savings account is convenience. For instance, these accounts are easily established at your local bank. Moreover, they allow for virtually limitless transactions that can be undertaken in person or remotely through checks or automated teller machines. This accessibility makes savings accounts a decent place to stash your emergency funds. What's more, they typically come with low minimum balance requirements. And on top of that, they come with FDIC insurance, so long as the bank you're working with is federally or state chartered

(be sure to check the status of your financial services firm if you bank with an online company or an overseas-based bank).

There are a number of disadvantages to savings accounts. For instance, in exchange for the limitless access, savings accounts typically pay out among the lowest interest rates around. For example, in the spring of 2006, many cash accounts were paying out more than 4 percent interest as the Fed was raising rates. But bank savings accounts were paying out less than 1 percent at that time. In fact, according to Bankrate.com, a research firm that tracks interest rates, both the average passbook savings account and the average statement savings account were yielding less than 0.6 percent interest in April 2006.

MONEY MARKET ACCOUNTS

Think of money market accounts as savings accounts on steroids. Like savings accounts, money markets are FDIC insured. But they often pay out considerably more than simple statement savings accounts. In the summer of 2006, the typical money market account was paying more than 3 percent interest, and money markets with a $10,000 minimum were yielding even more—3.5 percent.

Because they pay significantly more than savings accounts do and their yields are competitive with short-term CDs, money markets are an ideal place to stash your emergency fund.

However, keep in mind that there are some drawbacks. For starters, money market accounts aren't as liquid as savings accounts. Indeed, money markets place restrictions on how many transactions you can make in any given month. Typically, you will only be allowed to withdraw money from a money market account three to six times a month, depending on the bank. Any more activity may lead to penalty charges. Of course, the odds of your needing to tap this account for emergencies more than three to six times a month are slim.

MONEY MARKET MUTUAL FUNDS

Money market *mutual funds* are not to be confused with money market *accounts* at a bank. A money market mutual fund is an investment vehicle that buys and trades short-term and ultra-short-term debt.

Although these are technically mutual funds, money funds are an extremely safe vehicle. For starters, they allow investors to redeem their money on a daily basis, which means they are as liquid as most other cash accounts. By law, the average maturity of debt purchased by money market mutual funds cannot exceed 90 days, so there's very little interest rate risk. And most money funds invest 95 percent or more of their assets in U.S. Treasury bills and private securities with the highest credit ratings.

Still, money funds providers—typically banks and mutual fund companies—cannot guarantee with absolute certainty that your money fund investments will be 100 percent protected. Depending on market circumstances, there is still a possibility that you might not recoup 100 percent of your investment in a money fund. Unlike a money market account, money funds are not FDIC insured.

However, throughout the long history of these cash accounts, there have been only a handful of instances where money funds have failed to return every last dollar that investors have put into these accounts. If a financial services firm were to "break the buck"—in other words, fail to protect money fund investor assets—that would be a huge blow to its reputation. So even if your money fund loses value, many large, established money fund managers are likely to make you whole, even if it costs them money. Just to play it safe, though, investors are better off sticking with large, healthy fund companies with established track records like Fidelity or Vanguard or Schwab.

To compensate investors for this slight degree of market risk, money funds will typically pay out highly competitive interest rates. For example, during the summer of 2006 when bank money market accounts were paying out around 3 percent, money funds were averaging nearly 5 percent. Of course, those rates aren't locked for any period of time. When market interest rates fall, money fund yields will fall in lock step. And when rates rise, money funds will climb with them. A money market account, on the other hand, may not respond as quickly to changes in market interest rates since banks have discretion over those interest-bearing accounts.

Because they are highly liquid and pay out competitive rates, money funds are an ideal place to park the cash you are using to rebalance your investment accounts. It's also an ideal place to keep money that you intend to eventually work back into stocks and bonds.

Quiz for Chapter 5

1. What role does cash play in a financial portfolio?
   a. Cash is a liquid asset that can be used to purchase other assets.
   b. Cash is a source of capital preservation.
   c. Cash is a source of ballast for your portfolio during stock market storms.
   d. All of the above.

2. Which of the following is not considered a cash vehicle?
   a. Passbook savings accounts
   b. Money market mutual funds
   c. Treasury notes

3. What is the purpose of "laddering" your bank certificates of deposit?
   a. To reduce interest rate risks associated with investing in CDs
   b. To diversify the banks through which you purchase your CDs
   c. To hedge against inflation

4. Which of the following savings products is not federally insured?
   a. Bank CDs
   b. Money market funds
   c. Treasury bills

5. If you are selecting a money market mutual fund, what feature should you focus on?
   a. Low fees
   b. Past performance
   c. FDIC insurance

6. Which of the following cash accounts can be counted on to beat inflation?
   a. Jumbo CDs
   b. Money market mutual funds
   c. Treasury bills
   d. None of the above

7. Money market funds are safer than money market accounts because money funds invest in a diversified basket of different bank money market accounts.
   a. True
   b. False

8. Money market accounts are like money market funds in that they allow you to access your money freely.
   a. True
   b. False

9. Money market funds give you a fixed rate of interest.
   a. True
   b. False

10. Which of the following forms of risk does cash expose you to?
    a. Interest rate risk
    b. Inflation risk
    c. Risk of not being in the market
    d. All of the above
    e. None of the above

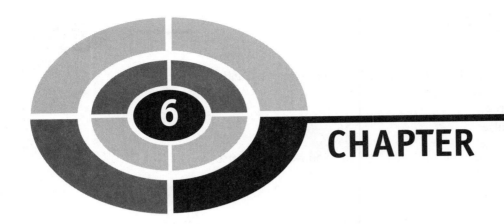

CHAPTER 6

Government Securities

What Are Government Securities?

So far, we've discussed how you can use *corporate* securities—be they stocks, bonds, or cash—as part of your long-term financial plan. One of the reasons why we often hitch our financial wagons to corporate securities is that private-sector companies are the real engines of growth in this economy.

As we discussed earlier, over the long sweeping history of the twentieth century, corporate earnings have tended to grow around 7 to 10 percent annually, which is why equity investors tend to earn around 10 percent a year on their money. Moreover, there are times when the private sector expands at an even faster clip, and periods such as these offer investors an even greater opportunity to grow their nest eggs.

After the recession of 2001, for example, corporate America enjoyed profit growth of more than 20 percent (on a year-over-year comparative basis) for several

Figure 6-1. Corporate Earnings Growth

Time Period	Growth*
1st Quarter 2002	−11.5%
2nd Quarter 2002	1.4%
3rd Quarter 2002	6.8%
4th Quarter 2002	9.7%
1st Quarter 2003	11.7%
2nd Quarter 2003	9.5%
3rd Quarter 2003	21.3%
4th Quarter 2003	28.3%
1st Quarter 2004	27.5%
2nd Quarter 2004	25.3%
3rd Quarter 2004	16.8%
4th Quarter 2004	19.7%
1st Quarter 2005	13.9%
2nd Quarter 2005	11.7%
3rd Quarter 2005	16.0%
4th Quarter 2005	14.4%

*Measures profit growth versus the same period in the prior year.

Source: Thomson Financial

quarters. See Figure 6-1. Not surprisingly, this roughly coincided with another bull market in U.S. stocks, which began on October 2002.

Yet there are other types of investment securities beyond those issued by private-sector companies. Most notably, there are *government-issued securities.* Obviously, neither the federal government nor states nor municipalities are up for sale. Investors are not legally allowed to buy and sell interest in democratically elected government institutions. Therefore, there is no such thing as government stock to invest in.

However, from time to time, governments—like most companies and households—require additional financing over and above what they bring in annually through traditional means (for governments that means tax revenues). To raise that money, governments often issue and auction off bonds. Money raised through bond issuance may be used to help fund specific projects or services. At the municipal level, for example, a city may require funds to expand services such as new utilities. A school district might float a bond in order to raise funds to build a new high school. A state government may issue bonds to cover the costs of road and bridge improvements.

For its part, the federal government is a huge player in the fixed-income market, as Uncle Sam routinely raises money through the bond market to help finance the growing national deficit and debt. The fact is that the federal government, like many American families, often spends more in a given year than it takes in. Deficit spending isn't necessarily the soundest course of action from the standpoint of fiscal responsibility. But sometimes, there are bigger considerations at hand. During times of war, for example, the government will spend all that is needed to support the nation's military efforts. During major financial crises, such as recessions or depressions, Uncle Sam may spend more than he takes in to jump-start the economy and the labor market.

Just as families will turn to credit cards to finance their overspending, Washington often turns to the bond market to pay for its largesse. Ironically, since foreign banks and governments have become big buyers of U.S. Treasury bonds as of late, America now depends on foreigners to help pay for domestic government services. Regardless, the fact that governments issue bonds gives investors of all stripes—including individual investors here at home—a chance to hitch their wagon to the stable income that government institutions can deliver.

Why Government Securities?

When investors put money into corporate securities, they are banking on the growth and health of the economy. In other words, investors of corporate assets are risk takers. They are willing to risk the loss of their original investments (remember: whether you own a corporate stock or a bond, there's a chance that the underlying company might go belly up) in exchange for the probability of seeing appreciable growth in their holdings.

Investors who purchase government securities, on the other hand, are not the betting type. In many cases, the reason investors put money into government bonds is because they want some assurance that they will at least recoup their original investment, even if the underlying investment doesn't work out. This is particularly true of Treasury bond investors, as Treasury securities are the purest form of government debt.

Unlike a corporation, the United States government cannot file for bankruptcy, which makes U.S. Treasury bonds the gold standard for safety seekers. In fact, the federal government will never go belly up because it has control over the national treasury. Even if the federal government were to face a financial crisis of historic proportions, it could always resort to printing more money through the Treasury Department to pay off its bond investors. No corporation in the world—not even the strongest AAA-rated firm—can offer investors this level of assurance. Therefore, there is a defensive appeal to government bonds that makes them highly attractive to certain investors, even if these bonds don't always yield as much as corporation securities do.

This goes back to the core principal of finances that we discussed earlier: the intrinsic relationship between risk and reward. Because Treasury bonds are so

CHAPTER 6 Government Securities

much less risky than corporate bonds, they do not have to pay bondholders a premium to entice them. Indeed, government bonds often throw off less income than corporate bonds of similar maturity. See Figure 6-2.

As a result, government bond investments tend to earn slightly less in total returns than corporate debt of similar maturities. According to Ibbotson Associates the average long-term government bond investment has returned 5.5 percent a year since 1926, while the average corporate bond of similar maturity has returned 5.9 percent. Over the course of a lifetime, this slight difference can be felt. A $100,000 investment in long-term corporate debt, for instance, made 30 years ago would have grown to nearly $560,000 today. That same $100,000 put to work in long-term government bonds would have grown to just under $500,000. See Figure 6-3.

Figure 6-2. Average Corporate and Government Bond Fund Yields (April 2006)

■ Corporate Bonds ▨ Government Bonds

4.15% 3.93% 4.82% 3.95%

Intermediate Term   Long Term

Source: Morningstar

Figure 6-3. Annualized Returns (1926–2003)

10.4% 5.9% 5.4% 5.4% 3.0%

Large Stocks | Long-Term Corporate Bonds | Long-Term Government Bonds | Intermediate-Term Government Bonds | Inflation

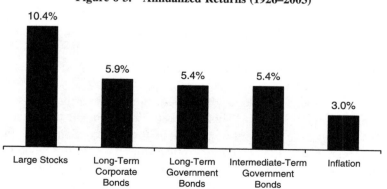

Source: Ibbotson Associates

Another Reason to Own Government Bonds

Safety isn't the only reason why investors gravitate to government bonds. Some government bonds come with a tax advantage. Interest income thrown off by corporate bonds is taxed as ordinary income at both the state and federal level. This makes corporate bond income far worse from a tax standpoint than corporate stocks. While the federal capital gains tax rate on long-term stock investments is capped at a maximum of 15 percent, ordinary income tax rates on bonds can go as high as 35 percent.

But a big advantage to owning Treasury bonds over corporate bonds is that they are free of state income taxes (the income is still subject, however, to federal taxes). As for municipal bonds, they're federal income tax free. Moreover, investors who purchase so-called munis issued by government bodies within their home states will also often get a state tax break. This is why municipal bonds often appeal to high net worth investors in the highest tax brackets.

This is not to say that government bonds do not, from time to time, outperform corporate bonds or even stocks. Indeed, the fact that government bonds sometimes lead the market means investors probably should have at least some exposure to government debt as well as corporate bonds at all times.

In periods when investors crave safety over speculation—such as the depression-era 1930s, the recession-riddled 1970s, and the bear market years of 2000–2002—government bonds have historically outperformed corporate securities. Indeed, you'll often witness a "flight to quality" among investors during uncertain economic or geopolitical periods. When the nation is headed to war, for instance—as was the case in 2003, when the United States went to war in Iraq—investors will often race to the safest assets around. And 9 times out of 10, that means Treasury bonds. See Figure 6-4.

Another environment in which government bonds perform well is in periods of falling market interest rates. This was especially true in the period following the 1970s, when interest rates peaked in the United States. In fact, since 1980, government bonds have delivered returns that have far exceeded their long-term historical averages. While the average annual gain for long-term government bonds has been 5.5 percent, government bonds generated total returns of 12.6 percent a year throughout the 1980s. They turned in another spectacular decade in the

Figure 6-4. **Government Bonds Versus Corporate Bonds**

Investment	1920s	1930s	1940s	1950s	1960s	1970s	1980s	1990s	2000s
Long-Term Corporate Bonds	5.2	6.9	2.7	1.0	1.7	6.2	13.0	8.4	9.9
Long-Term Government Bonds	5.0	4.9	3.2	−0.1	1.4	5.5	12.6	8.8	9.9

Source: Ibbotson Associates

1990s, producing average total returns of 8.8 percent a year. And between 2000 and 2005, government bonds generated annual gains of 9.9 percent. By historical standards, those are stocklike gains.

When Bonds Have the Upper Hand

How can you tell which asset, stocks or government bonds, are a better deal at any moment in time? One way is to compare the yield being paid out by 10-year Treasury notes versus the so-called *earnings yield* of the equity market. What's the earnings yield? It's a back-of-the-envelope calculation that lets you know how much earnings stock investors are purchasing for every dollar they're investing in the company. Here's the formula to calculate it:

Earnings per Share/Price per Share = Earnings Yield

So for example, let's say that companies in the S&P 500 Index (one of the broadest measures of the U.S. equity market) are collectively earning $75 per share. And let's say that the S&P 500 is trading at around 1,500. Let's plug in the numbers:

Earnings per Share/Price per Share = Earnings Yield

$75/1,500 = 5\%$

What does this mean? If 10-year Treasuries are yielding more than 5 percent, then it could be argued that bonds are a better buy, since they're paying out more per dollar in the form of interest than stocks are paying out in the form of profits. Conversely, if 10-year Treasuries were yielding less than 5 percent, then you could argue that stocks would be the better bet.

Risks in Government Bonds

Like any other investment, there are risks associated with investing in government bonds. For example, all types of government bonds subject investors to *interest rate risk*. If market interest rates should climb shortly after you purchase your government bonds, the price on your older, lower-yielding government debt will fall. And if those prices fall more than the bonds themselves are yielding, then you could be faced with negative total returns in your government debt.

Just as with corporate bonds, interest rate risk in government bonds can be mitigated in a couple of ways. For starters, investors can simply choose to hold their government bonds until maturity, at which point they will recoup their original investment in full (regardless of what price the bond trades at before maturity). Secondly, investors can reduce the impact of interest rate risk by sticking to short- and intermediate-term bonds. The shorter the maturity of your bond, the sooner it will come due. And when interest rates are on the rise, the sooner you get your money back, the quicker you can turn around and reinvest it at higher market rates.

Government bonds also expose investors to *inflation risk*. That's the risk that you won't be able to outpace inflation if you invest all your money in fixed-income securities. To be sure, government bonds have historically outperformed inflation over long periods of time. In fact, according to Ibbotson, the average government bond investment has outpaced the rate of inflation by nearly twofold. But there have been several periods in history when government bonds lagged the rate of inflation. In fact, this took place throughout the 1940s, 1950s, 1960s, and 1970s. In the 1940s, for example, government bonds returned 3.2 percent, but inflation surged 5.4 percent. That meant that government bonds lost 2.2 percent in real terms during that decade. In the 1970s, government bonds did reasonably well, returning 5.5 percent in nominal terms. But factor in inflation, which was running at an annual rate of 7.4 percent that decade, and the 1970s proved to be a bad time to be investing in the government.

In fact, it was only starting in the 1980s that government bonds began to outpace inflation in a meaningful fashion. And this period, starting in the early 1980s and extending through 2005, was considered one of the greatest bull markets for bonds. That's because market interest rates, after peaking in the late 1970s and early 1980s, began a gradual and long descent that continued throughout the 1980s, 1990s, and the 2000s. See Figure 6-5.

Finally, we come to the topic of *credit risk*. As we just discussed, Treasury bonds will never expose investors to so-called credit risk because such bonds are backed by the full faith and credit of Uncle Sam. In fact, never in the modern history of the country has the federal government defaulted on its obligations. Nor will it.

Figure 6-5.   **Government Bonds Versus Inflation**

Investment	1920s	1930s	1940s	1950s	1960s	1970s	1980s	1990s	2000s
Long-Term									
Government Bonds	5.0	4.9	3.2	−0.1	1.4	5.5	12.6	8.8	9.9
Inflation	−1.1	−2.0	5.4	2.2	2.5	7.4	5.1	2.9	2.6

Source: Ibbotson Associates

But this does not mean that all government bonds are free of credit risk. In fact, there are a few types of popular government bonds and bond funds that do expose investors to some degree of default risk. So now might be a good time to go over the various types of government bonds available to individual investors.

Different Types of Government Bonds

TREASURY BONDS

Among the most widely held—and widely trusted—government bonds are Treasury securities. Treasury securities come in a variety of maturities. For example, ultra-short Treasuries, those that mature in six months or less, are called *Treasury bills.* T-bills are considered one of the most popular cash vehicles provided by the government. Treasury securities that mature in 2 to 10 years are referred to as *Treasury notes.* And Treasury securities that mature in more than 10 years are called *Treasury bonds.*

There is a tremendous advantage to investing in this form of government bond. To reiterate, because these bonds are backed by the full faith and credit of the federal government, Treasury securities do not expose investors to any credit risk. Think about it: If the federal government ever defaulted on its debt, it would cripple the country's ability to borrow money in the bond market in the future. If foreign investors fear that there is even the slightest degree of credit risk in owning U.S. bonds, then demand for these securities would shrivel, and the United States would have to start offering significantly higher rates on its bonds to attract willing investors. Because higher bond rates will translate into higher borrowing costs, there is a built-in incentive for Uncle Sam to make good on its obligations.

Another reason why individual investors favor Treasury bonds is that they can be purchased directly through the Treasury Department, without the aid of a brokerage (although, you can buy these bonds on the secondary market through a broker, as well).

One of the difficulties for small investors in the corporate debt market is to get good pricing on small lots of bonds. The bond market still tends to favor large, institutional traders. This is why many small investors choose to utilize professionally managed mutual funds and exchange-traded funds to gain their bond exposure. But as we pointed out in the previous chapter, bond fund investors do not have the ability to circumvent interest rate risks by buying and holding their debt to maturity (again, this is because bond mutual funds, unlike individual bonds, don't come with a single maturity date at which you are guaranteed recouping your original investments).

Because the federal government allows individuals to purchase Treasury bonds, notes, and bills, for as little as $1,000 at a time, they are an easily accessible investment for many financial plans. To learn more about what types of bonds can be purchased through the government, go to the Treasury Department's online site, www.treasurydirect.gov.

The stability, dependability, and accessibility of Treasury securities make them a core holding in most financial plans. In fact, the 10-year Treasury note is viewed as the benchmark bond for the entire U.S. fixed-income market.

This distinction used to be held by the 30-year Treasury bond, but for about four years, at the start of this decade, the federal government stopped issuing new 30-year Treasuries because it no longer felt it needed these long-term bonds to finance the national debt. This was at a time when the debt was shrinking since the federal government was running budget surpluses for a few years. But after the recession of 2001, Uncle Sam began running larger national deficits again, and the federal government felt that 30-year bonds were a cost-effective way to raise money to finance the U.S. deficit. Despite the resurrection of the 30-year bond, though, the 10-year Treasury note is still considered a core holding of safety-minded investors who want to be assured of a sure-and-steady stream of income throughout a long period of time.

Another reason why Treasury bonds are so popular is that they are easily accessible through mutual funds. According to Morningstar, there were around 100 different mutual funds that specialized in Treasury bonds in the spring of 2006.

Treasury Bond Funds

Government bond fund investors should always keep fees in mind. A mutual fund's fees and expenses are always deducted from its total returns. So a fund

Figure 6-6. Percentage of Lowest-Fee Funds That Generated Better-Than-Average Returns

Type of Fund	1 Year Returns	3 Year Returns	5 Year Returns
Government Bond Funds	89%	100%	100%
Corporate Bond Funds	67%	81%	64%
Municipal Bond Funds	78%	88%	100%

Source: Financial Research Corp.

that earns, say, 10 percent in real terms but charges 2 percent in fees will deliver total returns of 8 percent to its shareholders. These fees are pernicious to all investors, but particularly so for bond fund investors. Why?

While stocks might return 10 percent a year on average, bonds are likely to produce gains of only around 5 percent. If a bond fund were to charge 2 percent in fees and gain only 5 percent in the marketplace, those fees would eat away at a huge chunk of the fund's gains. In this case, this fund's after-tax returns would be only 3 percent, which is about the rate of inflation. This is why bond fund investors must be particularly mindful of fees.

Indeed, as a result of this dynamic, fees are actually one of the few consistent predictors of mutual fund performance. That's what Financial Research Corp. concluded in a recent study. FRC discovered that government bond funds that had the lowest fees among their peers were most likely to outperform their peers. That's because low-fee funds have a much shorter hurdle to overcome. The results of the FRC study are shown in Figure 6-6. The study divided each fund category into 10 segments based on total expense ratios. In most cases, funds in each of these five categories that ranked in the lowest decile in fees produced better-than-average returns.

INFLATION-PROTECTED TREASURY BONDS

As we've discussed, in addition to credit risk and interest rate risk, bond investors must be mindful of inflation risk, which is the possibility that your core fixed-income holdings won't be able to outpace inflation in a meaningful way over long periods of time. But Uncle Sam has recently introduced different types of Treasury bonds that allow investors to circumvent inflation risk altogether. Fixed-income investors can use these new-fangled Treasury inflation-protected bonds in their portfolios to outpace inflation at all times. A discussion of your options follows.

Option 1: TIPS Bonds

The first basic option for inflation-wary investors is to buy individual *Treasury Inflation Protected Securities,* or TIPS, as they are known. TIPS can be purchased directly from the federal government's Treasury Department, through its Web site, www.treasurydirect.gov. The good news is that Uncle Sam allows individual investors to purchase these intriguing securities without the need of a separate brokerage account. TIPS can be purchased in varying maturities of 5, 10, and 20 years. And they can be purchased for as little as $1,000, so even small investors can take part.

What are TIPS? They're the first government bonds that not only promise to give you back your principal in full at maturity but also guarantee that the buying power of that principal investment will remain in tact, regardless of how fast inflation is growing. As a result, investors who utilize these bonds in their portfolios can expect to do quite well during periods of hyperinflation, such as we witnessed in the 1970s. After all, TIPS, which protect your investments from the ravages of rising prices, are likely to become quite popular in periods of hyperinflation, as investors will be looking for shelter from the inflation storm. If that should come to pass, the growing popularity of these bonds should send their prices rising during inflationary times, which means you could do quite well on a total return basis.

How do TIPS work? These bonds have a unique, though simple structure. In a normal Treasury, investors might buy a bond at par value of $1,000. And so long as they decide to hold that debt to maturity, they can expect to receive $1,000 back per bond when the security comes due. But with a TIP, the federal government will adjust the par value of these bonds annually to reflect the rate of inflation, as measured by the Consumer Price Index. In other words, if inflation were to keep rising at the historical annual rate of 3 percent, the par value of these bonds would be adjusted higher by 3 percent a year so that the underlying value of the fixed-income security will always keep pace with inflation.

What if instead of inflation, the economy goes through a bout of deflation? Deflation is a rare economic phenomenon in which prices fall over time instead of rising, as demand for goods and services shrivels. When prices fall significantly over long periods of time, corporate profits are likely to tumble, and that could mean trouble for American households. For starters, their investments in the stock market are likely to lose ground during such periods, as equity prices tend to track corporate earnings growth. Moreover, if companies aren't able to turn a profit on their sales, they're likely to lay off workers to cut costs, in which case household incomes could drop severely. In the United States, the last meaningful period of deflation took place during the Great Depression. However, other global economies have experienced the ravages of deflation more recently, such as Japan.

Should deflation strike, the par value of your TIPS bonds will decrease accordingly since this value is pegged to the Consumer Price Index. However, if you hold these bonds to maturity, you are guaranteed to get back either the original par value of the bond or the inflation-adjusted par value—whichever is higher. In other words, you cannot lose your original investment in these securities, even if deflation becomes the real threat to the economy.

There's another way in which TIPS bonds protect investors from inflation. Like other Treasury bonds, the income that TIPS generate is based on a fixed rate of interest. So a 5 percent coupon rate on a $1,000 bond will generate $50 of annual income. But remember that every year the par value of these bonds is being adjusted higher based on the rate of inflation. So instead of being calculated off of the bond's original $1,000 par value, the income thrown off by these bonds will be based on the rising inflation-adjusted principal value.

For example, by the time these bonds may be nearing maturity, their par value could rise to $1,200. Based on that same 5 percent coupon rate, this would mean you would receive $60 of interest income per year per bond, not the $50 you were getting based on the original par value. So, in a period of rising inflation, you are likely to receive higher payouts to offset rising prices in addition to your increased principal value.

There is one big downside to investing in TIPS bonds, however. And it has to do with taxes. Remember, as long as inflation is on the rise, the federal government will increase the par value of your bond every year. Of course, you won't get to enjoy this bump in par value until you redeem the bond at maturity, perhaps 5 or 10 years down the road.

Unfortunately, the Internal Revenue Service will tax you on what's known as the *implied income* you receive thanks to the annual inflation adjustments. As a result of the relative tax-inefficiency of these instruments (relative to traditional Treasury bonds), you're probably better off holding them in a tax-deferred account such as an individual retirement account.

Option 2: TIPS Mutual Funds

If you don't want the hassle of buying and managing a portfolio of TIPS on your own, there are a growing number of professionally managed mutual funds that specialize in these inflation-adjusted bonds. Indeed, according to Morningstar, there were around 100 of these types of mutual funds in existence in the summer of 2006.

The advantage of going through a mutual fund is that you can get a whole basket of different TIPS—maturing at different dates—for a small initial investment.

In some cases, you can start an investment in a TIPS fund for as little as $2,000. And that money will buy you instant diversification of dozens if not hundreds of different TIPS. By comparison, a $2,000 investment will only buy you two TIPS bonds if you invest on your own.

Of course, if you invest in TIPS through a mutual fund, you will expose yourself to some degree of interest rate risk because funds do not have a single maturity date. Among some of the most popular funds are: Vanguard Inflation-Protected Securities Fund (www.vanguard.com), Fidelity Inflation-Protected Bond Fund (www.fidelity.com), and American Century Inflation-Adjusted Bond Fund (www.americancentury.com).

Option 3: I-Bonds

So far, we've discussed government bonds that can be purchased directly from Uncle Sam, and that can also be traded on a secondary market. But there is another type of government bond that doesn't trade on an exchange. These bonds are simply bought from the government and redeemed through the government.

They're called *savings bonds*. You're probably familiar with the old-fashioned Series EE savings bonds that grandparents have traditionally purchased for their grandkids. Recently, Uncle Sam began to issue an inflation-adjusted version of these savings bonds known as I-bonds.

If you want some inflation protection but don't have the wherewithal to buy an entire portfolio of TIPS for $1,000 a piece, I-bonds can be a decent alternative. Like TIPS, I-bonds can be purchased directly from the Treasury, at www.treasurydirect.gov. But unlike TIPS, I-bonds can be bought for as little as $50 a piece. These savings bonds are sold in denominations ranging from $50 to $10,000, though many small investors will opt to buy I-bonds in $100, $200, or $500 increments.

How do I-bonds protect your investment from inflation? Well, the interest rate on these bonds is determined by a couple of factors. The first is a fixed-rate of interest that is set and controlled by the federal government. But the other portion of your interest rate is determined by fluctuations in the Consumer Price Index. This means that during periods when inflation is running hot, the CPI-pegged portion of your interest rate will rise. And that means the overall interest thrown off by these savings bonds will grow too. Meanwhile, the principal value of these bonds is guaranteed by the Treasury Department.

Because I-bonds do not trade on an exchange, there is no price per se on these securities other than the face value. While I-bonds do not come with a specific maturity, you are required to hold them for at least one year. And if you redeem these bonds within five years of purchase, you will face a penalty (equal to roughly the three most recent months of interest income you collected). After five years, you can redeem your I-bonds without penalty at any time. Keep in mind that I-bonds earn interest for a maximum of 30 years and individual investors cannot purchase more than $30,000 worth of I-bonds in any calendar year.

TREASURY STRIPS

All bonds are loans that an investor extends to an institution in exchange for a promised rate of interest. But some bonds, by design, do not pay investors any interest during the life of the loan. Instead, these bonds agree to pay the investor all of the interest income that would have accrued over the life of the loan in a lump sum at maturity on top of the principal investment that the investor is owed.

These types of bonds are called *zero-coupon bonds,* and the government versions of these securities are known as *Treasury STRIPS* (which stands for Separate Trading of Registered Interest and Principal of Securities).

Why would a bond investor purchase an I.O.U. that doesn't pay any interest for several years, if not decades? Remember, some investors put money in bonds not because they need the annual income today, but because they want to preserve their money and ensure that an even bigger pot of money will be there for them for a specific use at a specific date in the future. For example, a parent who knows that college bills are due for a child a decade from now may not need to generate bond income in years 1 through 9. Instead, such investors may simply be interested in knowing that a decade from now, they will get their principal returned to them plus a known amount of accrued interest.

Investors in zero-coupon bonds, however, should be warned that they will face the same tax disadvantage as TIPS investors. In other words, even though STRIPS won't pay you any annual interest income, the federal government will still make you pay taxes on the *implied income*—in this case, the money you would have earned every year had your bond thrown off annual interest like a traditional fixed-income security.

MORTGAGE-BACKED SECURITIES

The whole point of investing in a Treasury bond is to avoid any form of credit risk. But not all government bonds shield investors from the risk of default or economic turmoil. Take certain *mortgage-backed securities.*

While a corporate bond is backed by the assets of the issuing company and while a Treasury bond is backed by the full faith and credit of Uncle Sam, mortgage-backed securities are a little different. They are in essence bonds created by bundling together pools of mortgage loans issued to families and institutions. Those loans are frequently sold and then packaged into mortgage-backed securities by a number of players in the mortgage market.

For investors, these types of bonds offer the potential for higher yields, since the interest rate generated by this debt is linked to the cash flow of the underlying mortgages. These yields can be especially attractive relative to Treasury bond yields in periods when the economy and housing market are going strong.

Some mortgage-backed securities do come with government guarantees. For example, if you are investing in mortgage-backed bonds approved by the Government National Mortgage Association, otherwise known as "Ginnie Mae," then these securities are backed by the full faith and credit of Uncle Sam. Ginnie Mae is, after all, a part of the U.S. Department of Housing and Urban Development.

On the other hand, some mortgage-backed securities are sold by quasi-government agencies that are classified as *government-sponsored enterprises* (GSEs). Both the Federal National Mortgage Association (otherwise known as "Fannie Mae") and the competing Federal Home Loan Mortgage Corporation ("Freddie Mac") were created years ago to promote liquidity and efficiency in the mortgage market. Both GSEs function in much the same way. They were set up by the government to purchase mortgages in the secondary market and to securitize those loans in hopes of expanding the mortgage lending market. By doing so, the two firms, which are actually publicly traded companies today, hope to increase the availability of home loans to the general public and to reduce the costs of mortgages.

Investors should understand that mortgage-backed securities issued by these government-sponsored enterprises are not backed by Uncle Sam. While both Fannie Mae and Freddie Mac are regulated by the U.S. government, they are also public corporations that raise their own funds in the capital markets and are responsible for their own balance sheets. Therefore, one of the risks that investors in these mortgage-backed securities may face is the credit risk of Fannie and Freddie.

An additional risk that arises with all mortgage-backed securities is the risk of home owners prepaying their loans faster than expected. For instance, a 30-year Treasury bond will guarantee that over the course of its life, it will pay a consistent and constant stream of interest income. But mortgage-backed securities cannot always make that promise. If interest rates were to fall, for instance, home owners who took out mortgages may start to refinance their loans or sell their homes quickly to take advantage of the cheaper borrowing costs. As mortgages are prepaid in advance, the amount of income thrown off by these bundles of loans could diminish.

MUNICIPAL BONDS

Treasury bonds are issued by the federal government. Municipal bonds, on the other hand, are issued by states, counties, municipalities, local agencies, and school districts to fund a variety of projects. These can include anything from highway repair to school construction.

The "muni" bond universe consists of a couple of different types of bonds. *General obligation bonds,* for instance, are issued by states, counties, or local governments for general purposes. Because they are issued by governments that have taxing authority—in other words, if the municipality runs into a budget crisis, it could always raise funds by increasing property taxes—these types of municipal bonds are considered reasonably safe. *Revenue bonds,* on the other hand, are typically floated by an agency of a state or local government for a very specific project. While revenue bondholders are typically paid from the receipts generated from that project, like highway or tunnel tolls, there is no explicit promise that the state or municipality will bail out these bond issuers should the projects run into financial difficulties.

This brings us to a critical point when it comes to municipal debt: such debt exposes investors to credit risk. Remember, if push comes to shove, Uncle Sam can literally print money. So you know that Treasury bonds are safe. But states and local governments, while they have taxing authority, do not circulate their own currency. So they don't have the authority to print more money if they are falling behind in their obligations to lenders. This means that in a real financial crisis, municipalities and states might default on their bonds.

Think back to the early 1990s, when Orange County, California, was forced to file for bankruptcy in part as a result of bad investment decisions that went awry. To be sure, defaults are rare in the municipal bond world, much rarer than in the corporate fixed-income market. But municipal budgets, like corporate profits, are influenced by the economy. Indeed, when household incomes are rising, property values are soaring, and when consumers are spending, tax receipts collected by cities and states are likely to overflow. During such times, muni bond investors are comforted by the strong financial conditions of the issuing government bodies.

However, when the economy sours, income tax receipts are likely to drop off, property tax revenues are likely to plateau, and sales taxes aren't likely to generate quite as much as they did during the boom times. It's during economic slowdowns such as these when fears of muni bond defaults rise.

As a result of this credit risk, municipal bond investors must always be mindful of the financial health of the state or municipal government whose bonds they are thinking of purchasing. The good news is, just as the major credit rating agencies grade the risk level of corporate debt, they also provide ratings for muni debt.

While munis expose investors to a layer of credit risk, they compensate them through a key tax advantage. The interest income generated by munis is federally tax free, in much the same way that Treasury bonds are state income tax free. Moreover, if you invest in a municipal bond that was issued by your home state, interest on that bond is also likely to be state tax free as well. This is why muni bonds are often a favorite investment for investors in high tax brackets and in states with high taxes.

As a result of the tax advantage, however, munis don't yield as much interest as Treasuries do, at least not on paper. In fact, sometimes, the spread between muni and Treasury yields can look quite large. But you have to keep in mind that the muni yield is tax free, while the Treasury yield is subject to federal taxes.

To figure out whether a lower-yielding muni is more or less attractive than a Treasury bond, you have to figure out its so-called *taxable-equivalent yield*. The formula is simple:

Muni bond yield/(1 minus your tax bracket)

= Taxable equivalent treasury yield

For example, let's say you own a muni that's yielding 3 percent. And say you fall in the 35 percent federal tax bracket. Let's plug in the numbers:

Muni bond yield/(1 minus your tax bracket) = Taxable equivalent treasury yield

$$0.3/(1 - 0.35) = 0.4615, \text{ or } 4.62\%$$

Based on this calculation, if your muni is yielding 3 percent but Treasury bonds are yielding less than 4.62 percent, it may well be worth it to consider that tax-free muni bond. However, if Treasuries are yielding more than 4.62 percent (in this particular scenario), you may be better off in safer Treasury bonds. See Figure 6-7 for a comparison of taxable yields of municipal bonds and Treasury securities. For example, if you are in the 25 percent tax bracket, a muni bond yield of 3 percent is the equivalent of a Treasury yielding 4 percent.

Government Cash

In addition to bonds, the government also issues cash-equivalent securities that short-term investors should also consider. The most common government cash vehicle is a Treasury bill, or T-bill. A T-bill is a short-term security that comes with a set maturity. But unlike notes and bonds that mature anywhere from two

Figure 6-7. Municipal Bond Taxable Equivalent Yields

Muni Bond Yield	Tax Bracket				
	15%	25%	28%	33%	35%
2%	2.35%	2.67%	2.78%	2.99%	3.08%
3%	3.53%	4.00%	4.17%	4.48%	4.62%
4%	4.71%	5.33%	5.56%	5.97%	6.15%
5%	5.88%	6.67%	6.94%	7.46%	7.69%
6%	7.06%	8.00%	8.33%	8.96%	9.23%
7%	8.24%	9.33%	9.72%	10.45%	10.77%

years to 30 years, T-bills mature in six months or less. In fact, they are technically auctioned off in maturities of 4 weeks, 13 weeks, and 26 weeks.

Like TIPS, notes, and bonds, T-bills can be purchased directly from the Treasury Department (in increments of $1,000) or through a traditional brokerage account. And like TIPS, notes, and bonds, T-bills are backed by the full faith and credit of Uncle Sam. This means T-bills are as safe if not safer than other guaranteed cash accounts, such as federally insured savings accounts, money market accounts, and certificates of deposit.

But unlike most government bonds, which pay interest throughout the life of the loan, T-bills are structured somewhat differently. Contrary to popular opinion, T-bills do not pay out any direct form of interest. Instead, these bills are sold at auction, by the government, at prices that are below par value.

So for instance, the government may sell you a T-bill with a face value of $1,000 for only $950. Now, when the bill matures in 4, 13, or 26 weeks, you can redeem the security though the government and receive the full $1,000. The difference between what you paid for the bill (in this case, $950) and the par value of the security (in this case, $1,000) represents the interest you earn on the account. So for instance, in this case, you would have earned roughly 5 percent on your money.

T-bills are a great place to park money if you know precisely when you will need to spend it. That's because like bank certificates of deposit, T-bills come with a set maturity. But because they tie up your money for 4, 13, or 26 weeks, they might not be the most appropriate place to stash your emergency cash. While T-bills, like other government bonds, can be sold before maturity on the open market, you may not be able to get your full par value back, which means you will be leaving some interest income on the table by selling early.

Quiz for Chapter 6

1. Investors often put money into government bonds to avoid which type of risk?
    a. Credit risk
    b. Interest rate risk
    c. Inflation risk
    d. All of the above

2. Why are United States Treasury bonds considered among the safest form of investments?
    a. The U.S. government has one of the highest credit ratings in the industry.
    b. Treasury bonds are backed by the U.S. government, which unlike companies cannot file for bankruptcy.
    c. They are bonds, and bonds are inherently safe.

3. One reason why investors favor U.S. Treasury bonds is that interest earned on these securities is not subject to federal income taxes.
    a. True
    b. False

4. During what circumstances are government bonds likely to perform well?
    a. Periods of economic uncertainty, such as times of war
    b. Periods when interest rates are falling
    c. Both A and B
    d. None of the above

5. How can investors minimize interest rate risk on a government bond?
    a. Buy longer-term government debt.
    b. Buy shorter-term government debt.
    c. Invest in a diversified bond mutual fund.

6. Which of the following forms of debt offers investors the most inflation protection?
    a. TIPS
    b. High-yield bonds
    c. Short-term T-bills

7. Since they are government bonds, municipal debt is as safe as Treasury bonds.
    a. True
    b. False

8. What distinguishes Treasury STRIPS from other types of government bonds?
    a. Interest is paid annually instead of semiannually.
    b. Interest is paid semiannually instead of annually.
    c. Interest is paid in a lump sum when the bond matures.

9. Mortgage-backed securities issued by government-sponsored enterprises are as safe as Treasury bonds.
    a. True
    b. False

10. Which of the following government securities offers the shortest maturities?
    a. Treasury bonds
    b. Treasury bills
    c. Treasury notes

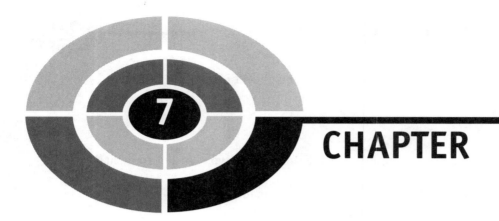

CHAPTER

Real Estate

What Is Real Estate?

Of all the investments that go into your financial plan, real estate will probably play the biggest role. In fact, one particular form of real estate investing—the purchase of your primary home—is likely to be the single-largest investment you will ever make in your life. Think about it: In what other investment arena are you likely to commit possibly half a million dollars or more in a single financial transaction?

While about half of all American households own stocks—in most cases indirectly through mutual funds—70 percent of Americans own real estate directly, in the form of their homes. This makes home ownership the single most prevalent form of investing in America. It has also proven itself to be a highly effective way to build wealth for your financial plan. According to a recent study by the Joint Center for Housing Studies at Harvard University, American homeowners enjoyed median net wealth (defined as the total value of their financial and nonfinancial assets minus all their debt) of nearly $172,000 at the start of this decade. By comparison, the typical renter enjoyed net wealth of less than $5,000.

Figure 7-1.   Median Wealth of Households Based on Home Ownership

	Home Owners	Renters	All Households
Under 65	$154,100	$4,500	$67,900
65–74	$249,700	$6,000	$176,700
74 or older	$243,000	$7,000	$151,400
All Ages	$171,800	$4,800	$86,100

Source: 2001 Survey of Consumer Finances, Joint Center for Housing Studies, Harvard University

Among older homeowners, those 65 to 74, their investment in residential real estate made an even bigger difference in terms of the health of their financial plan. The median homeowner 65 to 74 reported net wealth of around $250,000, versus just $6,000 among their counterparts who don't own their own homes. See Figure 7-1.

The irony is that until recently many homeowners did not view the purchase of a single-family home as an investment. And even today, following one of the biggest bull markets in residential real estate, many families still regard home ownership as distinct from, say, investing in stocks or bonds. Some of this has to do with the fact that home ownership is one of the few investments that serve a dual purpose. Your home isn't only a financial asset; it provides your family with shelter. So even if the home never appreciates in value throughout your holding period, the transaction will still have served a useful purpose.

But it's important to realize that every purchase of real estate—whether it's residential real estate, rental properties, or shares of commercial real estate ventures—is a form of investing.

For starters, real estate purchases represent a bet on the health of the economy, just like stocks. In fact, it is a bet on many different economies. First and foremost, it is a bet on the national economy. For your home or any piece of real estate to appreciate in value, there must be a market of potential buyers who are willing to take the property off your hands. And only when times are flush—for instance, when would-be buyers are fully employed, are enjoying rising incomes, and are seeing real gains in their other investments, such as their equity holdings—are other investors likely to step into the market and bid up your property.

But real estate is also a hard asset. It is also an immovable asset. Whether it's a piece of land, a home, or a commercial rental building, real estate investments are tied to their location. This means that by definition, your real estate investment is a bet on the local economy.

Indeed, the national economy could be doing just fine, creating a sufficient number of jobs to spur demand in real estate around the country. But if your state or local economy is suffering through a slowdown, would-be buyers might be in short supply in your immediate region. Moreover, if your region is suffering through a recession, outsiders are unlikely to move to that area, which means your potential pool of would-be buyers isn't likely to grow. This poses a significant risk to any real estate investment. And it raises a key point: The housing market is far less liquid than the equity or fixed-income markets. On Wall Street, you can always find a buyer for the securities you own or a seller for securities you want. On Main Street, it may take days, weeks, months, or even longer to find even a single interested buyer for your property.

To be sure, there are things that investors can do to improve the outlook of their properties. If you own a home, you could make improvements to the house itself by updating the kitchen, renovating the bathroom, or adding a garage. But those improvements won't be converted into appreciable profits unless there is sufficient pent-up demand for properties in your city, neighborhood, and block.

Finally, real estate is also a bet on your personal economy. This is certainly true for homeownership. Again, while financial assets like stocks or bonds are portable, physical real estate is not. This means that just as your home is fixed to its location, you are financially attached to the home. Indeed, buying a home in a particular location requires some sense of confidence in your own employment situation. After all, if you were to lose your job, you'd risk falling behind on your mortgage. To be sure, you could always sell the house if you lose your job, but you might not be able to sell it at a beneficial price given your need to sell quickly. This possibility adds an additional layer of risk to real estate investing.

Why Real Estate?

There are a number of reasons to add real estate to your financial plan. For starters, real estate is a hard asset. And like other physical assets such as commodities, home prices have historically risen faster on average than the overall rate of inflation.

Indeed, the median sales price on a single-family home sold in the United States has risen from $130,500 in 1975 (based on current dollars) to $219,000 at the end of 2005. This means that over this 30-year stretch, the average home price has appreciated roughly 1.7 percentage points above the annual rate of inflation each year. Of course, other major assets have risen faster than that. See Figure 7-2. Long-term government bonds, for example have grown around 2.5 percentage points faster than the rate of inflation since 1926. Equities have climbed more than 7 percentage points faster than consumer prices.

You should also keep in mind that the residential real estate market is composed of dozens of separate major metropolitan regions. And in many regions of the country, home prices have increased at a significantly faster rate than the

Figure 7-2.   Median Sales Price on Existing Single-Family Homes, 1975–2005

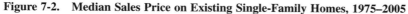
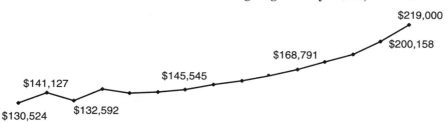

1975 1980 1985 1990 1995 1996 1997 1998 1999 2000 2001 2002 2003 2004 2005

Source: Joint Study for Housing Studies, Harvard University

national average. The Los Angeles metropolitan region, for example, saw its properties rise around 3 percentage points faster than the overall rate of inflation between 1990 and 2005. During that same period, the New York housing market appreciated 3.5 percentage points faster. And Miami's housing market soared nearly 5.3 percentage points higher than CPI. So real estate, like equities, can be a decent inflation hedge over the long-term.

However, for many homeowners, inflation is a secondary reason for buying a house. For many families, the decision to purchase a home boils down to this: You have to live somewhere, so why not kill two birds with one stone and purchase the property in which you reside? And why pay rent to a landlord when you can build equity in an investment while enjoying the shelter it provides.

Fortunately, owning a home—or other forms of real estate—can actually shelter your financial portfolio from market storms as well. This is because owning real property can help diversify a broader financial portfolio of stocks and bonds.

Indeed, history has shown that home prices tend not to move in lock step with the equity market. Between March 2000 and October 2002, for example, the S&P 500 Index of large U.S. stocks lost nearly 50 percent of its value, during one of the worst bear markets in equities in recent history. The Nasdaq composite index of growth stocks fell even harder, losing nearly 75 percent of its market value. But during this stretch, the median sales price for existing single-family homes actually rose. See Figure 7-3.

Nationally, home prices climbed nearly 20 percent between March 2000 and October 2002, according to data compiled by the National Association of Realtors.

Figure 7-3.   Housing Market versus Stock Market*

Performance
March 2000–October 2002

U.S. Housing Market	+19.7%
Northeast	+26.6%
Midwest	+18.6%
South	+21.9%
West	+19.7%
S&P 500 Index	−49.2%

*Housing market data based on sales of existing single-family homes.

And in some regions of the country, the gains were even more pronounced. In the Northeast, for example, median sales prices on single-family homes rose nearly 27 percent. Many economists credit the strong gains enjoyed in the housing market for propping up consumers and consumer spending during what turned out to be one of the worst periods for stocks since World War II.

Single-family homes aren't the only types of real estate investments that can be used to diversify a portfolio. Investors can also gain exposure to real estate through shares of real estate investment trusts (which we'll discuss in a moment) as well as mutual funds that invest in REITs.

There are a couple of ways we can measure this diversification factor. For starters, we can look at the *correlation* between real estate investments and other assets like stocks and bonds. Statistically, any two investments that enjoy a correlation factor of 1.0 are said to move in lockstep with one another. For example, large-cap U.S. stocks and mid-cap U.S. stocks enjoy a correlation of 0.96 percent, according to Morningstar. This means that when large stocks zig, mid-cap stocks zig as well. But real estate funds are only 0.49 percent correlated with U.S. stocks, according to Morningstar. And they are even less correlated—0.26 percent—to bonds. What's more, real estate funds have a negative correlation with cash, meaning there's no relationship between the two assets at all. See Figure 7-4.

Investors also rely on a second statistical measure to gauge portfolio diversification. It's called *R-squared*. This is simply a mathematical estimation of how

Figure 7-4.   Real Estate's Correlation to Other Assets (May 2006)

	Correlation Factor*
U.S. Stocks (S&P 500 Index)	0.49%
Foreign Stocks (MSCI EAFE Index)	0.41%
Bonds (Lehman Brothers Index)	0.26%
Cash (Money Market Funds)	−0.11%

*A correlation of 1.00% means the two assets move in lockstep.

Source: Morningstar

Figure 7-5.   Correlations to the S&P 500

Investment	R-Squared (May 2006)
Large Growth Stocks	79
European Stocks	76
Emerging Markets Stocks	73
Technology Stocks	64
Telecommunications Stocks	60
Financial Stocks	60
Precious Metals	36
Healthcare Stocks	30
Real Estate	24

Source: Morningstar

much of an investment's behavior can be explained by the movements of a benchmark index. Recently, Morningstar calculated the R-squared readings of various asset classes against the S&P 500 Index of large stocks. Since the typical large-cap growth stock fund invests in many companies found in the S&P 500, you would expect it to have a fairly high R-squared. And in fact, it does. The average large-cap growth stock fund sports an R-squared of nearly 80 percent. But when Morningstar studied other types of funds, it found that across the entire fund universe, real estate portfolios had among the lowest R-squared readings against the S&P 500: 24 percent. This means that less than one-fourth of the movements of real estate-oriented stocks can be attributed to fluctuations in the S&P 500. From a diversification stand point, this is a huge factor. See Figure 7-5.

Different Types of Real Estate

PRIMARY HOMES

After the bear market in stocks in 2000, investors shifted gears. The equity markets were no longer viewed as the surest way to financial success. Between 2001 and 2005, that distinction belonged to home ownership.

During that stretch, a record number of American families purchased homes. Indeed, the number of existing single-family home sales jumped 31 percent, new home sales grew 41 percent, and sales of condominiums and co-ops ballooned 49 percent between 2001 and 2005. Not surprisingly home prices set record highs during this stretch. The median price on single-family homes, for example, jumped 28 percent to $220,000 in this period. And as for condos, their median prices rose 43 percent to nearly $224,000.

There are myriad reasons to own a home. For starters, homes are the only asset class that offers tangible control. You can literally see your house, touch it, and step into it. You can physically improve it too. Anyone can add value to this asset by repairing it, fixing it, renovating it, redecorating it, and beautifying it. In fact, between 2004 and 2005, Americans put more than $420 billion worth of fixes and renovations into their properties.

Perhaps the biggest advantage to investing in your home is that you can literally live in this asset. From an investment standpoint, this offers families tremendous flexibility. For instance, if you owned a portfolio of stocks that did nothing over the course of a decade, you'd probably start to get antsy. And you'd probably look for reasons to sell. But in a home, you can afford to be patient. After all, if the housing market stalls out, you can always just live in the home and enjoy it for what it is—a shelter—even if it takes years for home prices in your neighborhood to rise. This makes primary homes an ultimate buy-and-hold vehicle.

Of course, there are other reasons to favor home investments. Among them are leverage, tax benefits, and cash-flow flexibility.

Leverage

The modern mortgage industry now allows millions of potential homebuyers to purchase a home with as little as 5 percent down. In fact, many loan programs will allow buyers to put zero down and to actually borrow more than 100 percent of the value of the property. As we discussed earlier, this is known as leverage. And this ability to borrow large sums of money so that you can invest in an asset that you are reasonably certain will appreciate in value over time can be an effective tool to grow your financial plan.

For example, say you bought a home in 2003 for $178,800 (this was the median price on a single family home in the United States that year). And say you put 5 percent down, or $8,940. Now say you sold it in 2005, at the median sales price of $219,600. On paper, this house appreciated 23 percent (that's from $178,800 to $219,600). But your actual investment in this house went up 356 percent. After all, you only put $8,940 of your own money down and turned it into a gross profit of $40,800. (Of course, you also paid mortgage bills during this time, but had you not purchased the home, you would have had to pay rent to live somewhere.)

Tax Benefits

In an earlier chapter, we discussed how interest expenses on home mortgages are tax deductible, provided that the total value of your mortgage does not exceed $1 million. But there's another big tax advantage to investing in a primary home.

If you sell your primary residence at a profit, you are allowed to exclude from capital gains up to $250,000 if you're single and $500,000 for married couples filing jointly.

That's how much *appreciation* you can exclude from capital gains taxes, not the sale price of the home. So in theory, if you and your spouse purchase a home for $500,000 and sell it for $1 million, the entire profit—$500,000—can escape capital gains taxes. This gives home ownership a huge advantage over stock investing. There is a caveat, however. To claim this tax break, the property in question has to have been your primary residence for two of the past five years. And you can only take advantage of this tax break once every two years.

Cash-Flow Flexibility

While it's not always advisable to pull equity out of your home—in fact, many financial planners criticized homeowners for using their homes like a cash machine at the start of this decade—the fact remains that homes do provide families with an emergency source of cash. The two easiest ways to access this money is through a home-equity loan or a home-equity line of credit. In a home-equity loan, you borrow a specific amount of money against your home value, and pay back the loan amount in monthly installments. A home-equity line of credit, on the other hand, works much like a credit card. It is a line of credit that you do not necessarily have to tap but is there for you in case an emergency arises. Because both loans are secured against the house, lending rates on both borrowing instruments are not too much higher than mortgage rates. Interest on home-equity debt is also tax deductible, up to loan values of $100,000. The tax deductibility of home-equity loan interest is one reason why many families with credit card balances choose to pay off their cards using home equity. This way, you can pay off your cards at favorable interest rates while taking advantage of the tax benefit of these loans.

Housing Market Risks

Of course, as with all investments, there are risks associated with home ownership. For example, when investors put their money to work in the equity markets, they typically do so in a diversified fashion, often through a mutual fund. This way, if a handful of their individual investments go south, the remainder of the portfolio should remain in tact. But in the housing market, homeowners will typically purchase one property at a time. This exposes homeowners to a couple of forms of risk. One is the risk that your home in particular will lose value. This could happen for any number of reasons, including environmental or aesthetic concerns

specific to your home or lot. Or more likely, the metropolitan region in which your home resides may be soft, even if the national housing market is flourishing.

The fact is that there are no guarantees that your home will enjoy the type of price appreciation that the national housing market experienced at the start of this decade. And there are no guarantees that your home values will rise—period. It all depends on the local market in which you purchase the property.

For example, between 1990 and 2000, the U.S. housing market appreciated by about 10 percent, based on home-sale prices. But not all regions of the country took part in this growth. Average home prices in the Northeast, for example, were flat throughout this decade, meaning investors saw zero percent gains on their real estate investments. And there were many individual cities that saw average home prices fall substantially. Homes in Baltimore, for example, lost 4 percent of their value between 1990 and 2000. Buffalo's housing market fell more than 10 percent. And homeowners in Allentown, Pennsylvania, saw their investments plummet more than 13 percent, on average, during that decade. Syracuse, N.Y., residents, lost $1 out of every $5 they put into their home during this troublesome stretch in housing. So the risks are very real.

There is a tendency among all investors to believe that things will always be the way they are today. It's a quirk of behavioral finance. For instance, when technology stocks were doing well in the late 1990s, many investors assumed that technology stocks would always be a fast path to easy money. But after the Internet bubble burst in 2000, investors understood that tech stocks, like all investments, run in cycles. And there will be times when they underperform other assets.

Homeowners need to be similarly mindful that just because housing prices soared between 2001 and 2005, it doesn't mean that home prices will always appreciate in that fashion. The Los Angeles housing market offers a perfect illustration. Investors marveled at how quickly home prices rose in the L.A. market between 2001 and 2005. During this brief period, the average price of a single-family home sold in Southern California jumped 86 percent, dwarfing gains achieved in most other asset classes. But to focus only on this four-year window of time is to miss out on the bigger picture. Between 1990 and 2000, home prices in L.A. actually tumbled 21 percent, on average. It's only when you look at the long history of home prices do you get a clearer picture of how this asset performs over time—and is likely to perform for you. What you'll find is that prices will likely rise over time, but much more modestly than you might expect.

SECOND HOMES

In recent years, the number of investors who've purchased second homes has grown considerably. Between 1995 and 2005, the ranks of second-home owners swelled by 1.2 million, representing a 22 percent increase. Part of the allure of second-home ownership is certainly tied to the rapid rise in real estate prices since 2001.

However, other factors have contributed to this rise. For instance, historically low interest rates at the start of this decade made borrowing significantly cheaper, enhancing the leverage that second-home owners could enjoy. Moreover, the federal government has made it tax advantageous to own two properties. Mortgage interest is tax deductible for second-home loans, just as it is on primary homes, provided that the total value of your combined home-acquisition mortgages doesn't exceed $1 million. (There is no deduction for mortgage interest on third homes or beyond).

Instead of encouraging the purchase of second homes, the federal government used to encourage home owners to purchase ever-larger properties. Prior to 1997, the government only gave a capital gains tax break on home-sale profits if the money was used to purchase a more expensive house within two years of the original sale. But after 1997, the government broadened the favorable treatment on capital gains for primary homes. And many housing experts believe that this has encouraged homeowners to use the proceeds of the tax break to purchase second homes, rather than simply larger primary residences.

Ironically, second homes both add and remove risk to your overall financial plan. If the second home is purchased in a separate community, away from your primary residence, it could be viewed as a vehicle through which you're diversifying your real estate portfolio. To a certain extent, this could remove some of the single-property risk and single-market risk posed by owning just one property. On the other hand, it will concentrate your financial plan's dependence on the health of the national housing market.

RENTAL PROPERTIES

The way most homeowners make money on their properties is through price appreciation over time. But homes are also an investment through which you can generate income. The most common strategy is to purchase rental property or convert an existing property into a rental unit.

Rental property can be anything from renting out a room in your existing single-family home or buying an entire multifamily property and becoming a landlord. What makes these investments appealing is that they generate wealth in a couple of ways. For starters, you can take advantage of the exact same leverage that primary homeowners receive through a mortgage. But instead of living in the home while you wait for the property to appreciate, you rent it out and receive monthly income in the form of rent checks.

The additional income you can expect to receive from a rental property will likely help you obtain financing for that investment. Lenders will consider the cash flow from anticipated monthly rent checks when assessing your ability to cover monthly mortgage payments on the rental property. In the best of all possible worlds, the amount of money you collect from your renter or renters will cover most of your mortgage. If your rental income exceeds your mortgage payments, then you are literally being paid to wait for your property to appreciate.

Even if your rental income does not cover your entire mortgage, as a landlord you would be eligible for a number of deductions, including tax breaks on the following expenses:

- Real estate taxes
- Insurance costs (including liability, fire, and flood insurance)
- Maintenance fees for building upkeep
- Depreciation of the building
- Depreciation of appliances and other furnishings in the building
- The cost of any repairs you made to the property
- Advertising costs to attract tenants
- Commissions paid to brokers to attract tenants
- Cleaning supplies
- Transportation to and from the property (if you don't live on site)
- Legal fees
- Court costs for evictions
- Professional fees for tax advice

However, investors who decide to become landlords need to realize that they are choosing to become small businesses. And just like any other business, there are a number of risks and headaches associated with dealing with customers—in this case, your renters.

For starters, all landlords must consider the risk of not being able to find renters in their local regions. What's more, even if you manage to attract renters, there are no guarantees that those tenants will always be on time with their rent checks. For some landlords, even missing a few months of rent checks could be a blow to their cash flow.

And even if you are able to attract responsible renters, there are no guarantees that you will consistently be able to charge the amount of rent that you would like. Just as the housing market is cyclical, so is the rental market. And if the economy slows considerably, you have to factor in the possibility that you may have to reduce rents to get business. Unfortunately, one of the expenses that Uncle Sam will not let you deduct is the cost of losses caused by vacancies in your property.

This means that before you decide to buy rental property, you should determine how many months of vacancy you can afford, based on the monthly mortgage you

owe on the property. And you need to do your homework on the neighborhood in which you are thinking of buying rental property. The next sidebar offers a checklist of issues that you need study before taking this plunge.

Checklist for Would-Be Landlords

- Neighborhood vacancy rates
- Neighborhood rental rate
- Renovation and repair costs for building
- State and local building requirements for apartment owners
- State and local fire code requirements
- State and local eviction and collection laws
- Property and liability insurance requirements
- Insurance costs
- Maintenance costs
- Costs for professional building management and maintenance service
- Utilities
- Parking restrictions or requirements
- Property taxes
- Legal consultation
- Tax and accounting consultation

Real Estate Investment Trusts

WHAT ARE REITs

So far, we've discussed ways investors can purchase physical real estate. But there is an alternative way to invest in real estate that does not require you to commit to a 30-year mortgage worth hundreds of thousands of dollars. It's called a *real estate investment trust,* or REIT, for short.

A REIT is a company whose sole purpose is to invest in and manage large real estate ventures. Typically, REITs will own stakes in commercial properties, such as shopping centers, office buildings, warehouses, and hotels. And individual real estate investment trusts often specialize in a particular segment of the commercial market. For example, AMB Property is a REIT that owns industrial buildings; Simon Property Group focuses on buying and building shopping malls. Some REITs, like Essex Property Trust, even invest in large apartment buildings, giving shareholders indirect exposure to the residential real estate market.

REITs have been around since 1960 to give small investors the ability to gain exposure to the commercial real estate market. But only recently—thanks to the rapid growth in the industry and the rise in investor interest in real estate— have REITs been embraced as a mainstream investment. In fact, 11 of the 500 companies in the S&P 500 Index are now real estate investment trusts. See Figure 7-6.

According to the National Association of Real Estate Investment Trusts, there are approximately 200 publicly traded REITS in the United States, managing about $475 billion in assets. This universe can be broken down into three general categories. Those companies that own and manage residential and/or commercial properties are called *equity REITs* (these REITs dominate the marketplace). Those that extend and purchase mortgages used by other firms to invest in real estate are called *mortgage REITs* (mortgage REITs also invest in mortgage-backed securities). And *hybrid REITs* are those that do a little bit of both.

Because a REIT is a publicly traded real estate company, its shares trade on major stock exchanges, just like any other stock. This means REITs are highly liquid investments that are accessible to small investors. In addition to individual REIT shares, investors can access this market through specialized mutual funds or

Figure 7-6.   REITs in the S&P 500

Company	Ticker Symbol	Date Added to S&P 500
Equity Office Properties Trust	EOP	10/1/2001
Equity Residential	EQR	11/1/2001
Plum Creek Timber	PCL	1/16/2002
Simon Property Group	SPG	6/25/2002
AIMCO	AIV	3/31/2003
ProLogis	PLD	7/16/2003
Archstone-Smith	ASN	12/17/2004
Vornado Realty Trust	VNO	8/11/2005
Public Storage	PSA	8/18/2005
Boston Properties	BXP	3/31/2006
Kimco Realty Corp.	KIM	3/31/2006

exchange-traded funds that invest in a basket of REITs. According to Morningstar, there are more than 300 REIT funds for investors to choose from.

WHY REITs?

There are two reasons why investors should consider adding a small exposure to REITs—perhaps 5 to 10 percent—to their financial plans. For starters, REITs have been among the best-performing asset classes over the past 30 years. Indeed, between December 1975 and December 2005, the average REIT has delivered annualized total returns of 13.8 percent. That's more than a full percentage point better than the S&P 500 performed during this same period. Meanwhile, REITs trounced the Dow Jones industrial average, which has returned less than 9 percent a year during this stretch. See Figure 7-7.

Although there are no guarantees that REITs will be able to consistently out-perform the S&P 500 in the future, REITs do serve another purpose—and that is to diversify a broad portfolio of stocks and bonds and cash. As we noted earlier in this chapter, the value of real estate is that it is an uncorrelated asset. It will not move in tandem with your other investments, including equities. As a result, a small, diversified dose of real estate investment trusts can help smooth out the ride in your financial plan.

A recent study by Ibbotson Associates confirms this. Ibbotson researchers compared three basic portfolios. The first invested 50 percent of its assets in stocks, 40 percent in bonds, and 10 percent in cash. The second portfolio invested some-what similarly, but took 5 percent of the money out of bonds and another 5 percent from stocks to create a 10 percent REIT exposure. The third portfolio took another

Figure 7-7.   Annual Total Returns for REITs versus Other Asset Classes (December 1975–December 2005)

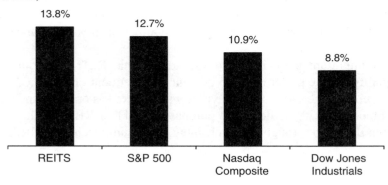

Figure 7-8.   **Performance of REITs in the S&P 500 from 1972 to 2004**

	Portfolio 1	Portfolio 2	Portfolio 3
Stocks	50%	45%	40%
Bonds	40%	35%	30%
T-Bills	10%	10%	10%
REITs	0	10%	20%
Return	10.9%	11.2%	11.6%
Risk	10.6%	10.3%	10.1%

Source: Ibboston Associates

5 percent out of stocks and another 5 percent out of bonds and created a 20 percent REIT exposure (see Figure 7-8).

Between 1972 and 2004, Portfolio 1 returned a respectable 10.9 percent a year, with a risk measure of 10.6 percent. On the other hand, Portfolio 2, which invested 10 percent of its assets in REITs, did even better. It returned 11.2 percent a year. And more importantly, it did so with slightly less risk. Finally, the third portfolio, which had the most REIT exposure, did the best of all. It returned 11.6 percent a year. And just as importantly, it did so with the least amount of volatility.

So why not invest 20 percent or more of your money in REITs? Some investors do. But it's important to understand how REITs generate their returns.

The vast majority of REIT returns come in the form of income, otherwise known as dividends. As owners of commercial properties, REITs are landlords. The shopping malls, office buildings, hotels, and apartments they own all have tenants. And every month, those tenants pay the REIT rent.

By law, REITs must pass along to their shareholders at least 90 percent of the income they generate, to preserve their tax status. The high dividend payouts of REITs make them a quasi-income vehicle, like bonds, rather than a growth vehicle like stocks. But REITs are more volatile than bonds, because the business they're in, being landlords, is highly economically cyclical. After all, in a downturn, the buildings that REITs own are likely to see a number of greater vacancies, which means lower rent income.

Another important point is that the dividends that REITs pay out generally do not qualify for the preferential 15 percent tax treatment on qualified corporate dividend income. Therefore, these payouts will be taxed as ordinary income based on your bracket. So if you decide to purchase a REIT or REIT fund, you should think about doing so through a tax-advantaged account, such as an IRA.

Quiz for Chapter 7

1. Real estate will likely be the single safest investment in your financial plan.
    a. True
    b. False

2. Real estate will likely be the single largest investment in your financial plan.
    a. True
    b. False

3. Real estate helps diversify an investment portfolio because...
    a. it represents a bet against stocks.
    b. it represents a bet against the economy.
    c. it has historically moved independently of stocks and bonds.

4. Investing in a primary residence ...
    a. is not risky because a home is a hard asset.
    b. is not risky because a home is an asset that you can purchase with leverage.
    c. can be risky, depending on where you live and when you live there.

5. Investing in real estate is a hedge against ...
    a. inflation risk
    b. interest rate risk
    c. market risk

6. Capital gains treatment on your primary home is similar to profits booked in your stock portfolio.
    a. True
    b. False

7. It is never wise to take equity out of your home through a home-equity loan.
    a. True
    b. False

8. An Equity REIT invests in which of the following assets?
    a. Stocks of real estate companies
    b. Commercial and/or residential properties

    c. Stocks

    d. Single-family homes

9. Real estate investment trusts are a leveraged vehicle through which investors can gain exposure to commercial real estate deals.

    a. True

    b. False

10. REITs are not as economically sensitive as stocks because...

    a. they must distribute more than 90 percent of the interest they receive through rental income, making them more like bonds.

    b. they own a diversified collection of real estate properties.

    c. they are highly economically sensitive.

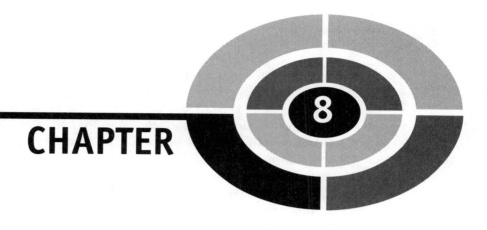

CHAPTER 8

Commodities

What Are Commodities?

We've already addressed the three major financial assets that make up the core of most investment portfolios: stocks, bonds, and cash. And we've just discussed a fourth, real estate. Yet there is yet another asset that can be used within an investment portfolio that also deserves some attention, commodities.

While stocks are shares of companies that produce goods and services, commodities are the *basic raw materials* that those companies use to make the goods that will eventually be brought to market. The most heavily traded commodities include things like crude oil, steel, copper, and gold. But commodities are an even broader asset class than just metal and energy inputs. The universe of commodities also encompasses agricultural products like pork bellies, wheat, soybeans, corn, orange juice, coffee, cotton, and even timber.

Indeed, any unfinished input that can be mined, smelted, harvested, raised, or grown—and can then be sold to companies in bulk for processing or packaging—are potential commodities that can be utilized in an investment portfolio.

Of all the asset classes that can go into a financial portfolio, commodities, on their own, are probably among the riskiest. Why? Think about what

a commodity is. The literal definition of a commodity is a raw material that can be traded on an exchange in bulk. This means there's nothing special about the underlying commodity itself. If you went out and purchased 100 ounces of gold, for example, and if your neighbor did the same, the two batches of gold would be identical. An ounce of gold is an ounce of gold no matter who owns it or whom they bought it from.

This distinguishes commodities from other asset classes like stocks, bonds, and even real estate. A stock investor, after all, can always improve his odds of success by doing his homework about the company he's investing in, the industry in which that company operates, the countries in which that firm operates, and the management team and directors who run the organization.

Moreover, the managers of that firm can also add value to your stock by improving the fortunes of the company. If you own shares of a publicly traded company that has fallen on hard times, for example, the managers of that firm could always improve profits by squeezing out additional cost savings. They could lead the company into new business ventures that can improve the long-term prospects of the firm. They might choose to enter new markets in hopes of expanding the firm's sales. And even if the management team fails, the company's board of directors can always elect to find new management and restructure the firm.

Similarly, if you own residential real estate, there are a host of things that you can do to improve the value of your investment in the open market. You could landscape. You could repair problem areas in your property. You could remodel. You could renovate the entire home and add on an extra bedroom. You could install a pool in the backyard or a state-of-the-art kitchen.

But when it comes to commodities, there's no value that an investor can add to the holding. It's up to the global economy to determine what an ounce of gold or a barrel of oil is worth at a given moment in time. Moreover, commodities, unlike stocks and bonds, don't pay investors any dividends or interest. So there's no income generated from these investments to protect investors should the underlying asset suffer principal losses. This is why commodities are much more volatile than stocks or bonds.

You'll recall that in a previous chapter, we discussed a statistical measure of volatility that investors often rely on called the *standard deviation*. Just as a reminder, the standard deviation is a mathematical expression of the ups and downs of an investment over time. The higher the standard deviation, the more volatile an investment is said to be. Well, between 1924 and 1970, commodities, as an asset class, were among the most volatile investments around. According to an analysis by Ibbotson Associates and the asset management firm PIMCO, the average standard deviation for commodities during this 35-year stretch was 19.88 percent. Only international stocks were more volatile during this period. Between 1970 and 1981, commodities were even more volatile, with a standard

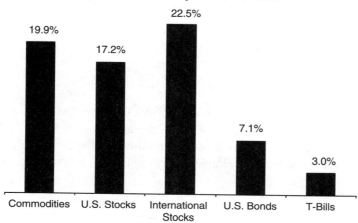

Figure 8-1.   Volatility of Various Assets*

*Based on standard deviation results from 1970 to 2004. The higher an asset's standard deviation, the more volatile it is said to be.
Source: Ibbotson Associates

deviation that was more than five times higher than that of U.S. bonds. See Figure 8-1.

One of the reasons why commodity prices tend to fluctuate so much is that they are wholly dependent on only a couple of factors—the first being the health of the economy. Remember, since commodities are manufacturing inputs, demand for items like oil, steel, and copper will always be dependent on economic activity. For example, the more cars consumers want to buy, the more steel will be needed to build those automobiles. The hotter the housing market, the greater the demand for timber for homes and furnishings.

Another factor at work within the commodity market is the basic principle of supply and demand. It's true that commodities tend to do best in periods of rapid economic growth. Indeed, the global markets witnessed a tremendous bull market in commodities between 2003 and 2006 as economies in Asia (led by China), Latin America, Europe, and North America were all expanding in synch with one another. But certain individual commodities can thrive even in an economic slowdown so long as tepid demand continues to outpace supply. In other words, commodities that are in short supply globally—and are therefore considered precious by the markets—will see their prices rise even if the overall economy is shaky.

This is why markets for certain commodities are managed to a great extent. Take crude oil. In an effort to ensure that prices and profits remain reasonably high no matter what the demand for oil, the Organization of the Petroleum Exporting Countries (better known as OPEC) has long established production targets for its

member nations so that supply will never outstrip demand by so much that prices per barrel of oil begin to fall significantly.

Why Commodities?

If commodities are so risky, why should individual investors consider including them in their long-term financial plans? The answer is simple. All long-term financial plans require assets that can beat inflation for the long haul. And history has shown that commodities, so long as they are held in a diversified mix, can do quite well.

In fact, in the 35-year period between 1970 and 2004, commodities actually outperformed both U.S. and foreign equities, posting double-digit annual gains. To be sure, commodities were still among the riskiest holdings during this time period, with a high standard deviation of nearly 20 percent. But so long as you held commodities for the long haul, and held them in a diversified manner, you would have enjoyed average annual gains of more than 12 percent during this time. By comparison, domestic equities delivered gains of around 11.2 percent a year. See Figure 8-2.

THE DIVERSIFICATION ARGUMENT

The interesting thing about investing is that sometimes when you mix different risky assets together the combination can actually serve to reduce the overall level of volatility in your portfolio. Think about it this way. Let's say you owned two investments. The first one soars 20 percent in year 1 and then falls 10 percent in year 2. Your other investment, meanwhile, falls 10 percent in year 1 and then surges 20 percent in the next year. On their own, each of these investments could be described as volatile. But because the first investment zigged when the second

Figure 8-2.	Commodities for the Long Haul
Asset	**Compound Annual Return (1970–2004)**
Commodities	12.38%
U.S. Stocks	11.22%
International Stocks	11.09%
U.S. Bonds	8.74%
T-Bills	6.27%
Average Rate of Inflation	*4.74%*

Source: Ibbotson Associates, PIMCO

one zagged, your overall returns were quite stable and your portfolio turned out to be far less risky than its component parts.

Well, that's what commodities held in small doses—say, 5 to 10 percent of your overall portfolio—can do for your equities and bonds. Consider this hypothetical example that researchers at Ibbotson Associates documented. Say you held a portfolio composed of 50 percent stocks (specifically, 25 percent large caps, 15 percent foreign equities, and 10 percent small caps), 45 percent bonds, and 5 percent cash. Between 1970 and 2003, this generic portfolio would have earned 10.4 percent a year, on average, according to Ibbotson. And it would have enjoyed a standard deviation of 9.63 percent.

Now, let's say that you took a mere 10 percent of the money in your equity stake and shifted that into a diversified basket of commodities. Had you done that in 1970, your new portfolio (consisting of 40 percent stocks, 45 percent bonds, 5 percent cash, and 10 percent commodities) would have delivered slightly higher gains—in this case, 10.5 percent a year. But more importantly, it would have achieved those returns with significantly less volatility during this three-decade stretch. In fact, this hypothetical portfolio's standard deviation would have been just 7.63 percent, according to Ibbotson. In other words, held in modest doses, commodities can reduce risk in your overall financial plan.

The reason that commodities act this way is that movements in commodity prices are not correlated with any other asset class. In fact, as Figure 8-3 shows, commodities are *inversely* correlated with U.S. stocks, U.S. bonds, foreign equities, and even cash. Indeed, the correlation between commodities and U.S. stocks is a negative −0.24 percent. Any reading near zero means that the two assets don't move in lockstep with one another. But a negative correlation means that when one asset falls, the other is likely to rise and vice versa.

History shows that this is literally true. Let's go back to the period between 1970 and 2004. How do you think other assets performed in years when U.S. equities fell? As it turns out, there is a decent degree of correlation in all equity markets. So even though foreign stocks aren't directly impacted by the U.S. economy,

Figure 8-3. Commodity Correlations (Based on Returns between 1970 and 2004)

Asset Class	Commodities	U.S. Stocks	International Stocks	U.S. Bonds	T-Bills
Commodities	1.00	−0.24	−0.07	−0.32	−0.10
U.S. Stocks	−0.24	1.00	0.58	0.24	0.03
International Stocks	−0.07	0.58	1.00	−0.03	−0.12
U.S. Bonds	−0.32	0.24	−0.03	1.00	0.23
T-Bills	−0.10	0.03	−0.12	0.23	1.00

Source: Ibbotson Associates

Figure 8-4.   When Stocks Zig, Commodities Zag

Asset	Compound Annual Return*
Commodities	19.02%
U.S. Bonds	7.34%
T-Bills	6.85%
International Stocks	−11.49%
U.S. Stocks	−12.28%

*Based on returns in the eight calendar years between 1970 and 2004 when U.S. stocks have lost money.

Source: Ibbotson Associates, PIMCO

foreign shares tend to fall when U.S. stocks do. And this was the case over the past 35 years. In the eight calendar years in which domestic equities lost ground between 1970 and 2004, international stocks also fell—and by nearly as much.

But what was surprising was how well commodities fared during these years. As it turns out, commodities soared more than 19 percent a year, on average, in the eight calendar years when stocks got crushed during this period. This means commodities actually proved more valuable, from a diversification standpoint, than bonds and cash. As you would expect, bonds and cash held up well in those years when equities cratered, but they rose only around 7 percent annually. See Figure 8-4.

Moreover, it seems that commodities can also play a role in diversifying a portfolio when bonds lose ground. Indeed, in those years in which U.S. bonds fell on a total return basis between 1970 and 2004, stocks rose. But commodities soared even more. While U.S. equities returned more than 10 percent annually in years when bonds lost value, commodities soared 21 percent annually in these periods. See Figure 8-5.

Figure 8-5.   When Bonds Zig, Commodities Zag

Asset	Compound Annual Return*
Commodities	20.97%
International Stocks	17.68%
U.S. Stocks	10.54%
T-Bills	4.49%
U.S. Bonds	−1.87%

*Based on returns in years between 1970 and 2004, when U.S. bonds have lost money.

Source: Ibbotson Associates, PIMCO

THE INFLATION ARGUMENT

Another reason to have some exposure to commodities at all times is that this asset class offers investors a tremendous hedge against inflation. In fact, commodities tend to do best in periods when inflation is running rampant. Why?

Commodities are the basic inputs that go into the production process, like oil and steel. If producer and consumer prices are rising (which happens in inflationary periods), chances are it's because the raw materials needed to produce those goods and services are climbing. So commodities are actually beneficiaries of inflation, since that's when their prices tend to appreciate.

Conversely, corporate assets like stocks and bonds tend to eschew inflation because rising prices hurt corporate profits and eat into investment returns.

Take the hyperinflationary period of the 1970s and early 1980s. This was a difficult time to be an equity investor for sure, as rising inflation was hurting the economy, which in turn impacted the U.S. stock market. It was also a difficult time to be a fixed-income investor. Even though bonds and cash were generating solid returns (bonds, in fact, rose 6.3 percent a year while cash was up nearly 7.5 percent annually between 1970 and 1981) inflation was actually rising at an even faster rate. This means that bond and cash investments were posting *negative* real returns throughout this inflationary period. But had you invested in commodities back then, you'd have earned eye-popping gains of more than 17 percent a year between 1970 and 1981. See Figure 8-6.

Indeed, had you invested $25,000 in a broadly diversified basket of commodities starting in 1970, you'd have seen that money grow 9.18 percent a year on an inflation-adjusted basis (that's the 17.09 percent gain for commodities minus the 7.91 percent rate of inflation). So by the end of 1981, your original $25,000 would have become nearly $72,000. By comparison, that same amount invested in bonds, on an after-inflation basis, would have shrunk to $20,600. And $25,000 invested in stocks during this 12-year period would have fallen to $24,000 by 1981.

Figure 8-6.   Commodities during Periods of High Inflation

Asset	Compound Annual Return (1970–1981)
Commodities	17.09%
International Stocks	10.24%
T-Bills	7.48%
U.S. Stocks	7.36%
U.S. Bonds	6.31%
Average Rate of Inflation	*7.91%*

Source: Ibbotson Associates, PIMCO

Figure 8-7.   Commodities during Periods of Low Inflation

Asset	Compound Annual Return (1982–2004)
U.S. Stocks	13.29%
International Stocks	11.53%
U.S. Bonds	10.02%
Commodities	10.00%
T-Bills	5.64%
Average Rate of Inflation	*3.12%*

Source: Ibbotson Associates, PIMCO

Of course, it stands to reason that if commodities thrive in inflationary periods, they probably don't do as well when prices are falling. And this turns out to be the case. Consider the period between 1982 and 2004, when the Federal Reserve finally wrung out hyperinflation from the U.S. economy. As inflation fell throughout this 23-year period, stocks soared 13.3 percent a year between 1982 and 2004. For their part, bonds climbed 10.02 percent annually. But commodities didn't fare that badly during this stretch. In fact, while they trailed the annual returns of U.S. stocks, foreign stocks, and U.S. bonds, commodities still managed to post a respectable average annual gain of exactly 10 percent during this period. See Figure 8-7.

How to Own Commodities

If commodities are such a great deal, why aren't they considered one of the main pillars of an investment plan? Part of it has to do with the fact that stocks, bonds, and cash can provide decent growth, diversification, and inflation protection on their own. Part of it has to do with the volatility and risk associated with any specific commodity. But a lot of it has to do with the fact that up until recently, small investors didn't have as much direct access to commodities as they did stocks and bonds.

To a large extent, the commodities market is still dominated by institutional and high-net-worth investors. This is true for most individual commodities, with the possible exception of gold and silver, since individuals can tap into those commodities at the retail level through coins and even jewelry. But some commodities are simply too difficult for most small households to trade. After all, are you prepared to take possession of 1000 barrels of oil or 500 bushels of corn?

Probably not. The good news is that there are ways for small players to invest in this market today.

DIRECT OWNERSHIP

For most individual investors, the easiest way to gain direct exposure to commodities is through the so-called futures market. *Futures* are contractual agreements in which buyers and sellers consent to trade a specific amount of a particular commodity (be it soybeans or coffee or oil) at a future date at an agreed-upon price. Futures contracts have made the commodities market much more fluid and efficient, since the transaction is conducted on paper and sellers aren't required to bring the actual commodity to the trading floor.

The good news is that futures contracts give small investors access to direct commodity purchases through various exchanges, including the New York Mercantile Exchange, the Chicago Mercantile Exchange, the Chicago Board of Trade, and the Chicago Board Options Exchange. While you will need to open a special futures account through a brokerage, the minimum amount of money you'll need to start trading could be fairly small. Some brokers may let you get started for as little as $10,000 (though they will require you to have a certain amount of assets in your portfolio to qualify to trade commodities).

But there are big risks associated with these types of accounts. For starters, it is highly risky to be trading individual commodities, as opposed to a diversified basket of raw materials. Indeed, a sudden geopolitical crisis in the Middle East or in Russia could send oil prices soaring or falling. And when it comes to agricultural commodities like orange juice or corn, an unexpected shift in the weather could ruin your investment.

Moreover, futures contracts are traded *on margin*. This means that you will be borrowing money from your brokerage to leverage larger transactions. While you may be using only $10,000 of your own money to instigate a trade, that money may be a fraction of the true value of the transaction. If the trade is successful, buying on margin will amplify your gains. But one wrong bet on a commodity futures contract could set you back tens of thousands of dollars. So you really must be careful.

A new alternative for direct exposure to commodities are so-called TRAKRS, a type of exchange-traded futures contract introduced recently by Merrill Lynch. The firm's Commodity TRAKRs trade on the Chicago Mercantile Exchange and are designed to give you broad-based exposure to a basket of around 20 different commodities found in the Dow Jones-AIG Commodity Index. This particular type of futures contract is not leveraged and can be purchased without a separate

futures contract. Merrill Lynch also offers a Gold TRAKR which should give you direct exposure to the precious metal.

INDIRECT EXPOSURE

The safest, and in many cases the smartest, way to gain exposure to commodities is indirectly, for instance, through a mutual fund. There are actually a couple of different levels of indirect commodity ownership.

First, there are mutual funds that offer investors exposure to *actual commodities* by buying and selling futures contracts linked to these assets. For example, the Oppenheimer Real Asset mutual fund is designed to give investors broad-based ownership of the raw materials found in the Goldman Sachs Commodity Index. The PIMCO Commodity Real Return fund tries to mirror the Dow Jones-AIG Commodity Index. And there are a few diversified mutual funds that use a portion of their assets to purchase and hold real commodities. The Permanent Portfolio, for example, is an open-end mutual fund that buys and holds stocks, bonds, and currencies, as well as physical gold.

In addition, there's an even more indirect way to gain exposure to commodities. And that's through mutual funds that buy and sell *shares of companies* that produce, grow, or mine commodities. Some of these funds, like the Van Eck Market Vectors Gold Miner's exchange-traded fund, give you exposure to a single commodity (in this case gold, through ownership of shares of gold-mining companies). For most do-it-yourself investors, single-commodity funds might not be the best course of action, since specific commodities are far more volatile than a diverse basket of different raw materials.

But there are also nearly 200 different so-called *natural resources mutual funds* that invest in a variety of basic materials companies, energy firms, gold miners, and traditional smoke-stack companies. The good news is that many of these sector funds will include shares of large blue-chip industry giants like Alcoa (aluminum), DuPont (chemicals), Georgia-Pacific (paper), U.S. Steel (metals), and Weyerhaeuser (timber).

Though natural resources sector funds are often a safer way to gain exposure to this asset class because of their diversification, they're not pure commodity plays. To be sure, whenever you invest in a gold-mining company or an oil concern, you will participate in a good deal of the movement in the prices of the underlying commodity. After all, as gold prices rise, the profits enjoyed by gold-mining companies will likely climb too. And when oil prices fall, profits at energy companies are likely to tumble as well.

However, be forewarned. You will never be able to fully capture all the movements in a commodity's price by betting on stocks that benefit from those assets.

A gold-mining company, after all, is still a company whose performance will also be impacted by its execution, management decisions, and competition from other gold miners. Moreover, publicly traded companies that are involved in commodities typically hedge their bets against falling commodity prices to protect their profits. So you'll find that stock and stock funds that give you commodity exposure won't rise as much, or fall as much, in value as the underlying commodity itself.

More Indirect Plays

Keep in mind that if you invest in a general stock mutual fund, there's a good chance that you already have decent exposure to commodity-oriented stocks. According to Morningstar, the mutual fund tracking firm, the average large-cap stock fund invests around 20 percent of its assets in a mix of energy stocks and shares of industrial firms. The typical small-cap portfolio actually invests slightly more, nearly 25 percent, in those two sectors.

Even an emerging market stock fund is likely to give you some indirect exposure to commodities, because many companies that are based in countries like Brazil, Mexico, and Russia are commodity producers. In fact, there's around a 70 percent correlation between movements in emerging markets stock funds and natural resources stocks, according to Morningstar.

Gold and Silver

Gold and silver are unique commodities. While most commodities like oil, timber, and steel are pure bets on the global economy—in other words, their prices will tend to rise when the economy is firing on all cylinders—gold and silver can also be used to bet *against the economy*. That's because these precious metals are considered de facto currency by investors in many nations.

To be sure, gold and silver have numerous industrial applications. For instance, a tiny amount of gold is used to seal air bags that go into automobiles. Gold is also used in the manufacturing of numerous electronic devices. Silver, for its part, goes into a whole host of products ranging from batteries to photographic equipment to X-ray machines.

Figure 8-8. Historic Gold Prices*

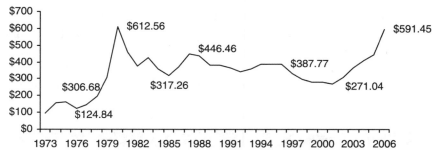

*Based on average annual gold prices for each calender year between 1973 and 2006.
Source: KITCO

However, investors gravitate to these so-called precious metals during uncertain economic times: for instance, when inflation is running rampant and when geopolitical crises are taking place. Indeed, historically gold has been held by investors who are fearful of inflation, currency instability, and economic uncertainties. This is probably why gold prices rose so much during the so-called stagflationary period of the 1970s and early 1980s. See Figure 8-8.

Another reason why gold and silver are popular among commodity investors is that these assets can be purchased rather easily, and in small units, through a variety of means. This distinguishes gold and silver from the industrial and agricultural commodities that trade mostly on exchanges.

For starters, you can buy gold coins through retail stores and exchanges. You can even buy gold directly through the United States mint (www.usmint.gov). Currently, the U.S. Mint is selling a 24-karat, 1-ounce "American Buffalo" coin that's 99 percent pure gold, alongside a 1-ounce "American Eagle" coin that's 92 percent pure. Foreign countries mint similar coins of similar purity. In Canada, for instance, you can purchase the 99 percent pure "Maple Leaf" gold coin. Australia mints the 99 percent pure Kangaroo nugget. And South Africa is famous for its 92 percent pure Krugerrand.

Keep in mind that if you buy gold directly, you're going to have to factor in storage costs—for instance, renting a safe deposit box at a bank—as well as insurance. And if you're buying gold coins in small lots on the secondary market (as opposed to directly from the U.S. mint), then you will be hit with hefty transaction costs.

As a result, some investors favor owning gold through a precious metals mutual fund or an exchange-traded fund that gives them either direct or indirect exposure to the asset. Of course, you can also elect to invest directly in gold- and silver-mining stocks such as Barrick Gold, Newmont Mining, and Freeport-McMoRan Copper & Gold.

Quiz for Chapter 8

1. Commodities are considered one of the three pillars of an investment portfolio.
    a. True
    b. False

2. Commodities tend to be more volatile than stocks.
    a. True
    b. False

3. Why are commodities risky?
    a. Individual commodities are highly economic sensitive, and they are also subject to major price swings due to supply disruptions.
    b. Unlike stocks and bonds, commodities don't pay investors any dividends or interest income to protect investors.
    c. Both A & b.
    d. Neither.

4. The reason to invest in commodities is that …
    a. they can improve the risk-reward characteristics of your investment portfolio.
    b. they offer capital preservation.
    c. unlike stocks, these are investments that most households understand, such as gold and oil and coffee.

5. Commodities offer a hedge against inflation.
    a. True
    b. False

6. As an investor, buying the stock of an oil company like ExxonMobil is the same as buying oil by the barrel.
    a. True
    b. False

7. Commodities tend to perform better in …
    a. a high-inflation period.
    b. a low-inflation period.
    c. either period.

8. Commodities are useful primarily to institutional and high-net-worth individuals.
   a. True
   b. False

9. Since commodities are the raw materials that are used to produce goods in the industrial economy, all commodities are a bet on economic growth.
   a. True
   b. False

10. If you add a small percentage of commodities to a diversified portfolio, it will ...
    a. increase your returns, but increase your risk.
    b. lower your returns, but increase your risk.
    c. increase your returns, but lower your risk.

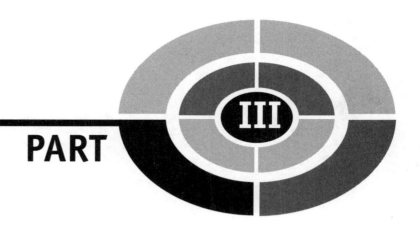

PART

III

Your Financial Accounts

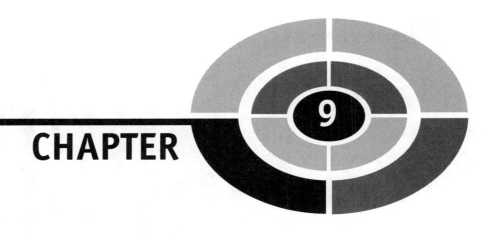

CHAPTER 9

Your Managed Funds

What's a Mutual Fund?

Mutual funds, which have been around for nearly a century, are among the most popular investments in this country. It's easy to see why. Funds are the most user-friendly investment vehicle available to individual investors. They can be used for virtually any purpose within a financial plan—for college savings, for retirement savings, or even as a rainy-day fund. And you can find any number of ready-made portfolios to suit your short-, intermediate-, and long-term financial goals.

Indeed, you can use a money market mutual fund as your primary cash account. You can use bond mutual funds to satisfy the fixed-income portion of your investment portfolio. And you can invest in a handful of stock mutual funds to provide growth for your long-term financial goals.

It's no wonder that collectively, the nation's 10,000 or so funds control roughly $9 trillion in wealth, making them by far the investment of choice for Middle America. In fact, as of the end of 2005, half of all households owned shares of at

CHAPTER 9   Your Managed Funds

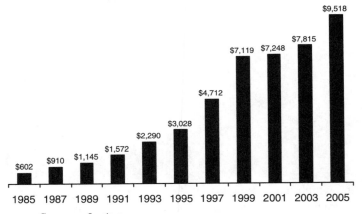

Figure 9-1.   Household Ownership of Mutual Funds

Year	Percentage
1980	5.7%
1984	11.9%
1988	24.4%
1992	27.0%
1996	37.2%
1998	44.0%
2000	49.0%
2002	49.6%
2003	47.9%
2004	48.1%
2005	47.5%

Figure 9-2.   Total Mutual Fund Assets (in Billions)

1985	$602
1987	$910
1989	$1,145
1991	$1,572
1993	$2,290
1995	$3,028
1997	$4,712
1999	$7,119
2001	$7,248
2003	$7,815
2005	$9,518

Source: Investment Company Institute

least one fund. And Americans placed more than 20 percent of their total financial investment in these portfolios. See Figures 9-1 and 9-2.

Despite all of this, many investors still don't understand what a mutual fund really is.

For starters, many believe that funds are a core asset, like a stock or a bond or a commodity. They're not. Instead, funds are vehicles that allow individual investors to gain easy and broad access to large portfolios of those stocks, bonds, and commodities, as well as cash. Think of a fund like a bucket that holds a mix of investments. The asset is what's in the bucket, not the bucket itself.

This is not to say that the bucket, that is, the funds, can't add value. Mutual funds are, after all, *managed* investment vehicles. All funds are led by either a manager or team of managers, whose job it is to investigate investment options and ultimately to put your money to work for you. (Technically, funds are classified as businesses whose sole purpose is to invest money for shareholders. This is why you'll sometimes hear people refer to mutual funds as *investment companies.*)

Ultimately, you the shareholder profit if the stocks and bonds and other assets that your fund invests in appreciate over time. Conversely, if for some reason your manager is unable to turn his or her holdings into gains, the losses suffered by the fund will be borne by its shareholders.

One of the reasons funds are so popular among middle-income families (the vast majority of fund investors, in fact, earn between $35,000 and $100,000 a year) is that they allow small investors to put modest amounts of money to work in a reasonably safe manner in the stock and bond markets. Funds can do this because they literally pool together the assets of thousands of small investors to create a single, powerful fund. Now, when you invest in that fund, you will own a portion of the total value of the portfolio, alongside thousands of fellow shareholders. Hence, the name *mutual* fund. But as with all things that are jointly owned, there are pros and cons, which we will discuss in a moment.

Another reason individual investors favor funds is that they are single-decision solutions. Once you choose a particular fund that invests in a particular type of asset, the fund itself will do the work for you. It will research the investments, buy the securities that it deems appropriate, initiate the trades, manage those securities over time, and eventually sell those securities on your behalf. Given how little time Americans have, and spend, to craft their long-term financial plans, funds would seem to be an ideal choice for the vast majority of investors who don't have the time, interest, or skill to manage their own portfolios. See Figure 9-3.

Figure 9-3.   Mutual Fund Share of Total Financial Assets

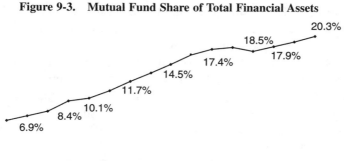

Source: Investment Company Institute

Different Types of Funds

STOCK FUNDS

The 10,000 different funds available invest in virtually every type of asset and offer every style of investing. But many investors associate funds with equities. That's because the vast majority of fund assets are deployed in the stock market. Indeed, 45 percent of fund assets are currently invested in domestic stocks and another 10 percent hold international equities. By comparison, only 15 percent of the mutual fund universe is made up of bond funds.

Now, there are a number of ways to slice and dice the stock fund universe. For starters, there are two broad categories of equity portfolios: general funds and specialized funds.

General funds are diversified stock portfolios that invest across various sectors and industries of the economy. Within this grouping, you will find another subdivision, between those funds that specialize in *foreign stocks* and those that invest *domestically*. Though foreign investing has become popular since the bear market of 2000, U.S. investors still put the majority of their assets in U.S. equities. Not surprisingly, domestic stock funds outnumber foreign portfolios by nearly five to one.

Funds that invest overseas are known either as foreign/international funds or as world/global funds. There's a slight distinction between the two. While a foreign fund must invest almost entirely overseas, a world fund can invest anywhere around the globe, including in North America. Furthermore, among foreign funds, you will find some that specialize in the *developed* economies of Western Europe and Japan. These are typically regarded as relatively safe investments as the size and strength of the equity markets in Europe and Japan are starting to rival that of the United States. There are also foreign stock funds that focus on *emerging market equities,* which are shares of publicly traded companies based in volatile economies found in Latin America, Asia, Eastern Europe, and the Middle East.

Emerging markets stock funds are considered among the most volatile investments around, as they expose investors not only to market risks, but political risks due to the unstable nature of many governments in the emerging world. Still, the fact that an emerging markets stock fund will invest in a diverse collection of these volatile assets for you makes them a safer vehicle through which to gain exposure to the emerging markets than owning these foreign shares directly. These funds also happened to have produced some of the mutual fund industry's biggest gains between 2003 and 2006.

As for *U.S. general equity funds*—those that invest in a cross-section of different industries and sectors here at home—they are generally divided into nine different categories. Those categories are based on the size of the stocks these funds favor (for instance, large caps, mid caps, or small caps), and the style of investing they adhere to (value or growth). For example, the Janus Twenty Fund invests in a few dozen of the largest growth-oriented stocks in this country, shares of companies like Google and Apple and Goldman Sachs. This makes it a *large-cap growth stock fund.* Meanwhile, the Fidelity Small Cap Value Fund invests in—you guessed it—shares of small stocks that are undervalued or overlooked by the market. In all, the nine styles of general domestic equity portfolios are: large-cap growth, large-cap value, large-cap blend; mid-cap growth, mid-cap value, mid-cap blend; and finally small-cap growth, small-cap value, small-cap blend. See Figure 9-4 for a list of stock fund categories as defined by Morningstar, the investment research company.

Unlike general funds, *specialized* or *sector funds* as they're sometimes called invest in a single sector of the economy, making them a risky (but potentially higher returning) type of investment vehicle. Indeed, because these funds concentrate their bets on a single sector such as technology or energy, they tend to be extremely volatile compared with general funds. According to Morningstar, the average standard deviation of a sector fund in 2006 was nearly 21. By comparison, the typical general stock fund sported a volatility measure of less than 16, making them about 25 percent less risky.

Among the more popular sector funds in the late 1990s, for example, were *technology-sector stock funds.* But in recent years, investors have gravitated to sector funds that focus on commodities and other hard assets that have done

Figure 9-4.   General Stock Fund Categories as Defined by Morningstar

General Stock Funds

Large Growth Funds
Large Blend Funds
Large Value Funds
Mid-Cap Growth Funds
Mid-Cap Blend Funds
Mid-Cap Value Funds
Small Growth Funds
Small Blend Funds
Small Value Funds
World Stock Funds
Foreign Large Growth Funds
Foreign Large Blend Funds
Foreign Large Value Funds
Foreign Small/Mid-Growth Funds
Foreign Small/Mid-Blend Funds
Foreign Small/Mid-Value Funds

Figure 9-5. Specialized Stock Morningstar Fund Categories as Defined by Specialized Stock Funds

Technology Funds
Health-Care Funds
Financial Funds
Utilities Funds
Natural Resources Funds
Communications Funds
Real Estate Funds

well lately. These include *natural resources funds* (which invest in energy- and commodity-related stocks); *precious metals funds* (which invest in gold and silver along with shares of gold- and silver-mining companies); and *real estate funds* (which invest in shares of real estate–oriented companies and real estate investment trusts). The other sector funds that are available to most investors include *health-care sector funds* (which invest in hospitals, health insurers, and drug and biotechnology companies); *telecommunications funds* (which invest in telecom, media, and cable stocks); *utility funds* (which invest in utility companies); and *financial services funds* (which invest in all sorts of financial firms ranging from banks to brokers to insurers). See Figure 9-5.

BOND FUNDS

Bond funds are generally divided into two camps. There are *taxable bond funds* and *municipal bond portfolios*. Taxable bond funds are themselves broken out into two general categories: *Corporate bond funds,* which invest in private-sector debt, and *government bond funds,* which invest in Treasury securities or mortgage-backed securities or both. Within each of these categories, you will find a whole variety of portfolios that specialize in either long-term, intermediate-term, or short-term debt. For example, there are long government and long corporate bond funds, intermediate government and intermediate corporate bond funds, and short government and short corporate bond portfolios. See Figure 9-6.

For its part, the municipal bond fund universe typically appeals to a narrower audience: high-net-worth or tax-conscious investors who favor munis because they are free from federal income tax. As we discussed earlier, residents of a state who purchase in-state munis will often also get a state tax break. As a result, there are now a host of *single-state municipal bond funds* available to investors. For instance, there are funds that simply buy municipal debt issued by governments or

Figure 9-6. Bond Fund Categories as Defined by Morningstar

Taxable Bond Funds

Long-Term Bond
Intermediate-Term Bond
Short-Term Bond
Ultra-Short-Term Bond
Multisector Bond
Long Government
Intermediate Government
Short-Term Government
World Bond
Emerging Markets Bond
High-Yield Bond
Stable Value
Bank Loan

Municipal Bond Funds

Muni National Long Term
Muni National Intermediate Term
Muni National Short Term
Muni Single State Long Term
Muni Single State Intermediate Term
Muni Single State Short Term
High Yield Muni Bond
Muni California Long
Muni California Intermediate/Short
Muni New York Long
Muni New York Intermediate/Short
Muni New Jersey
Muni Pennsylvania
Muni Minnesota
Muni Florida
Muni Ohio
Muni Massachusetts

agencies in California, New York, or Alabama. But some investors may consider this risky, since you would be betting on municipal debt issued entirely from a single state. This would mean all your bonds would be impacted by a financial crisis in that state's economy. Therefore, some investors prefer *national municipal bond funds*, which are also available.

HYBRID FUNDS

Finally, there are so-called *hybrid funds* to consider. A hybrid fund is one that is allowed by prospectus to invest in a combination of stocks and bonds. The most common form of a hybrid fund is an old-fashioned *balanced fund*. These are mixed portfolios that typically invest anywhere from 50 to 70 percent of their assets in equities, with the remainder going into bonds. Balanced funds typically give fund managers discretion as to how much of the fund's holdings belong in stocks versus bonds. So when managers believe times are ripe for equity outperformance, they might overweigh stocks and shift from a normal mix of, say, 60 percent equities and 40 percent fixed income to 70 percent stocks and 30 percent bonds. Conversely, if managers think bonds are likely to do better, they might dial down that portfolio's risk profile to a 50–50 mix.

In recent years, the fund industry has created other, more customized versions of hybrid funds. They are known as *asset-allocation funds*. Like balanced funds, these portfolios invest in a mix of stocks and bonds, but they tend to invest in preset combinations that appeal to specific audiences. For instance, there are so-called *static risk–based asset allocation funds* that appeal to self-described "conservative," "moderate," or "aggressive" investors. The conservative portfolio might be 40 percent stocks and 60 percent bonds, while the aggressive fund might be 80 percent equities and only 20 percent bonds.

Recently, fund companies have also launched a different type of asset allocation fund that's called a *life-cycle fund*. Like other hybrid funds, these managed portfolios are designed to appeal to investors who want a single-fund solution to their stock and bond needs. These funds will invest in all the major asset classes for you. But life-cycle funds differ in one major way: over time, their mix of stocks and bonds will grow more conservative as their shareholders age.

For instance, these portfolios come with a "target date." If you're planning on retiring in, say, 30 years, you might choose the Vanguard Target Retirement 2035 fund. Today, this fund will be primarily invested in equities, since you won't need this money for another three decades. But as time marches forward, this fund will gradually and automatically adjust for you by reducing its equity holdings and buying more bonds.

This feature makes life-cycle funds among the most user-friendly mutual funds around. With a life-cycle fund, you don't have to choose individual equity and fixed-income portfolios. You don't have to decide how much of your money should go to stocks versus bonds (the fund will do that for you). And you don't have to gradually become more conservative in your mix of stocks and bonds as you age, as the fund will do that for you too.

Why Funds?

INSTANT DIVERSIFICATION

As we discussed earlier, academic research tells us that we may need to own as many as 50 different stocks to achieve adequate diversification in our financial plans. Anything below that number and our portfolios might not be able to wring out the *stock-specific risk* we discussed in Chapter 3.

Well, the average stock mutual fund invests in around 175 different stocks at any given time, according to Morningstar. Meanwhile, the average bond mutual fund holds more than 425 individual separate securities at once. This means that the moment you put money into a fund, you will be instantly and sufficiently diversified. See Figure 9-7.

LOW BARRIER TO ENTRY

If you tried to replicate the diversification of the average stock fund, you'd have to purchase shares of around 175 different securities. Even assuming you went through a low-cost brokerage firm charging $20 a trade, this would work out

Figure 9-7.   Average Number of Holdings by Stock Fund Categories

Stock Fund Categories	Average Number of Holdings
Small Blend Funds	343
Large Blend Funds	228
Mid-Cap Blend Funds	204
Small Value Funds	194
Small Growth Funds	137
Mid-Cap Value Funds	115
Large Value Funds	103
Large Growth Funds	100
Mid Cap Growth Funds	95
Natural Resources Funds	95
Health Care Funds	86
Utilities Funds	76
Technology Funds	75
Financial Funds	74
Communications Funds	73
Real Estate Funds	63
Average Domestic Stock Fund	174

Source: Morningstar

to brokerage fees of $3,500. And that's not counting any principal investment. Assuming stocks are trading at an average share price of, say, $50 apiece, to purchase even 10 shares each of 175 different companies would require another $87,500. Obviously, this isn't a course of action that many families are willing (or can afford) to take.

This brings us to one of the biggest advantages that mutual funds have over direct investing: their low barrier to entry. Indeed, many portfolios managed by some of the best-known mutual fund companies, such as Fidelity, American Century, Legg Mason, MFS, and AIM, will allow investors to start with as little as $1,000 to $2,500. In fact, some funds will let you make a minimum initial investment of as little as $500. And if you sign up for an *automated investment program*, where you agree to transfer small amounts of money into the fund every month automatically from your checking account, many funds will let you get started for as little as $25 or $50.

PROFESSIONAL MANAGEMENT

There is a lot more to investing than picking stocks and bonds. Not only must you know which securities to invest in, you need to know when is the best time to buy them; what price to buy those investments for; how long to hold them; when to sell them; and when to add to your positions, depending on market conditions. For many families, this is a huge undertaking. So many households elect to hand over these responsibilities to a professionally managed mutual fund.

Remember that a mutual fund is an investment company, with a formal structure. In addition to professional investment managers, mutual funds will likely be guided by an investment committee to ensure that your fund manager is investing in the right assets, securities, industries, and regions at all times. Moreover, behind the scenes, funds also typically enjoy the support of a team of securities analysts whose job it is to assess the credit-worthiness and growth prospects of various investments. While some fund managers and analysts will rely primarily on financial documents to make their stock picks, many will literally visit companies, speak with management, and walk the factory floors to assess whether a particular investment is worthwhile.

DAILY LIQUIDITY

Though mutual funds are designed to be long-term investing vehicles, you'll never be locked into any fund for any long period of time. By law, mutual funds are required to allow investors to redeem their money on a daily basis. If you place an order to sell some or all of your holdings, that fund must redeem your shares

based on the day's closing price. If your order is transmitted after hours, you will be redeemed based on the following day's close.

Why can't funds simply redeem you at the moment you place your order, like a brokerage account can with individual stocks? For starters, funds are structured differently than individual stocks. Stocks trade on an exchange throughout the day, which means their prices fluctuate constantly throughout the trading session as new buyers and sellers enter the market. But mutual funds shares aren't bought and sold on an exchange. Instead, they are sold directly to investors by fund companies. And when it's time to redeem, the fund company cashes you out.

Also, funds aren't single securities, but rather portfolios of different securities. During the day, fund managers will themselves be buying and selling stocks and bonds for their portfolios. Since managers aren't required to reveal in real time which securities they're currently trading, it's impossible to put a fair price on the fund's collection of stocks and bonds during the trading day. Only after the manager's trading is done at the end of the day can the fund company assess the true market value of all the securities that remain in the portfolio.

DOLLAR COST AVERAGING

You'll recall that one of the safest ways to invest in equities is to *dollar cost average* into the market. In other words, you can reduce risk by putting small amounts of money to work in the market at routine intervals, spread over time, rather than investing a large amount all at once. When investing in individual stocks through a brokerage account, dollar cost averaging often becomes costly, especially if you are investing tiny amounts every month into dozens of different stocks. After all, each purchase would trigger another round of brokerage commissions.

In a mutual fund, though, you don't have to go through a brokerage. If you invest in a so-called *no-load fund,* which sells its shares directly to investors without financial advisers or commission costs, then the fund company will let you dollar cost average into the portfolio with no transaction fees to worry about. In other words, you can put $500 every month into the Vanguard 500 Index Fund for the next 10 years, and each of those 120 small monthly purchases will be commission free.

Now, you can also purchase mutual funds through brokerage platforms. For instance, brokers like Charles Schwab, E*Trade, and Fidelity operate what are essentially *mutual fund supermarkets,* offering investors a choice of thousands of different funds run by hundreds of different fund companies. Some of those funds will be *load funds,* which means the fund company itself will charge you a commission (some loads are as high as 5.75 percent of your investment). But in many cases, these fund supermarkets will also have a list of *no-load/no-transaction fee funds* whose shares can be bought and sold routinely without any commissions levied by either the brokerage firm or the mutual fund company.

The Drawbacks of Fund Investing

LACK OF CONTROL

Mutual fund investors can pick which type of fund they want to invest in. But the authority to make buy and sell decisions within the fund resides entirely with its manager. Any moral misgivings, for example, that you may have in terms of investing in liquor or tobacco stocks will not be respected by the manager. This is why some investors choose not to go with a fund. Moreover, mutual funds are only required to reveal to their shareholders the complete list of stocks and bonds they own twice a year. So there's no real way for fund investors to know, in real time, what their managers are specifically investing in.

ONCE-A-DAY PRICING

As we just discussed, mutual fund shares do not trade on an exchange. Therefore, they are priced only once a day. So if you place a "buy" or "sell" order for shares of a particular fund, the transaction will be completed at the end of the trading day. Many investors consider this a big disadvantage.

Why? Well, if there's a crisis in the markets and stocks are selling off at rapid speed, an individual-stock investor can call his or her broker and sell at the current price. But a fund investor would be forced to wait until the end of the trading day to get out of the fund—by which time stock prices may have lost another 2 or 3 percent (or possibly more) of their value.

Similarly, if stocks are rallying on a given day and you want to buy shares at the current price (to enjoy the run up), you won't be able to time your trade through a fund. Instead, you will be forced to wait until the end of the trading day to purchase your fund shares, by which time the rally may be over. This flaw in the mutual fund structure is one reason some fund investors prefer so-called exchange-traded funds (which we'll discuss in a moment) that trade like individual securities and therefore offer minute-by-minute pricing.

THE "MUTUAL" STRUCTURE

As has been discussed, mutual funds pool the collective wealth of thousands of investors to create a single, influential portfolio. Keep this "pool" imagery in mind. In many ways, a mutual fund is like a swimming pool. In fact, it's a public swimming pool. As a fund investor, you are but one of potentially thousands of other swimmers in the water. Unfortunately, you have no say as to how many more people can come into your investment pool or who can be kicked out.

Here's the problem: As your fellow investors jump into and out of this pool, they often make waves for you and the fund manager. For example, if too many people rush into a fund all at once, a flood of new money might flow so quickly into this fund that the manager may not be able to effectively put it to work in the market. This means the manager may be forced to hold that money in a cash account for a while, effectively slowing the returns of the fund. Or, the manager may be forced to invest the new assets in the second- or third-best ideas—simply to get the money into the market—rather than investing solely in top stock picks.

This is why "hot" funds often turn cold in subsequent years. After posting solid gains, many hot funds will start to see new money flow in thanks to advertisements and articles in the press. But if too much hot money flows in, the manager might not know what to do with it all. This is typically why the top funds in one year turn into some of the worst-performing portfolios in subsequent periods.

Conversely, if a number of fund shareholders decide to exit the pool all at once, this too can hurt the fund. In this case, the manager may be forced to sell stocks and bonds within the portfolio in order to cash those exiting investors out. Typically, a fund manager will keep a percent or two of the fund's assets in cash to meet redemptions without being forced to liquidate other holdings in the portfolio. But if too many folks leave at once, the manager will probably have to sell. And this causes problems.

Indeed, too many people exiting a fund can force a fund to underperform, since the manager might be forced to sell securities at inopportune times in the market simply to meet redemptions. Moreover, a fund manager who is fearful of mass redemptions might decide to keep more of the fund's assets in cash. And since cash typically underperforms stocks and bonds, this cash will create a drag on your fund's total returns.

TAX INEFFICIENCY

There's another problem that arises in a mutual fund when the fund manager is forced to sell securities to meet redemptions. The manager may be forced to sell stocks that have appreciated recently. And selling winning stocks will trigger capital gains taxes that the remaining shareholders in the fund will have to pay.

This is another reason why some investors don't like the "mutual" aspect of a mutual fund.

It's important for fund investors to understand that there are a couple of different ways that they can get hit with a capital gains tax bill through their fund. First, they will trigger capital gains taxes whenever they sell fund shares that have appreciated. So if you invest $50,000 in Fidelity Magellan and sell half your stake at a gain, you're going to have to pay Uncle Sam taxes on your profit from the fund.

But you can also get hit with a tax bill from your fund even if you don't sell. That's because while you're deciding what to do with your fund shares, the manager of your fund is buying and selling securities in the portfolio. And if the manager sells stocks that have appreciated, the fund will realize its own capital gains.

Unfortunately, by law mutual funds that realize capital gains in a given year must pass along those gains to their shareholders by the end of that year. Typically, a fund will distribute its gains—and the tax bill that comes with it—in late November or December. This means that even a buy-and-hold fund investor, who never sells any shares of his or her mutual fund, might still have to pay annual capital gains taxes simply because other shareholders in the fund forced the manager to sell.

Don't Buy an Immediate Tax Bill

The fact that funds often make capital gains distributions in November and December means that fund investors probably shouldn't put new money to work in mutual funds late in the year. After all, why step into an immediate tax bill, especially if you weren't invested in the fund at the time it realized those gains?

For instance, say you invest $5,000 into a new fund on December 1. And let's say that this fund had realized capital gains earlier in the year. So on December 15, it distributes those gains back to its shareholders. Even though you weren't in the fund when those gains were realized, you will receive a check in the mail for $250 from your fund. While getting money kicked back to you might sound good, it's actually not. That's because the $250 in capital gains distributions will actually lower the value of your own investments by the same amount. In other words, instead of having a $5,000 investment in the fund, you really have a $4,750 investment in the portfolio, along with a check for $250.

Worse still, that check comes with an immediate tax bill (this is why it's often smart to wait until January 1 of the next year to put new money to work).

How big your tax bill will be is dependent on how much selling your fund manager was forced to undertake throughout the year, how profitable the securities in the fund were, and how good a job the fund did at managing its tax liabilities.

FUND MANAGER RISK

While the notion of professional management sounds great, there are no guarantees that your fund manager will be able to consistently deliver solid returns for the long term. In fact, there are no guarantees that your managers will even beat the stock market averages that they're paid to outperform. History has shown that many fall short.

In 2006, Standard & Poor's conducted a study of how professional fund managers fare relative to their specific benchmarks (for instance, large-cap managers were compared against the S&P 500 large-cap index, while small-cap managers were pitted against the S&P 600 small stock index). Researchers found that in general, fund managers consistently underperformed their benchmarks over long periods of time. Indeed, in the three-year period through March 2006, only 38 percent of large-cap fund managers beat the S&P 500. And over five years, only 33 percent managed to outgain that benchmark. The track record was worse for small-cap fund managers. Only around one in five managed to beat their benchmarks over the past three- and five-year periods. See Figure 9-8.

Part of the reason why fund managers underperform is that they're human. Sometimes, they make mistakes. But some of it has to do with the flaws in the mutual fund structure. Because of the need to constantly meet redemptions, for instance, fund managers will often hold a few percentage points of their assets in cash. But doing so creates that cash drag that we talked about. The more cash a manager holds, the worse his performance is likely to be relative to his benchmark index. After all, those indexes are comprised entirely of stocks.

Figure 9-8. Percent of Mutual Fund Managers Who Have Beaten Their Benchmarks (Data as of March 31, 2006)

	1 Year	3 Years	5 Years
All Large Cap Funds	56.92%	38.1%	32.9%
All Mid-Cap Funds	38.9%	22.6%	12.7%
All Small-Cap Funds	45.2%	24.1%	21.3%
All Growth Funds	88.2%	73.4%	62.1%
All Value Funds	28.8%	26.5%	45.0%

Source: Standard & Poor's

Still another reason why funds might underperform their benchmarks is that they charge investors administrative and investment management fees for running the fund. And those fees, as we'll discuss, come right out of a fund's total returns, hurting their performance over time.

MUTUAL FUND FEES AND COMMISSIONS

Mutual funds charge a number of different types of fees. It's often hard to keep track of them, since funds don't present shareholders with a single itemized bill.

For starters, there are loads, or commissions paid to brokers and advisers who recommend specific funds to you. In general, there are three different ways to pay for this commission. They include *A share class funds*, which require you to pay the commission or load up front. Then there are *B share class funds*—sometimes referred to as back-end loaded funds—because they charge you the commission when you sell your shares. And finally, there are *C share class funds,* which charge you a so-called level load throughout the time you own the fund.

Loads often range from around 3 percent to 5.75 percent. As you would expect, over time, this makes a huge difference. For instance, say you invest in an A-share class fund charging a load of 5 percent. And say you want to invest $10,000 in the fund. In a front-end load fund, not all of your $10,000 investment will make its way into the market. Because the advisor or other intermediary is taking a commission off the top, 5 percent of your $10,000 in this example will be deducted before being invested. This means in an A share fund, you would start out investing $9,500, not the original $10,000 you had planned.

No-load funds, by contrast, do not assess any commissions for purchasing the investment. These funds are often referred to as *direct-sold funds*, since you do not need a separate brokerage accounts to purchase these shares—you can buy and sell them directly from the mutual fund company. The advantage of going the direct-sold route is that you can avoid two levels of commissions—the first to your brokerage account for the basic transaction cost, and the second involving the load that goes to the advisor or third party who recommended the fund to you.

This is why cost-conscious, do-it-yourself investors regard no-load funds as the most cost-effective vehicles for individual investors to invest in funds. Examples of classic no-load fund operations include those run by the Vanguard Group, T. Rowe Price, and Fidelity. See Figure 9-9.

In addition to loads, there are investment management fees. This money goes to cover the salaries of fund managers and the securities analysts who help those managers investigate investment opportunities. Investment management fees also

Figure 9-9. The Impact of Loads on Investor Returns (Assumes an Average Annual Return of 7 Percent)

	Initial Investment	Year 5	Year 10	Year 25
No Load	$100,000	$140,255	$196,715	$542,743
1% Load	$99,000	$138,853	$194,748	$537,316
3.25% Load	$96,700	$135,697	$190,322	$525,104
5.75% Load	$94,250	$132,191	$185,404	$511,536
No Load v. 5.75% Load		*$8,064*	*$11,311*	*$31,207*

go toward covering the cost of research. Depending on your fund, your management fees may range from between 0.25 and 1 percent of assets a year. In other words, if you were to invest $10,000 in a fund charging 1 percent management fees, the company would deduct $100 from your account each year. If you were to invest $100,000, it would deduct $1,000 a year.

In addition to investment management fees, funds also charge distribution fees to cover the cost of marketing the portfolio. And there are also so-called shareholder servicing fees to consider, which pay for basic administrative services. Those include record keeping, printing monthly statements, and mailing documents. Combined, these three basic fees represent your *total expense ratio,* which is deducted from your fund's returns.

The average expense ratio for a stock mutual fund was about 1.54 percent as of the end of 2005. This means that if you invested $100,000 in an average portfolio, that fund would deduct $1,540 from your account every year. (To look up the fees charged by your mutual fund, you can visit the Website of the mutual fund tracking firm Morningstar, www.morningstar.com, or visit finance.yahoo.com.)

Why are fees so important? It's because they are deducted straight out of your fund's total returns. This means the higher the fees that a fund charges, the more those fees will eat away at the long-term returns generated by your investments. And the lower your fund returns, the harder it will be to achieve your long-term goals.

Here's how it works: Say you invest in a fund whose manager achieves 10 percent gains through his investments. But say the fund charges 2 percent in total expenses. If that's the case, its total return would actually be 8 percent. To be sure, 2 percent of assets a year doesn't necessarily sound like a lot. But thanks to the laws of compound interest, it can actually turn into a huge sum over long periods of time. In fact, a fund that grows 8 percent a year over 25 years will turn $100,000 into $684,850 during this time. On the other hand, a fund that returns a full 10 percent a year during the same time period would grow that original $100,000 into nearly $1.1 million. That's a difference of nearly $400,000. See Figure 9-10.

Figure 9-10.   The Impact of Annual Expenses on Investor Returns

Stock Fund	Market Return	Expense Ratio	Net Return	Growth of $100,000 in 25 years
Low-Cost Fund	6.0%	0.50%	5.5%	$381,000
Average-Cost Fund	6.0%	1.50%	4.5%	$300,500
High-Cost Fund	6.0%	2.00%	4.0%	$266,500
Low-Cost Fund	10.0%	0.50%	9.5%	$967,000
Average-Cost Fund	10.0%	1.50%	8.5%	$768,500
High-Cost Fund	10.0%	2.00%	8.0%	$685,000

For an even more extreme example of how fees can cut into your financial plans, consider the following: Say you have two funds—one that charges 0.5 percent total annual expenses and another that charges 3 percent. And assume that both funds deliver the same gross market return of, say, 12 percent. The fund that charges 0.5 percent will report a total return of 11.5 percent. On the other hand, the fund that charges 3 percent will show after-fee returns of only 9 percent. A $100,000 investment that grows 9 percent a year for a quarter century becomes around $862,000. By contrast, a $100,000 investment growing 11.5 percent for 25 years becomes more than twice that: $1.5 million.

What to Look for in a Fund

STICK WITH LOW FEE FUNDS

Picking funds is almost as hard as picking stocks because there are many unknown variables that can affect a fund's performance over time. But there's one thing that we can say with absolute certainty: If fees come straight out of your total returns, the higher the fees your fund charges, the higher the hurdle it must overcome to deliver solid returns. This is why investors should start their search for stock, bond, and hybrid funds with those portfolios that charge below-average fees.

But wouldn't the best funds and the smartest fund managers charge the highest expenses for their services? In other industries, it may work that way. But because fund fees directly reduce fund performance, the best-performing funds are often among the cheapest.

Study after study shows that when it comes to mutual funds, low-fee portfolios tend to outperform high-fee funds on average because of the vagaries of how fund fees are deducted. In 2004, Standard & Poor's conducted an interesting study. It broke out several categories of general domestic stock mutual funds. S&P researchers then subdivided each category into those portfolios that charged higher fees than the category average and those funds that charged lower-than-average expenses. It then studied the historical performance of these "above average" and "below average" funds over short and long periods. In eight out of the nine general domestic stock fund categories that we spoke of earlier, the below-average-fee funds beat the above-average-fee funds consistently over the past 3, 5, and 10 years (see Figure 9-11).

Standard & Poor's concluded: "It is important for both investors and financial advisers to keep fund expenses in the forefront of their analysis when assembling a portfolio." But make sure you do what Standard & Poor's did. They compared the expenses of funds relative to their category averages, not against the general average of all mutual funds.

The fact is that certain types of funds cost more to run than others. A classic example is an emerging market stock fund. These portfolios invest in small, rather obscure companies that are domiciled in emerging economies in Asia, Latin America, and Eastern Europe. As a result, emerging market stock fund managers often have to spend weeks or months visiting those countries to check on the companies they're investing in as well as the general economic conditions in those countries. By comparison, a large-cap fund that invests in blue-chip stocks probably doesn't have to travel much.

Moreover, large-cap stocks are "covered" by dozens of analysts on Wall Street, so it's easy to get information on those types of equities. Small-cap domestic stock fund managers, on the other hand, often invest in tiny companies that aren't covered by Wall Street at all. Therefore, you should expect your small-cap stock funds to charge slightly more in annual expenses because it simply takes more leg work to investigate those investments.

See Figure 9-12 for a list of the average expenses for funds, according to Morningstar.

Fees are particularly damaging to lower-returning investments such as bonds, since expenses will eat up a greater percentage of their gross returns. So bond fund investors should be particularly mindful of the fees that their portfolios charge.

The good news is that investors are already following this advice. Even though the average stock fund charges around 1.5 percent in annual expenses, shareholders tend to gravitate to lower-fee funds. In fact, an analysis by the Investment Company Institute showed that the average expense ratio paid by fund investors, based on a weighted dollar average, was actually 0.91 percent at the end of 2005. See Figure 9-13.

Figure 9-11. Low-Fee Funds Outperform (Data through May 31, 2004)

	1 Year Returns	3 Year Returns	5 Year Returns	10 Year Returns
Large Growth				
Above Average Fees	14.75%	−6.97%	−5.04%	7.19%
Below Average	**16.07**	**−5.32**	**−3.37**	**8.90**
Large Blend				
Above Average Fees	14.93	−3.89	−2.50	7.93
Below Average	**17.27**	**−2.51**	**−1.26**	**10.01**
Large Value				
Above Average Fees	17.74	−1.53	0.84	9.19
Below Average	**18.79**	**0.01**	**1.81**	**10.53**
Mid-Growth				
Above Average Fees	21.03	−4.45	0.69	6.56
Below Average	**22.83**	**−3.14**	**2.39**	**9.47**
Mid-Blend				
Above Average Fees	23.35	3.38	8.37	12.13
Below Average	**25.47**	**4.93**	**7.99**	**12.12**
Mid-Value				
Above Average Fees	25.94	6.89	8.01	11.01
Below Average	**26.18**	**7.29**	**9.83**	**12.21**
Small Growth				
Above Average Fees	26.04	−2.58	2.88	6.47
Below Average	**27.50**	**−0.77**	**5.65**	**10.29**
Small Blend				
Above Average Fees	30.67	5.60	7.83	10.72
Below Average	**30.01**	**7.33**	**9.79**	**11.51**
Small Value				
Above Average Fees	30.73	9.39	12.20	11.36
Below Average	**31.78**	**11.22**	**13.33**	**13.40**

Source: Standard & Poor's

Figure 9-12. Average Expense Ratios Paid by Stock Fund Investors

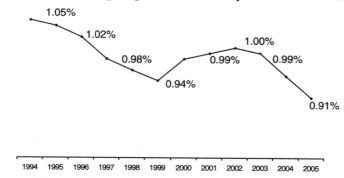

Source: Investment Company Institute

Figure 9-13. Average Expense Ratios for Mutual Funds by Category (As of April 2006)

Type of Fund	Average Total Expense Ratio
Large-Cap Growth	1.48%
Large-Cap Value	1.35%
Large-Cap Blend	1.34%
Mid-Cap Growth	1.59%
Mid-Cap Value	1.44%
Mid-Cap Blend	1.46%
Small-Cap Growth	1.67%
Small-Cap Value	1.55%
Small-Cap Blend	1.49%
Emerging Markets	1.92%
Technology Stock	1.87%
Financial Sector	1.70%
Real Estate	1.56%
Health-Care	1.77%
Natural Resources	1.54%
Long Government Bond	1.08%
Long Bond	1.03%
Intermediate Government Bond	1.08%
Intermediate Bond	1.05%
Short Government Bond	0.99%
Short Bond	1.00%
World Bond	1.28%
High-Yield Bond	1.23%

Source: Morningstar

Figure 9-14.   Comparison of Market Share of Stock Funds by Expense Fees

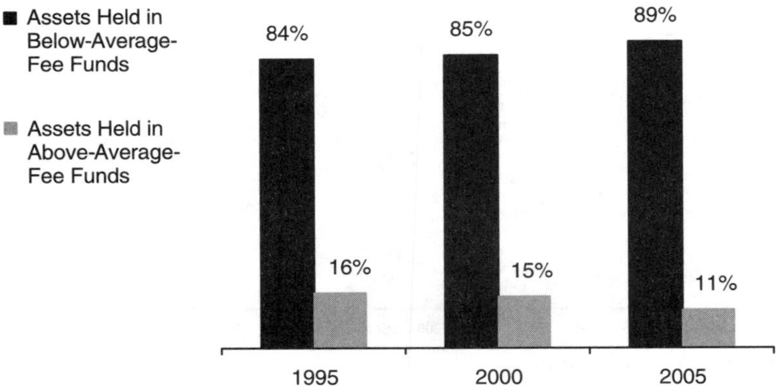

■ Assets Held in
Below-Average-
Fee Funds

■ Assets Held in
Above-Average-
Fee Funds

84%   85%   89%

16%   15%   11%

1995   2000   2005

Source: Investment Company Institute

In fact, in 2005, 89 cents of every dollar that was invested in a stock fund was held in a below-average-fee fund, according to the Investment Company Institute. Even better, this trend is growing. The 2005 results show a slight improvement from 1995, when 84 percent of every dollar was held in a below-average-fee fund and 16 percent of assets were held in expensive portfolios. See Figure 9-14.

STICK WITH LOW-TURNOVER FUNDS

The term *turnover* refers to the speed with which your fund manager will buy and sell stocks. For example, if your mutual fund has a 100 percent turnover rate, it means that in a one-year period of time, your fund is likely to have sold and replaced every single holding in its portfolio. The average stock fund, according to Morningstar, has a turnover rate of around 90 percent, which means stock funds tend to do a decent amount of trading.

But isn't trading good? Aren't fund investors paying their managers to trade securities on their behalf? That's true. But there are no guarantees that when your manager trades frequently, that he or she will make profitable decisions. Meanwhile, every time the manager does trade, there is something that takes place that is absolutely certain—and that's the fact that the fund will incur trading costs.

Every time your fund manager places a trade, he or she will incur the exact same type of *brokerage commissions* that individual stock investors must pay when they make an investment transaction. And your fund company will pass along those costs to shareholders. Ironically, even though brokerage commission expenses can sometimes rival investment management fees, they are not included

Figure 9-15.   Performance Based on Turnover Rates (Data as of April 2006)

Turnover Rate	5 Year Returns	10 Year Returns	15 Year Returns
Turnover Less Than 50%	**5.91%**	**9.42%**	**10.91%**
Turnover 50%–90%	4.59%	8.23%	10.38%
Turnover 90%–200%	4.24%	7.70%	10.03%
Turnover Greater Than 200%	2.27%	6.70%	8.65%

Source: Morningstar

in a fund's so-called total expense ratio. Nevertheless, these costs will be deducted from the fund's total returns. This means that over time, trading fees can be a huge drag on the performance of your fund.

Take a look at Figure 9-15. What this chart shows is that consistently, low-turnover funds have outperformed high-turnover funds over long periods of time. In fact, the lower the turnover rate, the better off the fund has performed over the past 5, 10, and 15 years, according to Morningstar. Indeed, the average stock fund with a turnover rate of less than 50 percent returned 10.91 percent a year for the past 15 years through the end of April 2006. By comparison, funds with turnover rates of 200 percent or greater gained just 8.65 percent a year.

To reiterate, these modest differences in annual returns can add up to huge gaps over time. For example, $10,000 earning 10.91 percent a year over 30 years would grow to more than $223,000. But if that same amount was put in a fund that gained 8.65 percent a year, it would grow only to roughly half that amount—$120,000.

It just goes to show how important all types of fees are to a fund investor. Indeed, a fund manager who trades so frequently that brokerage commissions grow to 0.5 percent of assets would have to improve his fund's total returns by more than 0.5 percent to justify the expenses. This goes back to an earlier point: the higher the fee that a fund charges, the higher the hurdle it sets for itself.

CONSIDER INDEX FUNDS AND MANAGED FUNDS

Most mutual funds—more than 90 percent, in fact—are classified as *actively managed portfolios*. Actively managed funds are led by stock pickers and bond pickers. These funds give their managers a decent amount of latitude (within the fund's prospectus) to pick whichever securities they want and to hold them in whatever proportion they deem appropriate. This means the fund's performance lives or dies based on the skill of the manager.

But in addition to actively managed portfolios, there are so-called *index funds*. Like an actively managed portfolio, an index fund has a manager. But this manager is more of an administrator than a stock picker. This is because index funds do not

ask—or allow—their managers to make stock selections. Instead, an index fund (as its name would imply) simply tries to mirror a stock or bond market index by buying and holding all of the securities found in that index.

The most popular index fund in the world is the Vanguard 500 Index, with total net assets of more than $105 billion. By prospectus, the manager of this fund, popular in many 401(k) retirement plans, will not attempt to beat the S&P 500 Index by betting on certain stocks and avoiding others. Instead, the manager agrees to simply buy and hold all 500 of the stocks in the S&P 500, in the exact proportion in which they are found in the index.

The only time an index fund will sell a stock is if the index that it is tracking jettisons a particular stock. For example, if a merger between two companies were to knock a stock out of the S&P 500 Index, the Vanguard 500 fund would have to dump that stock as well.

Beyond the S&P 500, there are index funds that track any number of different market benchmarks, ranging from the Russell 2000 index of small stocks, the MSCI EAFE international stock fund index, the MSCI emerging markets stock fund index, and the Lehman Brothers Aggregate Bond Index, just to name a few.

But isn't this a reckless strategy—to buy and hold every stock in a broad market index, losers and all? That was certainly the knock against indexing when the very first index fund, the Vanguard 500 index portfolio, was launched in 1976. But history has shown that index funds, on average, have performed as well, if not better, than many of their actively managed counterparts over long periods of time.

Indeed, in the 10-year period ending in July 2006, the Vanguard 500 Fund has managed to beat 73 percent of its actively managed peers, according to Morningstar.

Of course, the Vanguard 500 is only one fund. Take a look at Figures 9-16 through 9-19. The Morningstar data clearly show that the average index mutual fund has held up quite well compared with actively managed portfolios over long periods of time. In fact, in many stock and bond fund categories, the average index fund has actually beaten traditionally managed portfolios. Over the past 10- and 15-year periods ending in May 2006, for example, the average large-cap index fund slightly outpaced actively managed large-cap portfolios.

Figure 9-16. Index Funds versus Active Management: Large-Cap Funds (Data as of May 2006)

	5 Year Returns	10 Year Returns	15 Year Returns
Index Funds	1.25%	7.87%	9.78%
Actively Managed Funds	1.58%	7.16%	9.48%

Source: Morningstar

Figure 9-17. Index Funds versus Active Management: Small-Cap Funds (Data as of May 2006)

	5 Year Returns	10 Year Returns	15 Year Returns
Index Funds	10.17%	9.49%	12.92%
Actively Managed Funds	7.94%	9.07%	11.17%

Source: Morningstar

Figure 9-18.   Index Funds versus Active Management: Foreign Funds (Data as of May 2006)

	5 Year Returns	10 Year Returns	15 Year Returns
Index Funds	10.86%	7.42%	6.92%
Actively Managed Funds	10.84%	7.55%	8.95%

Source: Morningstar

Figure 9-19.   Index Funds versus Active Management: Bond Funds (Data as of May 2006)

	5 Year Returns	10 Year Returns	15 Year Returns
Index Funds	4.49%	5.80%	6.32%
Actively Managed Funds	5.10%	5.39%	6.27%

Source: Morningstar

And over the past 5-, 10-, and 15-year stretches, small-cap index funds have handily beaten the active managers. For example, over the past 15 years, the average small-cap index fund returned an impressive 12.9 percent, while professional managers could only muster 11.1 percent, on average.

While index funds haven't done as well in other categories, such as foreign stock funds, they've still been extremely competitive.

How is this possible? It goes back to a couple of themes we've already mentioned. For starters, because index funds do not require the services of an investment research staff (after all, there is no stock selection in an index fund), they tend to charge among the lowest fees in the industry. While the average domestic equity fund charges fees of around 1.5 percent a year, the average equity index fund levies fees of about half that—0.75 percent of assets per year.

Meanwhile, many specific index funds charge far lower fees than that. The Vanguard 500 Fund, for example, charges just 0.18 percent of assets per year. This means that a $100,000 investment in the Vanguard 500 would only cost you $180, whereas the typical stock fund would hit you up for $1,540.

Another reason why index funds do so well is that they simply buy and hold stocks found in a market benchmark. As a result, they have extremely low turnover. For example, the average actively managed stock fund has a turnover rate of around 90 percent. But the average index fund has a turnover rate of less than half that—40 percent. And there are a number of index funds with even lower turnover rates. The T. Rowe Price Total Equity Market index fund, for example, which tracks an index of all U.S. equities, had a turnover rate of just 5 percent in 2006. This type of buy-and-hold strategy keeps transaction costs low at index funds as well.

Finally, there is a certain logic to indexing. True, your index fund will never be the absolute best-performing fund around. This is because an index fund must own all the stocks in a given index, which means the fund's total return will represent the *average* results of all of its holdings.

But history has shown that a majority of actively managed funds have fallen well short of average because they tried too hard to be better than average. This is why many investors have come to embrace indexing. Jack Bogle, founder of the Vanguard Group, which launched the very first retail index fund, has a saying: "Why look for the needle in the haystack when you can own the whole haystack?" In other words, why spend all your time trying to identify the absolute best-performing securities when you can simply own a piece of every security in a given market?

Again, your returns will only be average. But the point of financial planning is not to swing for the fences. It's to make sure your money is always growing. And since financial plans can do quite well based on the long-term historical rate of growth of stocks and bonds, why risk everything by trying to do better than stocks and bonds?

Exchange-Traded Funds

Exchange-traded funds (ETFs) were introduced in the United States in the early- to mid-1990s on the heels of two trends: the growing frustrations with the "mutual" aspect of fund ownership, and the growing acceptance of indexing as an investment strategy. See Figures 9-20 and 9-21.

State Street Global Advisers and Barclays Global Investors were among the first companies to launch exchange-traded funds in the 1990s, largely to compete against traditional mutual funds. But with their growing popularity, many ETFs are now being offered by mutual fund companies themselves, including Vanguard, Fidelity, and AIM.

What exactly is an exchange-traded fund? It's an index fund of sorts. Like a regular mutual fund, ETFs are baskets of stocks that offer investors instant diversification through a single investment. They often track traditional indexes like the S&P 500, the Russell 2000, or the MSCI EAFE index of developed market international stocks. (In the late 1990s, one of the most popular ETFs in the

Figure 9-20. Growth in Assets in Exchange-Traded Funds (in Billions)

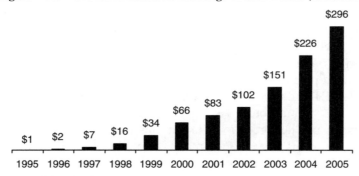

Source: Investment Company Institute

Figure 9-21. Growth in Number of Exchange-Traded Funds

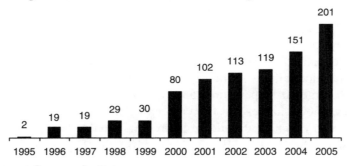

Source: Investment Company Institute

country was the Nasdaq 100 Trust Shares, a portfolio that tracks the technology-laden Nasdaq 100 Index).

But ETF providers are now taking indexing to the next level. Today, you can find dozens of specialty ETFs that not only track single-country indexes—Brazil, South Africa, Belgium, the Netherlands, and Malaysia—but highly specialized sectors of the economy. Barclays Global Investors, for example, offers so-called iShares ETFs that track everything from the Dow Jones U.S. Home Construction Index to the Comex Gold Trust Index. AIM's PowerShares ETFs offer investors the chance to invest in a wide range of specialty indexes, including those that track companies involved in water technology and nanotechnology.

What really sets ETFs apart is their structure. While ETFs look like index mutual funds, they are actually securities that can trade like an individual stock on an exchange (typically the New York Stock Exchange or the American Stock Exchange). This means that unlike mutual funds, ETFs can be bought and sold throughout the trading day.

In other words, if the stock market is in the midst of a sell off on a particular day, an ETF investor might be able to get out of his or her fund in the middle of the trading day, before things get too bloody. Conversely if, say, gold prices are starting to climb in a particular day, an investor in a gold ETF could step into the market mid-day, and theoretically capture some of the day's rise. This is something that a precious metals mutual fund investor could not do.

Even better, ETFs do away with another mutual fund flaw: the impact of other shareholders on your account. As we discussed, in a traditional mutual fund, a fund manager may be forced to sell securities within the portfolio—potentially triggering capital gains taxes—if too many shareholders exit the fund at once. But in an ETF, this really isn't a problem.

This goes back to the fact that ETFs are exchange-traded. When an investor wants to redeem from a traditional mutual fund, it's the fund company that takes back his or her shares and cashes the investor out. So the fund company has to find the money to meet the redemption. But an ETF is traded like a stock on an exchange, which means when people sell their ETF shares, another buyer (not the fund company) pays them the money and takes their place.

Another advantage to ETFs is that their fees are often as low, if not lower, than many traditional index mutual funds. For example, while the Vanguard 500 Index Fund charges 0.18 percent, Barclays iShares S&P 500 Fund, which also tracks the S&P 500, charges just 0.10 percent. This means that on an investment of $100,000, the Vanguard traditional index fund would charge you $180 a year, while the iShares S&P 500 ETF would cost $100. See Figure 9-22.

Figure 9-22. **Low-Cost Advantage of ETFs (Data as of July 2006)**

Name	Expense Ratio
Vanguard Extended Market Index ETF	0.08%
iShares S&P 500	0.10%
S&P 500 SPDR	0.10%
iShares Russell 2000 Index	0.20%
iShares Lehman TIPS Bond	0.20%
iShares Lehman Aggregate Bond	0.20%
iShares S&P 600	0.20%
MidCap SPDR	0.25%
Vanguard Health Care ETF	0.26%
Vanguard Information Technology ETF	0.26%
iShares Cohen & Steers Realty	0.35%
iShares MSCI EAFE Index	0.36%
iShares Dow Jones Dividend Index	0.40%
Fidelity Nasdaq Composite Tracking	0.45%
PowerShares Dividend Achievers	0.50%
PowerShares Dynamic Large Cap Growth	0.63%
Average Domestic Stock Mutual Fund	1.54%

Source: Morningstar

There is one big disadvantage to ETFs, however. Because these are exchange-traded products, you will need to open a brokerage account to invest in them. Moreover, every transaction you make in an ETF will cost you brokerage commissions. This means that any investor who is considering dollar cost averaging into an ETF should probably reconsider and instead select a traditional index mutual fund.

For example, say you decided to invest $100 a month in the iShares S&P 500 ETF, and you did so for 25 years. That would have amounted to 300 separate transactions over the course of two and a half decades. Even at a low commission cost of, say, $20 a trade, that would work out to $6,000 in unnecessary transaction fees. Now, had you put that same amount into the Vanguard 500 Index Fund, you would have gained exposure to virtually the same portfolio, with zero transaction fees.

Quiz for Chapter 9

1. What is a mutual fund?
   a. One of the valuable core assets available to small investors
   b. An investment company
   c. Both
   d. Neither

2. Because they are diversified investing vehicles, all mutual funds are considered reasonably safe to own
   a. True
   b. False

3. Specialized mutual funds invest in a diversified mix of sectors of the economy.
   a. True
   b. False

4. A hybrid fund...
   a. invests in a mix of stocks and bonds.
   b. invests in a mix of stocks and cash.
   c. is like a regular mutual fund in that it is diversified, but it trades like a single stock on an exchange.

5. One advantage to investing in a mutual fund is that they all offer active professional management.
   a. True
   b. False

6. Actively managed funds tend to outperform index funds because there is an active stock picker managing the funds.
   a. True
   b. False

7. High turnover within a portfolio tends to...
   a. result in lower returns.
   b. result in better returns.
   c. result in better returns relative to index funds.

8. If a mutual fund generates a total return of 7.5 percent and has a total expense ratio of 2.5 percent, what is the actually return?
    a. 10 percent
    b. 5 percent
    c. 7.35 percent

9. A fund's total expense ratio includes
    a. management fees, distribution fees, and transactional costs.
    b. shareholder servicing fees, management fees, and transactional costs.
    c. management fees, distribution fees, and shareholder servicing fees.

10. Exchange-traded funds are similar to index mutual funds, except that they...
    a. trade on a stock exchange.
    b. are actively managed.
    c. trade on a stock exchange and are actively managed.

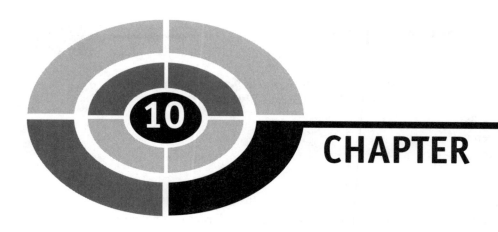

College Savings

Why We Must Plan for College

The purpose of any long-term financial plan is to start addressing tomorrow's needs today. That way, by the time those needs come due, you will have taken full advantage of the time value of money. In the next chapter, we will discuss ways families typically save for the most important (and expensive) goal of any financial plan—retirement. In this chapter, we will address what is fast becoming the second-most-expensive financial goal for most families: paying for your children's college education.

Surveys show that the vast majority of today's parents—97 percent, in fact—hope and expect at least one of their kids will attend college. And nearly 80 of those parents understand that they will have to pay for some, if not all, of those tuition costs. But there are several challenges for parents saving for college today:

- *Your time horizon is shorter.* While a worker might have as many as 40 years or more to save and plan for retirement (provided they start young), saving for college must typically be done within a much shorter time frame: 18 years at the most. And that's if you get started the moment your child is born. The reality is that most parents tend to wait until their children are at least two years of age to really get started. This means your time horizon is really closer to 16 years. The shorter your window of time, the more difficult the challenge. For example, if you were to save $1,000 today and had 45 years to let it compound, that money would grow 21-fold, assuming a 7 percent rate of interest. But that same amount, invested similarly for just 16 years, would barely triple. This means any type of college savings strategy that parents employ today must involve a greater percentage of their own personal savings—as opposed to investment gains—than even a retirement account may require.

- *College costs are rising faster than inflation.* When it comes to retirement, enemy number 1 is inflation. As you grow older and your money grows with you, you need to make sure that inflation won't eat away at the purchasing power of your nest egg faster than that nest egg is expanding. But when it comes to college savings, your enemy is even more insidious. While the historical rate of inflation has been growing at an annual pace of 3 percent, college expenses—including tuition, fees, room, and board—have been growing twice as fast. In other words, college inflation has been growing 3 percentage points on top of inflation each year. What this means is that if you want to grow your college fund at a faster rate than college prices are climbing, your assets will need to earn at least 6 percent annually. This means old ideas, such as traditional savings bonds (which in 2006 were paying out a modest 3.7 percent annual rate of interest) probably won't cut it. Nor will bank CDs (though a surprisingly large number of parents choose to use CDs to grow their college savings funds). Indeed, college inflation has even outpaced the annual historical rate of return for long-term government and long-term corporate bonds. This means stocks will need to play a major role in your plan.

- *Parents aren't starting early enough.* As with any long-term financial plan, the biggest challenge to a college savings plan is often inertia. Indeed, recent surveys have shown that a third of parents who say they expect to pay for at least some of their children's college bills haven't saved a dime. In addition, one in four parents have managed to save less than $5,000. In today's market, that simply won't get the job done.

Here's why: According to the College Board, the average tuition bill for a single year at a four-year private university is $21,235 (based on the 2005–2006 school year). Twenty years ago, tuition was about half that—$11,019 (and that's using current dollars). But the $21,235 price tag is only for tuition. The full cost of a single year's worth of tuition and fees, room and board at a four-year private

Figure 10-1.   Rising Cost of Tuition, Room, and Board at Private Universities (Prices in constant 2005 dollars)

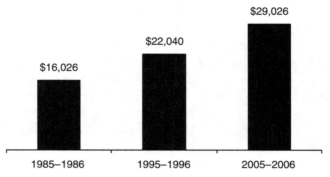

Source: College Board

college is just under $30,000. This means that four full years of private college for just one of your children will easily cost $120,000. See Figure 10-1.

Public universities are certainly an option, but public school education prices are growing almost nearly as fast as private education. Today, the full cost of sending your child to one year of a four-year public university is more than $12,100. This is about double what it was 20 years ago. See Figure 10-2.

The upshot of all of this is that some students are being forced to forgo their college dreams due to rising costs and their family's inability to keep up with those prices. Indeed, a recent Congressional report stated that as many as 48

Figure 10-2.   Rising Cost of Tuition, Room, and Board at Public Universities (Prices in constant 2005 dollars)

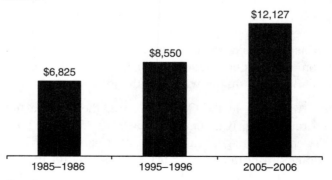

Source: College Board

percent of "college-qualified high school graduates" are unable to attend a four-year college because they cannot afford to. What's more, an additional 22 percent are prevented from attending any college at all.

Fortunately, parents do have options. For starters, while the average cost of college is certainly rising at a disturbing pace, families saving for college can still be good consumers. While you may be priced out of the most expensive private schools, you can still seek a good college education at a public university. And often, there are a number of public universities that charge well below the national averages.

Indeed, recent studies indicate that close to half of all students wind up attending a four-year university that charges under $6,000 a year. And the vast majority of students spend less than $9,000 a year for tuition and fees. See Figure 10-3.

Then there's always financial aid. Though it's not necessarily the wisest idea to bank on financial aid because you may not qualify, the fact is that the vast majority of students will qualify for some form of assistance, at least to cover a portion of their costs. According to the National Association of Student Financial Aid Administrators, two-thirds of all undergraduates receive some form of aid. And at private universities, this number is actually much higher. Nine out of 10 undergraduates at four-year private colleges receive at least some form of financial aid.

To be sure, some of that aid may come in the form of loans instead of scholarships or grants. But as was noted in Chapter 2, student loans are really a decent form of debt that's also tax deductible. And not all of your financial aid will come in this form. According to a study by the National Center for Education Statistics,

Figure 10-3. Where Full-Time Undergraduates Go to School (Based on 2005–2006 academic year)

Yearly Charges at Four-Year Colleges	Percentage Attendance
$33,000 and Higher	1%
$30,000–$32,999	5%
$27,000–$29,999	3%
$24,000–$26,999	3%
$21,000–$23,999	6%
$18,000–$20,999	5%
$15,000–$17,999	3%
$12,000–$14,999	2%
$9,000–$11,999	5%
$6,000–$8,999	21%
$3,000–$5,999	43%
Under $3,000	3%

Source: College Board

Figure 10-4.   Percentage of Undergraduates Who Receive Some Financial Aid (Based on 2004 academic year)

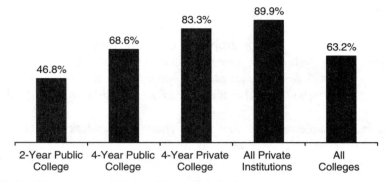

Source: National Association of Student Financial Aid Administrators

the average undergraduate who received financial aid in 2004 borrowed $5,800 in student loans, but received an additional $4,000 in the form of grants. Combined, these loans and grants typical cover about two-thirds of the average student's tuition and fees.

The situation is even better at private universities. In 2004, the average undergrad at a four-year private college who received aid took out $7,000 in student loans and received another $13,500 in grants for a grand total of $14,200 in financial aid. This helped more than 83 percent of undergraduates pay for tuition and fees. See Figure 10-4.

The most encouraging news is that the federal government has recently established several new tax-advantaged college savings vehicles to help parents cover that remaining gap. Since financial aid is such an important part of many families college savings plan, it's important to be mindful of qualifying for aid when you start saving. Thankfully, most of the federally sponsored college savings plans around are financial-aid friendly. Let's discuss them in detail.

529 Savings Plans

WHAT ARE THEY?

Though many parents refer to 529 savings plans as the "401(k) of college savings," these tax-sheltered investment accounts are really closer in structure to a Roth IRA. Just like in a Roth IRA, contributions are made with after-tax dollars (though there may be some state tax deductions available). Once in the plan, your

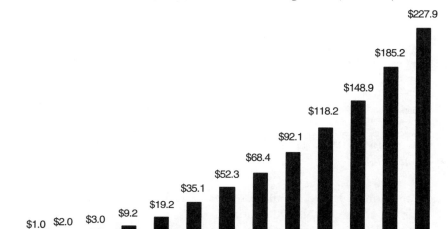

Figure 10-5.   Projected Assets for 529 Savings Plans (in billions)

Source: Financial Research Corp.

investments will be sheltered from taxes. And money that is eventually withdrawn from a 529 plan can be taken out tax free provided that the money will be used for *qualified educational expenses* at an accredited college.

Qualified expenses, according to the IRS, include tuition, fees, books, supplies, and any equipment that your university requires as part of enrollment. So for instance, if your child's college requires all students to purchase a computer, then you could use 529 money for that purpose. Moreover, money saved through a 529 plan can be used to pay for room and board as well, so long as the student in question attends at least half time at an accredited institution. See Figure 10-5.

Just as a 401(k) is considered the first option for retirement savings, many parents regard 529 plans as the best vehicle to start saving for school. The tax-deferral alone is a valuable commodity that parents should not overlook.

Consider the example in Figure 10-6. The financial services firm T. Rowe Price studied the importance of tax deferral on college savings. It compared two hypothetical examples: a parent who saves $5,000 a year for 18 years in a tax-deferred 529 account, alongside a parent who saves the same amount for the same amount of time, only through a regular taxable brokerage account.

Both parents end up putting aside $90,000 of their own money (that's $5,000 a year for 18 years). And the *capital appreciation* on their savings is similar. But the big difference is the fact that throughout this 18-year time period, the parent who saves in the 529 has completely shielded his or her assets from investment taxes. Meanwhile, assuming a 25 percent federal income tax rate and a 5 percent state

Figure 10-6.   529 Plans versus Taxable Savings (Savings period is 18 years)

	In-State 529*	Out-of-State 529	Taxable Account
Total Amount Invested	$92,250	$90,000	$90,000
Earnings on Investments	$131,386	$128,182	$127,126
Taxes before Withdrawal	$0	$0	$14,927
Taxes at Withdrawal	$0	$0	$10,626
After-Tax Total Savings	$223,636	$218,182	$191,574

*Assumes you receive a state tax deduction of $2,250 in each year, for a $1,000 tax savings.
This example also assumes that the parent makes a $5,000 annual contribution to these savings plans for 18 years; that the money is invested in a large-cap growth fund earning pretax returns of 8 percent a year; and that the parent is in the 25 percent federal tax bracket and at a 5 percent state tax bracket.

Source: T. Rowe Price

tax rate, the non-529 saver would lose nearly $15,000 of the account's value to taxes over the course of this time horizon.

Moreover, the taxable investor would have to pay another $10,600 or so when he or she needs to liquidate the account to obtain the cash to pay for school. That's because the moment investors sell an appreciated asset in a taxable account, they realize capital gains and capital gains taxes will be due. By contrast, when you sell an investment inside a tax-sheltered 529, it is not considered a taxable event. When you withdraw money out of this tax shelter, it will come out tax free.

So, in this example, T. Rowe Price researchers concluded that the taxable saver might accumulate around $191,500 over an 18-year period, based on an 8 percent rate of return in a hypothetical large-cap growth stock fund. But the 529 saver—using the same investment strategy and setting aside exactly the same amount of personal savings—would accumulate nearly $27,000 more, or around $218,200. Think about it: An extra $27,000 in savings, over the course of an 18-year college investment regimen would buy you possibly another full year at a private four-year university.

T. Rowe Price took its analysis one step further. Researchers at the firm asked the following question: How much additional money could be saved if the parent utilized a 529 plan that offered state residents a tax deduction on contributions (as many do)? In this case, T. Rowe Price concluded that the state income tax savings would allow a parent to stuff even more into his or her 529 and those savings could add up to a meaningful sum if allowed to compound for several years.

Based on the above example, a parent who uses his or her home state plan might be able to accumulate as much as $224,000 in his or her 529 (again, this is assuming $5,000 annual contributions and an 8 percent annual rate of return). The bottom line: If you go with your home state 529—assuming it offers a tax break—you might come out $32,000 ahead of the taxable saver. That's a lot of money.

Still, despite the clear advantages of 529 plans, there are a number of confusing elements to these accounts that parents don't always understand.

For starters, though 529s get their name from the section of the federal tax code that gave birth to them in 1996, these plans are actually sponsored by states. Today, virtually every one of the 50 states, plus the District of Columbia, has established at least one 529 savings plan. Many states, in fact, offer multiple 529s in partnership with financial services providers like Vanguard, American Century, and Fidelity. This makes the system even more confusing.

The good news is that you can invest in any 529 savings plan around, not just the one offered by your state. So for example, a resident of Illinois may choose to invest in Iowa's 529 savings plan. Why? Well, the parent might not like the financial services firms that manage the Illinois plans. Instead, he or she may prefer Iowa's plan because it is run by Vanguard, which is known as a low-cost leader in the industry. Or, the parent may simply prefer the investment options in one state's 529 plan over another.

If you are considering using an out-of-state 529, remember that many states offer their residents a state tax break if they participate in the home state plan, as we discussed earlier. In the case of Illinois, for example, in 2006 state residents could deduct as much as $10,000 per contributor per year for money invested in the Illinois 529. (For a full list of all 529 plans, visit www.savingforcollege.com. The details of every state's 529 are listed on this Web site, along with the fees they charge, the investment options they offer, and possible tax breaks.)

Keep in mind that you can invest in multiple 529 plans. Many families will choose to invest in a 529 plan run by their home state to take advantage of the state tax break. But after exhausting the tax deduction, they may divert the rest of their college savings into a different state's 529 plan.

WHY CHOOSE A 529?

A big reason why many regard the 529 as the family's first choice for college savings is the amount of money you can contribute and who can contribute that money. For starters, there are no income limits to participate in a 529, as there are in some other plans. So no matter how much the parents earn, they can take advantage of these college savings vehicles for their children.

You don't have to be a parent either. Grandparents and even friends of the family are permitted to open a 529 plan and contribute on a student's behalf. The only requirement is that the beneficiary must have a Social Security number (this merely means you can't open a 529 for your child before he or she is born).

Even better, the federal government does not impose any annual contribution limits to a 529. To be sure, most 529 plans will cap the total amount you can contribute to a single beneficiary over the course of your life. But the cap is extremely generous. In fact, many state plans will allow you to stuff as much as $250,000 (and in some cases even more) into these accounts. That should be more than enough to pay for your child's undergraduate and perhaps even graduate school bills.

There is a slight caveat, however. Though you can contribute as much as you want up to the state plan limit, the federal government will consider a contribution to a 529 as "a gift" to the beneficiary. And in 2006, any gift of more than $12,000 to a single beneficiary could subject the gift-giver to gift taxes. Fortunately, the 529 system provides a way for investors to get around this gift-tax issue. If you make a contribution of up to $60,000 to a 529 plan in a single year, the IRS will let you treat that contribution as if it were spread out over a five-year period ($12,000 a year), thereby avoiding the gift tax.

This means any parent who is trying to play catch-up when it comes to college savings could drop as much as $60,000 into one of these accounts in one year without worry. This $60,000 rule also makes 529s an ideal vehicle through which grandparents might consider gifting money to their grandkids in a tax-efficient manner.

Now, compare this to the contribution limits for a competing college savings vehicle, the so-called Coverdell Education Savings Account (which we will discuss at length in a moment). The Coverdell permits parents to stuff only $2,000 a year for their children's education (before 2002, the annual cap was even lower: $500). Try amassing $120,000 for four years of private college within an 18-year time frame, or shorter, through contributions of only $2,000 a year. It would be very difficult. This is why many parents naturally start with a 529.

FINANCIAL AID IMPLICATIONS

Another reason 529 plans are so popular is that from a financial aid standpoint, they are quite benign. To understand why, it's important to recognize how the financial aid system treats assets.

In general, it is much easier to qualify for aid if money is held in the parent's name, as opposed to the child's. For example, while the federal financial aid system assumes that 35 percent of a student's assets should go toward paying for college expenses, no more than 5.6 percent of parental assets are expected to be used for school costs (parent's should note that starting in the 2007–2008 school year, the student's expected contribution rate will drop to 20 percent, thanks to a recent change in law). This is in recognition of the fact that many families have additional obligations than simply worrying about one child's college expenses.

Even though the IRS considers a 529 contribution to be a gift to the beneficiary (in this case the student), the Department of Education has made it clear that

529 assets cannot be considered the student's for the purposes of applying for financial aid. If the 529 plan is established by the parent, it will be regarded as parental assets for financial aid consideration. And if the account is opened by a grandparent, then the assets are neither the parent's nor the student's, which is even better for aid purposes.

INVESTMENT OPTIONS

One of the criticisms of 529 plans is that there are limited investment options within these accounts, just like with a 401(k). In general, investors will find a handful of traditional mutual fund options from which to choose in addition to a set of so-called *life-cycle funds,* similar to those we discussed in Chapter 9. These *age-based investment options*, which attract the lion's share of 529 assets, are single-fund investment solutions (meaning they invest in a mix of stocks and bonds and cash) that are managed with different time horizons in mind. This way, depending on how old your child is when you open the account, you can find a customized age-based portfolio suited to your beneficiary's needs. Obviously, the younger your child is, the more aggressive these funds will be and therefore the more they will invest in equities. But as your child grows older, these portfolios will automatically reduce the amount of risk by buying more bonds.

There is yet another limitation with 529 investment choices. The mutual funds and age-based investment options you will find in your plan will almost certainly be products managed by one firm—most likely the financial services firm that partners with a particular state plan. For instance, in Massachusetts, Fidelity is the state's partner, managing and administering all aspects of the 529 (this includes services such as overseeing the investments, mailing quarterly statements, and providing customer service). Therefore, investors who sign up for the Massachusetts plan will get to choose only among Fidelity funds. Similarly, Maryland's plan is run by T. Rowe Price, so investors will be limited to investment options managed by T. Rowe Price.

DRAWBACKS TO 529s

In addition to the limited investment options, there are a couple of other shortcomings to 529 plans that should be discussed. The first has to do with fees. The fact is that many state-run 529 plans are sold to investors through financial intermediaries. And in recent years, there has been criticism that too many brokers are pushing high-fee 529 plans without disclosing the potential impact of those costs to consumers. Just as they do with mutual fund investing elsewhere, fees matter in 529 accounts because they eat away at the long-term potential market for your account.

Moreover, the federal government recently expressed concerns that brokers were not informing 529 customers of the potential tax breaks they could receive by taking advantage of their home state plans. Ultimately, it is up to consumers to decide which 529 plans to invest in. So these concerns over high fees are largely avoidable so long as you do your homework and stick with a low-cost 529 provider. You can find out how much each state's plan charges in fees at www.savingforcollege.com.

Up until recently, there was one other big drawback surrounding 529 plans. The one feature that makes these accounts so attractive—the tax-free withdrawals from these tax-sheltered plans—was technically scheduled to "sunset" on December 31, 2010. In other words, after this date, withdrawals from these plans were set to go back to being taxed at the child's income tax rate.

But recently, the federal government made the tax-free status of 529 plans permanent, thanks to the passage of the Pension Protection Act of 2006. The vast majority of college finance experts had always been confident that Uncle Sam would eventually make this move. After all, 529 plans have become such valuable vehicles for families saving for college that it's hard to imagine that Congress would turn its back on such a family-friendly issue. Now that the federal government has taken this step, many financial planners believe 529s should be the core savings vehicles for most parents saving for school.

Coverdell Education Savings Accounts

WHAT ARE THEY?

Like 529s savings plans, Coverdell Education Savings Accounts (ESAs) are tax-sheltered vehicles that allow parents to save money toward their children's education. Founded in 1997, Coverdell accounts used to be called Education IRAs. But since they have nothing to do with retirement, the name was changed several years ago.

The rules for Coverdell accounts are fairly similar to a 529. For starters, parents must fund a Coverdell with after-tax dollars. In other words, there are no federal tax deductions for funding an ESA. Once in the plan, money is allowed to grow tax free. And eventually, money is allowed to be withdrawn from an ESA completely tax free, so long as it is used for qualified educational purposes. Even better, these accounts always permitted tax-free withdrawals, so there was never any risk that this beneficial provision would expire (as was the case with 529s earlier on).

WHY CHOOSE A COVERDELL?

For starters, Coverdell accounts have a broader definition for what consititutes *qualified educational expenses*. For instance, Coverdells can be used to pay for basic tuition, fees, books, and room and board at accredited colleges—just like a 529. But in addition, these accounts can also be used to pay for elementary and secondary education. This means Coverdell accounts are particularly attractive to families who are also thinking of sending their kids to private elementary and secondary schools (K-12).

What's more, the IRS specifies that money held in an ESA can go toward paying for "equipment" associated with K-12 or college education, in addition to tuition, fees, and room and board. This means you can withdraw ESA money to pay for things like computer equipment or even possibly Internet service used in conjunction with elementary, secondary, or postsecondary education.

INVESTMENT OPTIONS

Another reason why many parents might choose to open a Coverdell instead of a 529 is that ESAs are not state-sponsored programs. This means Coverdell accounts can be established at banks, brokerages, or mutual fund companies of your choosing. For instance, if you're already a customer of Vanguard and like their mutual fund offerings, you could simply open a Coverdell through that fund company.

In this sense, Coverdells are a lot like individual retirement accounts. In an IRA, you can choose which financial services company to open the account with. And by doing so, you can invest in any number of different mutual funds, ETFs, or other investment vehicles. In fact, you could simply choose to invest your Coverdell assets in individual stocks through a brokerage.

DRAWBACKS

There are two big limitations when it comes to ESAs. For starters, not every parent is allowed to contribute, as the federal government imposes income restrictions for contributors. In 2006, those with modified-adjusted gross incomes of $110,000 or more were not eligible to establish a Coverdell account. For married couples filing a joint return, the income threshold was set at $220,000.

In addition, those who are eligible to contribute can only invest a maximum of $2,000 a year into these plans. As we discussed earlier, it would be difficult for a parent to save enough for four years of private university by setting aside only $2,000 annually. This is especially true if you get off to a late start. For example, if you start saving for your child's college education when he or she turns 10, $2,000 a year invested at 7 percent interest for just eight years would grow to only around $22,000.

Even worse, if the federal government does not extend or make permanent an earlier piece of Coverdell legislation, those annual contributions limits will fall to just $500 starting in 2011. (Moreover, if the federal government does not act in the coming years, the legislation that allows Coverdell money to be used for K-12 purposes will also expire starting in 2011.)

Because of the low contribution limits, parents who choose to save through a Coverdell should probably consider using this account in conjunction with another college savings vehicle. In years past, the federal government restricted parents from funding a Coverdell and a 529 savings plan for the same beneficiary in the same year. But recently, the government lifted that restriction, and many parents are using both plans.

Finally, Coverdells come with a ticking clock. According to the federal government, these funds must be used for the beneficiary's educational expenses by the time he or she turns 30. If money is left in these accounts after the beneficiary turns 30, the investment gains remaining in the plan will be taxed. They will also be subject to a 10 percent penalty. By contrast, 529 savings plans do not come with any age requirement. In fact, 529 assets can be held well into adulthood. And in fact, many plans are used by adults to pay for continuing education.

FINANCIAL AID IMPLICATIONS

Up until recently, Coverdell education savings accounts were at a distinct disadvantage to 529s when it came to financial aid. That's because money held in a Coverdell used to be considered the student's assets. But a recent ruling by the Department of Education changed all that, and Coverdell balances are now considered a parental asset. So for financial aid purposes, Coverdells are considered advantageous.

Custodial Accounts

WHAT ARE THEY?

Before the advent of 529s and Coverdell education savings accounts, a popular way for many parents to save for college was through old-fashioned custodial accounts. These included Uniform Gifts to Minors Act accounts, or *UGMAs,* as well as Uniform Transfers to Minors Act accounts, otherwise known as *UTMAs.*

Both accounts allow parents to transfer ownership of certain assets into their child's name through a trust. With an UGMA, parents can transfer cash, stocks, and other securities to their kids to help pay for college. The same is possible through an UTMA, though UTMAs also permit the transfer of other types of assets including art, collectibles, and even real estate. By law, the transfer of ownership must be irrevocable, meaning that parents cannot regain title to the assets. But because children are not legally allowed to manage their own finances, parents can still retain control over these financial assets until the child in question turns either 18 or 21, depending on the state.

WHY CHOOSE AN UGMA OR UTMA?

Unlike a 529 plan, a custodial account is not a tax-deferred vehicle. UGMAs and UTMAs are taxable accounts. But the whole point of investing in these accounts is to take advantage of your child's beneficial tax rate.

For example, in the past, a common strategy for parents saving for college was to transfer ownership of appreciated stock to the child. Then, when it was time for college, the child could sell the shares at his or her lower capital gains tax rate (typically 5 percent). The proceeds of the sale could then be used to pay for tuition. Without the custodial account, parents might be forced to sell the appreciated stock in their own name, which would trigger capital gains taxes of 15 percent.

But over the past couple of decades, Uncle Sam has made it harder to take advantage of your child's beneficial tax rate, which has made these accounts less appealing. First came the introduction of the so-called kiddie tax, in 1987. The purpose of the kiddie tax was to prevent wealthy parents from using custodial accounts simply to shield their own assets. So the federal government began to tax minors on unearned income, such as capital gains. Under the old kiddie tax rules, the first few hundred dollars of unearned income in an UGMA was tax free, the next few hundred dollars was taxed at the child's beneficial rate, and anything over that was taxed at the parent's rate (the actual threshold amount was adjusted for inflation annually). Only when the child turned 14 did he or she become eligible to take full advantage of his or her beneficial tax status. And once that occurred, all unearned income over a certain threshold was taxed at the child's lower rate.

But in 2006, the federal government raised the kiddie tax age limit from 14 to 18, effectively removing any substantive tax advantage to saving for college through these custodial accounts. Indeed, in 2006, the first $850 of unearned income in a custodial account was considered tax free, the next $850 was taxed at the child's rate, and anything above that limit was taxed at the parent's rate until the child turned 18. This means there is now little difference between parents saving and investing in their own name and doing so through a custodial account.

DRAWBACKS

The raising of the kiddie tax age has certainly damaged the usefulness of custodial accounts as college savings vehicles. In fact, parents are now much better off using 529 plans to fund their kids' college educations. This is what researchers at T. Rowe Price recently concluded. In this case, T. Rowe Price compared two hypothetical situations: a parent saving $5,000 annually in a growth stock fund (earning 8 percent a year) within a 529 savings plan and a parent investing similarly in a custodial account for the child. Under the new kiddie tax law, the parent utilizing the custodial account would see the child's account grow to $207,700 in 18 years. But the parent who opted for the 529 would enjoy an account balance of $218,200, or $10,500 more. See Figure 10-7.

There's one more drawback when it comes to UGMAs and UTMAs; it has to do with control. Let's say you established an account for your child when he or she was 10. And let's assume that you've used this vehicle as your child's primary college savings account. Once he or she turns 18 (or 21 in certain states), control over the assets in the account legally reverts to the child. So you as the parent would have no authority to force your child to use the proceeds of the account to pay for college. If your child wanted, he or she could take the money and go to Spring Break. This problem does not arise in a 529, since 529 assets are controlled by the person who opened the account, not the beneficiary.

FINANCIAL AID IMPLICATIONS

Another reason why parents may want to reconsider using a custodial account is that UTMAs and UGMAs are among the worst college savings vehicles when

Figure 10-7.   529 Plans versus Custodial Accounts (Savings period is 18 years)*

	529	UGMA/UTMA
Total Amount Invested	$90,000	$90,000
Earnings on Investments	$128,182	$131,854
Taxes before Withdrawal	$0	$8,873
Taxes at Withdrawal	$0	$5,251
After-Tax Total Savings	$218,182	$207,731

*This example assumes that the parent makes a $5,000 annual contribution to these savings plans for 18 years; that the money is invested in a large-cap growth fund earning pretax returns of 8 percent a year; and that the parent is in the 25 percent federal tax bracket and at a 5 percent state tax bracket.

Source: T. Rowe Price

it comes to qualifying for financial aid. That's because by law, the ownership of assets in a custodial account are transferred to the child. And assets held in the child's name are detrimental to qualifying for aid. As we discussed, colleges and universities expect a sizeable portion of student money to be used to pay for tuition and other expenses.

Parents who are currently using a custodial account do have an out. The federal government now allows parents to convert an UGMA or UTMA into a so-called custodial 529 savings plan. Technically, the assets held in a converted custodial account will still belong to the child. But the Department of Education will not consider assets held in a custodial 529 as the student's.

Prepaid College Tuition Plans

WHAT ARE THEY?

So far, we've discussed self-directed accounts that help parents save and invest on their own for college. But one type of college savings vehicle doesn't require parents to make any investment decisions. They're called *prepaid tuition plans.*

Technically, these state-run programs are also known as 529s, since they were born from the same part of the tax code that gave birth to 529 savings plans (as if the college savings system wasn't confusing enough). But prepaid tuitions plans are nothing like 529 savings accounts. Indeed, while 529 savings plans are similar to 401(k) plans, prepaid tuition plans are much closer in structure to traditional pensions. This is because prepaid tuition programs do not require any investment decisions on the part of parents. Moreover, parents do not bear financial risk in these plans.

Instead, a prepaid plan simply allows parents to purchase units or credits of education for use in the future based on today's prices. In some states, contributions to prepaid programs are state-tax deductible. And if educational costs rise at a faster-than-expected rate, parents stand to do quite well in these programs, since they will be locking in a high rate of return.

Prepaid plans are largely state-run programs. In fact, around 20 different states offer these plans to residents who intend to send their children to an in-state public college or university (to learn if your state offers a prepaid program and to find out the terms of those contracts, visit www.collegesavings.org).

Recently, a consortium of more than 200 private colleges created what's called the *Independent 529 Plan.* This nonprofit program allows parents to lock in future educational expenses at private schools such as Princeton, Vanderbilt, and Syracuse universities, based on today's prices. The member schools in the

Independent 529 have also agreed to discount tuition to would-be investors by at least one-half of 1 percent per year. (To learn more about this program, visit www.independent529plan.com).

WHY CHOOSE A PREPAID PLAN?

The benefit of a prepaid tuition plan is that parents don't have to spend years investing for their children's college fund. There are no mutual funds or other investment options to choose from. Prepaid plans simply require a commitment of money up front. Because these plans allow families to lock in educational prices, prepaid programs appeal to those families who want absolute assurance of being able to afford to send their children to college.

DRAWBACKS

There are, however, several drawbacks to prepaid plans. For starters, prepaid plans really cover only tuition and mandatory fees. Money contributed to these accounts cannot be used to pay for room and board. So parents who use a prepaid program might also have to fund a 529 savings account to cover noneducational expenses.

Moreover, state-run prepaid programs are designed to allow residents to pre-purchase educational costs at an in-state school. But what if your child doesn't want to attend a public school in your home state? What if your child prefers to go to a private university? What if he or she doesn't get accepted to a public college in your home state? In that case, you can seek a refund from the prepaid program, but the amount of the refund will depend on each plan's rules. Some state plans will refund only a small amount more than your original principal investment. This means you will have lost any opportunity to invest that money for gains on your own.

FINANCIAL AID IMPLICATIONS

Prepaid tuition programs used to be the worst savings vehicle for qualifying for financial aid. For years, money saved through a prepaid tuition program used to reduce financial aid eligibility dollar for dollar. But a recent change in the law now treats prepaid tuition the same way 529 savings assets are treated—as parental assets. This means prepaid plans can be used by families who are counting on financial aid eligibility.

Quiz for Chapter 10

1. What are the special challenges facing parents saving for college?
   a. They have a relatively short investment period compared to saving for retirement.
   b. They need to earn at least 6 percent annually just to beat the rate of college inflation.
   c. Both A and B.
   d. It is no harder to save for college than to save for other financial goals.

2. The 529 college savings plans let you...
   a. invest after-tax dollars and withdraw money tax free for qualified educational expenses.
   b. invest pretax dollars and withdraw the money at the student's beneficial tax rate.
   c. invest after-tax dollars and withdraw the money at the student's tax rate.

3. Because 529 plans are sponsored by states, parents are somewhat limited in their choice of investment plans.
   a. True
   b. False

4. What is the maximum lifetime contribution parents can make to a 529?
   a. $250,000.
   b. There is no restriction placed on contributions.
   c. It depends on the state plan.

5. What are the disadvantages of a 529 plan?
   a. Limited investment options.
   b. Parents may be hit with a gift tax.
   c. Assets in the plan could hurt your child's chances of getting financial aid.
   d. All of the above.
   e. There are no disadvantages.

6. 529 savings plans and Coverdell ESAs differ in which of the following ways?
   a. 529 money can be used for K-12 expenses as well as college costs.
   b. Coverdell money can only be used for tuition and fees.

    c. Coverdell money can be used for K-12 expenses as well as college costs.

7. As with 529 savings plans, money invested in a prepaid tuition plan can be spent on the following qualified educational expenses:
    a. Tuition and fees at an accredited college
    b. Tuition, fees, room and board at an accredited college
    c. Tuition and fees at an accredited primary, secondary, and post-secondary educational institution

8. You cannot contribute to both a 529 plan and a prepaid tuition plan in the same tax year for the same beneficiary.
    a. True
    b. False

9. From a financial aid standpoint, it is always better to have assets held…
    a. in the child's name rather than the parent's.
    b. in the parent's name, rather than the child's.
    c. in a custodial account.

10. The federal financial aid system assumes what percentage of the parent's assets will be used to pay for college costs?
    a. up to 5.6 percent
    b. 35 percent
    c. 20 percent

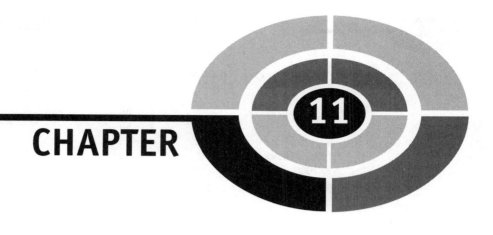

CHAPTER 11

Retirement Savings

Why We Must Plan for Retirement

From a financial planning standpoint, retirement is both a blessing and a curse. On the one hand, those of us who are planning for our golden years have been blessed with a big luxury: time. And a whole lot of it. For most Americans, a working career will typically last around 40 years. For some, it may be even longer. In theory, this length of time should give most households plenty of opportunity to allow compound interest to work on behalf of their long-term financial plans. See Figure 11-1.

But that's in theory. The fact is, around one in four American adults has yet to save anything for retirement. That's according to a recent survey by the Employee Benefit Research Institute. And among those who are saving, more than half have less than $25,000 amassed. That's hardly going to be enough to pay for a phase of life that could well last another 25 or 30 years, thanks to modern medicine. What's worse, barely more than a third of all workers in America have even tried to calculate how much they'll need to save for retirement. And without knowing

Figure 11-1.   Total Savings and Investments for Retirement

	All Workers	Ages 35–44	Ages 45–54	Age 55+
Less than $25,000	53%	49%	43%	43%
$25,000–$49,999	12	14	14	8
$50,000–$99,999	12	16	12	12
$100,000–$249,999	11	12	14	11
$250,000 or more	12	9	16	26

Source: Employee Benefit Research Institute

how much to save, it's impossible to determine if your financial plan is on track or not.

This brings us to the curse of retirement planning: Trying to save for one's golden years has become an absurdly expensive financial undertaking. And unlike, say, saving for college, the government provides no last-minute financial aid or student loans to help cover gaps that will invariably arise in one's retirement savings plan.

Surveys would indicate that most workers haven't a clue how much retirement actually costs. Estimates are all over the map. For example, around 30 percent of workers think they'll need less than a quarter of a million of dollars to live comfortably in retirement, according to recent surveys. Another 20 percent or so think they'll need between a quarter of a million dollars and half a million dollars to finance their golden years. Yet another 20 percent or so think they'll need between a half million and a million dollars. And yet another 20 percent or so think retirement will easily cost a million dollars or more. See Figure 11-2.

So what's the right answer? It depends on a number of factors. Among them: your current income; your current rate of savings; the speed with which your investment accounts can be expected to grow during retirement; and the speed with which you're likely to withdraw those funds to generate your annual income in retirement. Whatever your particular answer is, brace yourself for a big number.

Figure 11-2.   How Much Do Workers Think They Need to Save For Retirement?

	All Workers
Less than $250,000	30%
$250,000–$499,999	19%
$500,000–$999,999	21%
$1 million–$1.49 million	8%
$1.5 million or more	10%

Source: Employee Benefit Research Institute

For instance, according to a recent health-care study by the Employee Benefit Research Institute, a 65-year-old couple who retires today—and simply lives to an average life expectancy of 82 for men and 85 for women—will need to amass $295,000 for retirement. But that's just to pay for health-insurance premiums and out-of-pocket medical expenses for the remainder of their lives. Your other expenses—housing, food, clothing, transportation, and entertainment—could easily wind up costing you twice as much, if not more.

To determine how much you'll actually need, you really have to start with your current income and lifestyle. After all, the whole point of being able to fund a "comfortable" retirement is to sustain a level of income that will allow you to continue living as you do today. The last thing you'd want to happen is to go down in socioeconomic standing simply because you've quit working.

How Much Retirement Income Will You Need to Generate in Retirement?

There's been plenty of academic research over the years geared to answering this very question. For several years, in fact, researchers at Georgia State University and Aon, the insurance company, have studied trends in spending, taxation, and aging in an effort to determine how much income retirees really need in order to sustain a particular lifestyle. They've come up with some interest findings.

For example, a retiree who earns $70,000 a year during his or her working career might be able to lead a similar lifestyle in retirement for as little as $52,500 annually, which works out to around 75 percent of preretirement income. By contrast, it might require a worker who earns $150,000 today around 85 percent of his or her preretirement incomes, or $127,500 a year, to maintain that lifestyle in retirement.

Why might retirees require slightly less money in retirement to cover a similar lifestyle? Part of it is due to the fact that once you retire, you will no longer have to save money for retirement. But Georgia State researchers also discovered that spending patterns change in retirement. For example, once you leave the workforce, your budget for things like clothing and transportation and taxes are likely to diminish. Hence, retirees are generally able to get by with between 74 percent and 87 percent of their preretirement incomes, depending on how much they earn today. See Figure 11-3 for a complete breakdown based on incomes.

Of course, each situation is different. A person who can technically get by on 75 percent of their preretirement income may make decisions in retirement that will require even more funding. For example, many retired couples today choose

Figure 11-3. **Income Replacement Needed to Maintain Lifestyle in Retirement**

Preretirement Income	Replacement Percentage
$30,000	78%
$50,000	74%
$70,000	75%
$90,000	76%
$150,000	85%
$200,000	86%
$250,000	87%

Source: Georgia State University, Aon (2001 survey)

to relocate after they quit working. And if you decide to move to a different region of the country with a higher cost of living than your current situation, then your budgetary needs will change. Similarly, some retirees choose to travel and vacation early on in their retirement years. And if you were to choose to go to exotic—and expensive—locations, then your retirement income will need to reflect that.

How Big Must Your Nest Egg Be to Generate Sufficient Annual Income?

Simply knowing how much income you'll need to generate once you retire won't answer a more important question: How much must you save by the time you retire for your financial accounts to be able to generate that level of desired income safely? To find that out, we must turn to a different body of research.

Over the years, academics have been looking into the past success rates of various withdrawal strategies. In other words, economists have been studying how many years various types of portfolios tend to last, depending on how much money is withdrawn each year from those accounts to create a stream of income in retirement. For example, if you were to withdraw, say, 7 percent of the value of your retirement accounts annually, would that account be depleted in 20 years? Or might it last for 25 years or more, depending on how it was invested?

In the late 1990s, before the Internet bubble burst, many workers incorrectly assumed that they could tap around 10 percent of their retirement accounts annually. This means many workers actually thought that if they had $500,000 saved up, they could extract $50,000 a year from their accounts and still have money left over in 30 years. This wishful thinking arose at a time when stocks were gaining far in excess of 20 percent a year. And in that environment, conventional wisdom actually believed that spending one-tenth of your nest egg every year was a safe bet.

But after the stock market crashed in 2000, investors began to realize the folly of banking on 20 percent annual returns in their retirement portfolios. Instead, many workers have reset their expectations for equity market gains. Today, a portfolio representing a mix of stocks and bonds might only be counted on to grow 7 percent a year on average—and that's assuming you invest wisely.

Based on these more modest assumptions, what is a safe withdrawal rate? Three professors from Trinity University in San Antonio—Philip Cooley, Carl Hubbard, and Daniel Walz—crunched the numbers and came to a very sober conclusion. They studied the performance of various types of investment portfolios based on the historical returns for the stock and bond markets between 1926 and 1995. They then analyzed how many years those portfolios would have lasted historically, depending on how much money was withdrawn from those accounts annually.

It turns out that investors who want to be absolutely assured that their money will last at least 30 years can only withdraw 4 percent a year on an inflation-adjusted basis. That is to say, if you were 65 years and had an account worth $100,000, you could only withdraw $4,000 in year 1, if you wanted to be assured that you'd still have money left in your accounts by age 95. Then, based on a 3 percent inflation adjustment, you could withdraw $4,120 in year 2. Then in year 3, you would withdraw that amount plus another 3 percent inflation kicker.

Based on actual market returns, virtually every type of investment portfolio imaginable, ranging from all stocks to all bonds and most everything in between, managed to survive a 4 percent annual withdrawal rate for at least three decades, according to the findings of the Trinity professors. By contrast, a 50 percent stock/50 percent bond portfolio had only a 50–50 chance of lasting 30 years based on an 8 percent withdrawal rate.

But herein lies the problem: If you intend to withdraw only 4 percent of your retirement accounts each year to play it absolutely safe, you'd have to amass at least $1 million by age 65 in order to generate an income stream of $40,000. And $40,000 still doesn't sound like a whole heck of a lot of money to many would-be retirees. So doesn't this make retirement planning next-to-impossible for middle-income workers?

Not exactly. That's because you have to factor in your other sources of retirement income.

Other Sources of Retirement Funding

While much has been written about Americans' lack of confidence in the nation's Social Security system, the fact remains that this government safety net still generates a sizable percentage of income replacement in retirement. How much you

Figure 11-4.   Hypothetical Percentage of Preretirement Income Replaced by Social Security

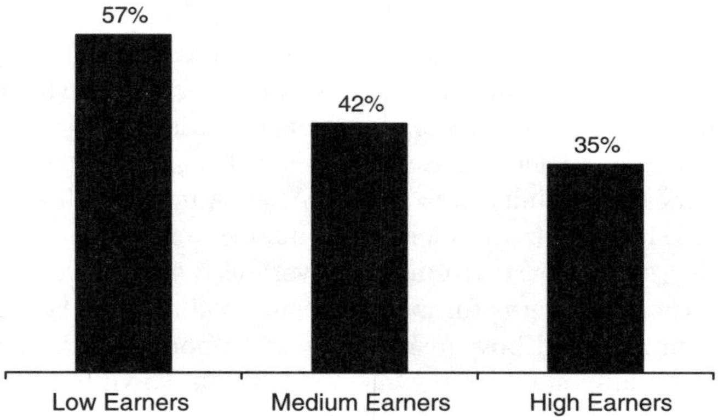

Source: U.S. Social Security Administration

can expect from Social Security will depend largely on the length of your working career and how much you've earned, and paid into the system, throughout your lifetime.

The United States Social Security Administration generally offers the following guidelines: Low-wage earners can expect to have more than half—57 percent, to be exact—of their preretirement salaries replaced by Social Security benefits. Meanwhile, middle-income workers can expect to have slightly more than 40 percent of their paychecks replaced by government benefits. Meanwhile, upper-income Americans can still expect around a third of their preretirement income to be covered by Social Security. See Figure 11-4.

Researchers at Georgia State University went one step further and studied the actual average Social Security payouts for workers in various income brackets. What they discovered is that most workers can expect to see anywhere from 10 to 53 percent of their preretirement salaries replaced. For example, while a person earning $200,000 might expect to see 13 percent of his or her preretirement salary covered by Social Security checks, a worker making $30,000 might see more than half of his or her paycheck replaced once in retirement. See Figure 11-5.

What this means is that your personal savings don't need to cover the entire amount of your retirement needs. Workers earning $30,000, for example, might need to replace 78 percent of their preretirement salaries to maintain their lifestyles in retirement, according to Georgia State University research. But if Social Security is likely to replace 53 percent of those workers' salaries, then they may only need to cover another 25 percent of their preretirement salaries to reach their overall goal. And 25 percent of $30,000 is just $7,500.

Figure 11-5. Income Replacement Provided by Social Security

Preretirement Income	Income Replaced by Social Security
$30,000	53%
$50,000	44%
$70,000	35%
$90,000	28%
$150,000	17%
$200,000	13%
$250,000	10%

Source: Georgia State University, Aon (2001 survey)

Using the 4 percent withdrawal rate, this means these workers may only need to amass $187,500 by retirement to be able to generate sufficient income. (If you're using the 4 percent withdrawal rate, just multiply your annual income needs by 25 to figure out how much you'll need to amass in your retirement accounts.)

Workers in different income brackets should expect to have different targets. Going back to the Georgia State models, we know that workers earning $50,000 will probably need to replace around 74 percent of their working salaries to be able to live as comfortably in retirement as they do today. Since Social Security is likely to replace 44 percent of these workers' incomes, this leaves them with a gap of only 30 percent to fund. And 30 percent of $50,000 works out to $15,000 in annual income needs. In this case, if you multiply that $15,000 by 25, you will find out exactly how much you'll need to amass to be able to generate sufficient income at a 4 percent withdrawal rate. Here, the answer is $375,000.

Of course, the higher your income, the more money you'll need to set aside to be able to fund your goals. Workers earning $90,000 a year, for instance, will probably need to replace 76 percent of their salaries to maintain their lifestyle in retirement, according to the Georgia State analysis. Since Social Security is likely to replace 28 percent of these workers' paychecks, they will need to cover a slightly bigger percentage of their preretirement incomes. In this case, their responsibility is to fund 48 percent of their preretirement incomes. Based on a salary of $90,000, this works out to $43,200 a year. Multiply that by 25 to figure out how much you'll need to amass in order to withdraw sufficient income at a 4 percent withdrawal rate. Here, the answer is $1.08 million. See Figure 11-6.

Again, this is only an estimate. Depending on your own particular circumstances, you may need to adjust this figure higher or lower. If you plan on leading a slightly more extravagant lifestyle in retirement than you did during your working years, then you will certainly need to do so. And if you anticipate higher health-care expenses due to an existing medical condition, it probably makes sense to adjust your goals higher.

Figure 11-6.   Income Needed From Sources Other Than Social Security to Maintain Lifestyle in Retirement

Preretirement Income	Non-Social Security Income Needed
$30,000	25%
$50,000	30%
$70,000	40%
$90,000	48%
$150,000	68%
$200,000	73%
$250,000	77%

Source: Georgia State University, Aon

Although the numbers get increasingly frightening the higher your income, and the more expensive your lifestyle, bear in mind that you don't have to rely solely on your personal savings to fund the gap. A minority of workers, for example, have access to *traditional guaranteed pensions* from their employers. These so-called *defined benefit* retirement accounts will typically base their payouts on the length of service workers have at a firm and what their peak salaries were. While the vast majority of Americans don't work for companies that offer traditional pension benefits—or have bounced around from job to job so frequently that their guaranteed pension payouts are expected to be paltry—workers with this benefit should make sure to include it when assessing their retirement income needs.

Don't Forget Your Home Values

As we discussed in Chapter 7, the vast majority of households today own their own homes. This has a couple of benefits. For starters, if you pay off your mortgage by the time you retire, your income needs may fall, as you won't be required to make ongoing monthly mortgages payments (or equivalent rent payments) in retirement.

Moreover, once your children leave the house, there are ample opportunities for would-be retirees to downsize. You could simply choose to sell your existing home and purchase a significantly smaller property, such as a condo, in the same community, thereby allowing you to pocket the difference in price. You could then apply that money to your retirement savings accounts. Or, you could sell your home and move to a similar-sized property in a significantly cheaper part of the country, also allowing you to lower your expenses.

Yet another option in retirement for those 62 and older is to consider a so-called *reverse mortgage.* Reverse mortgages, just like traditional mortgages, are loans secured by the value of your home. The proceeds of this loan can be paid to you in a lump sum or in monthly payments. So for many seniors, these vehicles can be used to supplement monthly retirement income.

The good news is that reverse mortgages do not require you to pay back the loan as long as you continue to live in the house against which the mortgage is applied. In fact, you can continue living in the home until you die, at which point the house itself will serve as repayment to the lender for the mortgage. Of course, if you choose to sell the house or move out of your primary residence before you die, you will have to repay the proceeds of the reverse mortgage at that time.

Because of the way these mortgages are structured, there are several requirements to consider. For starters, reverse mortgages are restricted to homeowners 62 or older. Moreover, the house that you intend to take the reverse mortgage out on must be your principal residence. And keep in mind that not all properties are eligible for reverse mortgages. For example, mobile homes are ineligible. And while most single-family homes qualify, there may be some question as to whether certain condominiums and some multifamily structures qualify.

Because the amount a reverse mortgage will pay you is tied to the equity you have in the home—as well as the value of the home, along with your age—these income-generating loans are best suited for older homeowners who have built considerable equity in their properties. Moreover, because the house you live in will be used to pay off the loan, this is not appropriate for homeowners who are considering bequeathing their properties to their kids.

Tax-Advantaged Accounts Help

In addition to your home, the single-most important savings vehicle you're likely to rely on to fund your retirement plan is a tax-deferred retirement account. Some of these tax-advantaged plans, such as your 401(k), are employer-sponsored, meaning your company sets up the account and administers the money. Others are government-sponsored entities, such as individual retirement accounts (IRAs), which you can set up through any number of financial services firms.

In recent years, many workers have begun to question the advantages of tax-deferred investing, given the fact that investment taxes across the board have been lowered in the past decade. Indeed, long-term capital gains used to be taxed as high as 20 percent. Today, the maximum rate for long-term capital gains is just 15 percent at the federal level. Similarly, corporate dividend income used to be taxed as ordinary income, at rates as high as 38.6 percent. But in 2006, the

Figure 11-7.   Taxable versus Tax-Deferred Investing*

Time Horizon	401(k)	Taxable Account
5 YEARS	$22,572	$21,555
10 YEARS	$55,737	$51,090
15 YEARS	$104,468	$91,709
20 YEARS	$176,069	$147,726
25 YEARS	$281,275	$225,135

*This example assumes the following: You invest $5,000 a year for each of the various time horizons. The money is presumed to be invested in a growth stock fund earning 8 percent annually. And the investor is assumed to be in a combined 32 percent federal and state income tax bracket.

Source: T. Rowe Price

top tax rate on qualified dividend income was capped at 15 percent. Meanwhile, income tax brackets have also been lowered, from a top rate of 38.6 percent to the current maximum rate of 35 percent.

Still, retirement investors need to keep a fundamental rule in mind: Not having to pay taxes beats having to pay taxes any day. And accounts that can be sheltered from taxes for decades are likely to be more useful to retirement savers than accounts that assess a modest level of taxes year in and year out.

The mutual fund giant T. Rowe Price confirmed this in a recent study. T. Rowe Price researchers took a hypothetical example, where an investor would put $5,000 into a growth stock fund on a pretax basis in a 401(k) every year for five years. Assuming the money grows 8 percent a year and is withdrawn in five years, the after-tax value of that 401(k) would be $22,572, according to T. Rowe Price. See Figure 11-7.

By comparison, if that same investor put $5,000 a year into a traditional broker-age account for five years, the investor would have turned that money into $21,555 during this time, based on a combined 32 percent federal and state income tax bracket.

Over longer periods of time, the gap widens even further. Over 25 years, for example, a $5,000 annual pretax investment in a 401(k) earning 8 percent a year would grow to $281,275. That's accounting for the fact that you would tap the account at the 25-year mark and have to pay taxes on it. That same amount, contributed into a taxable account, would grow to just $225,135. That's a difference of around 25 percent.

The bottom line: Tax sheltered accounts such as 401(k)s and IRAs allow investors to not only take advantage of compound interest but let their tax sav-ings compound over decades, which amounts to real money. So let's discuss the various tax-advantaged retirement accounts available to workers today.

Employer-Sponsored Retirement Accounts

401(κ) RETIREMENT ACCOUNTS

What They Are

When they were first created in 1981, 401(k) retirement accounts were supposed to be a supplementary account to guaranteed pensions. Yet over the years, pensions have fallen by the wayside and these tax-deferred retirement plans have become the primary savings vehicles for millions of American workers. Today, 401(k) accounts, which hold $2.1 trillion in retirement assets, are the largest source of retirement savings for two-thirds of American workers, according to the employee benefit consulting firm Hewitt Associates. That's up from 41 percent as recently as 1999. See Figure 11-8.

Technically, 401(k) plans are *self-directed defined contribution plans.* The self-directed part of their description is simple to explain. Unlike a traditional pension, where the company makes all the investment decisions for its workers, a 401(k) requires participants to make all the decisions. Among them: how much they're going to contribute, how they're going to manage the money invested in these plans, and when they plan on tapping the assets.

The term *defined contribution* refers to the fact that the only thing guaranteed in these plans is that if you choose to invest, say, 5 percent of your salary into a 401(k) investment account, 5 percent of your paycheck will be contributed into the plan. There are no guarantees regarding how quickly that money will grow or how much retirement income a worker can safely generate from that money. All of that will be determined by the worker's own investment performance.

Indeed, unlike "defined benefit" pensions where the company can tell you with absolute certainty how big your retirement checks will be, workers within defined

Figure 11-8.   Growth in Assets in 401(k)s

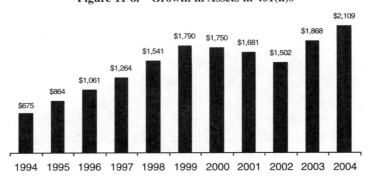

contribution 401(k) plans bear all the investment risk. Should you fail to meet your investment goals 20 years from now based on poor investment selection, for instance, you'd have to find another way to pay for retirement. On the other hand, if you're particularly savvy at investing, you could wind up earning more through a 401(k) than you might have received through a defined benefit pension. In that case, your "extra gains" would be yours to keep.

Ironically, while 401(k) plans have been credited with democratizing Wall Street—by allowing investors to stuff a small percentage of their paychecks every week or month into the stock and bond markets—millions of workers are not allowed to participate. This is because your employer must choose to establish such a plan and to keep it going throughout your working career.

Many small businesses, for example, citing the costs of establishing and running 401(k) plans, do not offer their workers access to these retirement plans. And there is no legal obligation requiring companies to do so.

The good news is, when 401(k) plans are made available to workers, those employees generally take advantage of them. In 2005, for example, 75 percent of all workers who were eligible to participate in a 401(k) did so. And this participation rate has remained relatively stable throughout the years. See Figure 11-9.

How They Work

Employer-sponsored 401(k) plans allow worker to invest pretax dollars into their investment plans. In other words, money that is contributed annually into these plans is tax deductible and will not be counted toward your annual income. So investing in a 401(k) has immediate tax benefits.

Figure 11-9. 401(k) Participation Rates Among All Eligible Workers

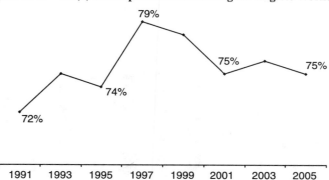

Source: *Hewitt Associates*

Moreover, once money is inside the plan, it is allowed to grow and compound tax-deferred. At retirement, after the worker turns $59\frac{1}{2}$, money withdrawn from these accounts will be taxable as ordinary income.

As for investment options, investors will typically have about a dozen or so to choose from, many of which are likely to be off-the-shelf mutual funds. If you're worried about being stuck with your original investment choices, don't be. Most plans these days allow for frequent trading. In fact, most plans will allow participants to move money into and out of various investment options once a day.

Another nice feature of these plans is that they are portable. So if you leave your employer, you have several options. Some companies will allow former employees to continue to utilize their 401(k) plans, though those former workers won't be able to put new money into their accounts. Some workers who switch jobs will simply choose to roll their former employer's 401(k) into their new employer's retirement plan, if the new company plan permits this type of tax-free rollover. Or, the government will simply allow workers to roll over their 401(k)s into tax-deferred individual retirement accounts if they leave their jobs, quit work, or retire.

In most cases, money inside a 401(k) can be tapped prior to retirement in the form of loans. Some workers, for example, may choose to take out loans against their retirement plans for a variety of purposes, such as to cover the cost of a down payment on a house. If you are thinking of taking out a loan against your 401(k), keep several things in mind.

For starters, in most cases, the proceeds of the loan will have to be paid back within five years or less, or it will be deemed an early withdrawal. And if money is pulled prematurely from these accounts, that is, before age $59\frac{1}{2}$, it will be taxed as ordinary income and subject to a 10 percent penalty. Moreover, you will owe interest on the loan from your 401(k). And finally, whenever you take out a loan against your 401(k), you will be forced to use after-tax dollars to repay your account, even though you funded your account with pretax dollars. So paying back the loan actually becomes more costly.

Eligibility

Because 401(k)s are employer-sponsored plans, your company must offer them for you to participate. The good news is, most companies that do sponsor 401(k)s will allow workers to begin contributing immediately upon starting work. A minority of plans, however, will impose a service requirement. For example, according to a recent survey by Hewitt Associates, around 5 percent of plans will only allow workers who have been at the company for at least three months to participate. Some plans, in fact, impose a one-year employment requirement before allowing employees to contribute.

How much can you contribute? There are a couple of factors that will determine this. For starters, the federal government imposes a blanket annual limit on 401(k) contributions. In 2006, that limit was set at $15,000. In subsequent years, that cap will rise with the rate of inflation. However, don't be surprised if you may not be allowed to contribute up to the federal limit. That's because all 401(k) plans are governed by company rules in addition to federal policy. And some companies may not permit full utilization of these plans by all workers.

Why wouldn't a company let all its workers take full advantage of their 401(k)s? It's a little-known fact, but companies that offer 401(k)s are required to meet certain so-called *nondiscrimination tests* by the federal government. These tests are designed to ensure that "highly compensated employees" (in other words, executives and managers) aren't benefiting disproportionately from these plans. To make sure this doesn't happen, the government requires 401(k) plans to measure the participation rates of both highly compensated employees and employees who are not highly compensated (in other words, the rank-and-file workers). If non-highly compensated workers are not participating in large numbers—and at sufficient contribution rates—managers and other highly paid workers at the firm may not be permitted to contribute to the federal maximum levels. So if you're only allowed to contribute, say, 8 percent of your income even though the federal government says you can contribute up top 15 percent, it's probably because other workers at your firm aren't contributing sufficiently to allow highly paid workers to take full advantage of their accounts.

There's one other thing workers need to remember. Thanks to a recent change in the law, the federal government will allow workers age 50 or older to stuff more money into these plans than other workers are allowed to contribute. These are referred to as *catch-up contribution rates*. The law was put in place to allow Baby Boomers who got a slow start saving for retirement to literally catch up and bring their accounts up to speed. In 2006, the annual catch-up contribution limit for 401(k)s was $5,000. Combined with the regular federal annual limit, this means that some workers might be able to contribute as much as $20,000 a year toward their retirement. In subsequent years, this catch-up contribution amount will be adjusted higher to reflect the rate of inflation.

Why They're Appealing

There are two hugely appealing aspects of 401(k)s. The first has to do with the fact that this is an automated form of savings that you can set and virtually forget. Once you establish participation, you can have your company direct 5 or 10 percent of each paycheck, before taxes, into your investment account. Since you get a paycheck every week or month, 401(k)s are an ideal way to dollar cost average money into the markets.

But there's one other feature that most other retirement plans don't come with. And that's a *company match*. The vast majority of 401(k) plans—around 70 percent to be exact—offer workers who participate a matching contribution into their accounts. In the most common situation, a company will invest 50 cents into your account for every $1 you contribute up to a certain amount, up to the first 6 percent of pay. This money is yours to invest and later withdraw.

Why do companies offer matches? It goes back to the nondiscrimination tests that we just discussed. In order for highly paid workers at a company to fully enjoy their 401(k)s, the rank and file must utilize these plans as well. And one way companies have discovered to encourage worker participation is to dangle the company match in front of them.

For workers, taking full advantage of a company match should be a no-brainer. That's because if you invest $1 and your company forks over 50 cents, you will automatically have earned 50 percent returns on your investment without taking any market risk. Any stock market returns you earn on your money will simply be icing on the cake. So the first rule of thumb for any worker eligible for a 401(k) that matches is to take full advantage of the match.

ROTH 401(K)S

Roth 401(k)s are a new twist on the traditional 401(k) retirement plan. While both types of accounts are fairly similar in contribution limits and investment options, there is one big difference. Instead of using pretax money to fund a Roth 401(k), workers use after-tax dollars to contribute to these employer-sponsored accounts. Once inside a Roth 401(k), money is allowed to grow tax sheltered. But at retirement, investors who use Roth 401(k)s will be permitted to withdraw money completely tax free, so long as they are over $59^{1}/_{2}$.

These new-fangled Roth accounts were first dreamed up in tax legislation that was passed in 2001. But companies were not permitted to implement Roth 401(k)s until January 2006. Because they are so new, many companies have yet to establish these accounts, so only a small fraction of workers have access to these plans. But recent surveys by Hewitt Associates indicate that nearly one-third of companies that offer traditional 401(k)s are considering the new Roth accounts as well.

If your employer offers such an account, is it better to go with a traditional 401(k) or a Roth? That depends on your current income and the income you expect to earn closer to retirement. Typically, the younger you are, the more a Roth 401(k) may make sense. For starters, that's because young workers have more time to make up for the money they'll lose on the taxes they'll owe up front by contributing to a Roth 401(k) instead of a traditional account. Remember, in traditional 401(k), your annual contributions will reduce your taxable income, thereby lowering your income tax bills in the years you participate. By contrast, in a Roth 401(k), the money you stuff into the account will still be counted toward your taxable income.

Moreover, younger workers are likely to be just starting out in the work force. This means that there's a great chance that they are in a low income tax bracket and will eventually earn more as they age. Because Roth 401(k)s require you to pay taxes up front but not at withdrawal, they make most sense for workers who are currently in a lower tax bracket than they expect to be at retirement. Conversely, an older highly paid worker may do better in a traditional 401(k) where new contributions will lower your immediate tax bill.

T. Rowe Price recently studied the numbers and found that whether or not a Roth 401(k) makes sense all depends on your income today versus your income closer to retirement. For example, say you're a 45-year-old worker who contributes $15,000 a year into a Roth 401(k) until you retire at age 65. And then, assume you continue to invest the money, earning 8 percent a year. But you begin to withdraw this money gradually over a retirement that lasts 30 years, until you're 95. Assuming you start out in the 25 percent federal tax bracket but gradually rise to the 35 percent bracket at retirement, you'd make out better with the Roth. According to T. Rowe Price's analysis, you'd generate $1.3 million in total lifetime income through your Roth 401(k) versus just $1.1 million in a traditional 401(k).

But if the situation changes, your strategy may not work. For example, in the hypothetical scenario just mentioned, if you drop to the 15 percent tax bracket at retirement (instead of rising to the 35 percent bracket), you'd actually do better in the traditional 401(k). In that case, you'd generate nearly $1.5 million in the traditional account versus $1.3 million in the Roth.

If you are considering a Roth 401(k), be warned of how matches will be treated. If your company matches your Roth contributions, by law that money will have to be kept in a separate account. This is because the IRS will still want to tax money obtained through company matches—and the earnings generated off those matches—at withdrawal. In a traditional account, this is no problem because withdrawals are all taxed as ordinary income. So a simple solution for younger workers may be taking full advantage of a traditional 401(k) up to the company match. Then you could use your remaining savings to fund the Roth without the match.

403(b)s and 457s

In addition to 401(k)s, the alphabet soup of tax-deferred retirement accounts includes so-called 403(b)s and 457s. Both vehicles allow workers to save and invest for their golden years through a tax-advantaged self-directed account like the 401(k). But they play to different audiences.

For example, 403(b)s are tax-sheltered savings accounts for teachers and employees of nonprofit organizations such as hospitals. The rules governing 403(b)s are somewhat similar to 401(k)s. For example, in 2006, 403(b) participants could save as much as $15,000 a year in pretax money, and older workers, depending on their status, could stuff additional sums in the form of catch-up contributions.

Once inside these plans, 403(b) money can be invested in a mix of different types of investments, including stock funds and bond funds. But there's a catch. While a 401(k) is actually established and managed by your private-sector employer, a 403(b) is more loosely overseen by nonprofit employers. Your school district or hospital, for example, will likely refer you to a list of financial vendors through which you can establish your 403(b) account. Be warned, however. Because many of the financial firms that offer 403(b) services are likely to be insurance companies, the fees associated with these plans tend to be much more expensive than 401(k) costs. As a result, 403(b) investors have to be particularly mindful of identifying low-cost investment options.

A 457, on the other hand, is a tax-advantaged retirement account that caters to employees of states and municipalities. The rules of these plans will differ greatly from state to state, but the federal limits for contributions are also similar to those of 401(k)s. This includes annual contributions of $15,000 a year in 2006, plus catch-up contributions of as much as $5,000 for older workers. In recent years, the federal government has improved the portability of all three plans so that workers who switch jobs can roll over their 403(b)s, 457s, or 401(k)s into IRAs upon leaving their employers.

Government-Sponsored Retirement Accounts

TRADITIONAL DEDUCTIBLE IRAs

What They Are

Individual retirement accounts, or IRAs, were founded more than 30 years ago, well before the creation of the 401(k). And over time, investors have amassed a sizeable sum in these accounts. At the end of 2005, these tax-deferred savings vehicles held around $3.7 trillion in retirement wealth. And approximately $3.3 trillion of that wealth is held in so-called traditional IRAs, making them by

Figure 11-10.   Growth in Assets in Traditional IRAs

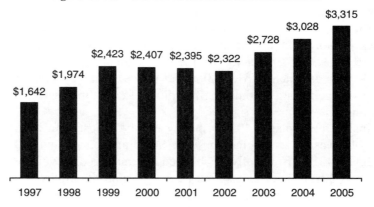

Figure 11-11.   Household Ownership of IRAs

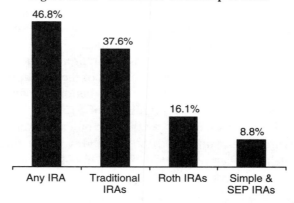

far the most popular type of individual retirement account in the country. See Figures 11-10 and 11-11.

Like 401(k)s, traditional IRAs are tax-deferred, self-directed retirement accounts that have proven themselves to be an effective tool for building retirement assets. Indeed, surveys indicate that workers who are utilizing IRAs—or 401(k)s for that matter—are far ahead of their counterparts who don't take advantage of these government-sponsored accounts. A recent study conducted by the Investment Company Institute, for instance, found that workers ages 35 to 49 who own either an IRA account or a 401(k) have saved $60,000 on average toward retirement. By comparison, the typical 35- to 49-year-old who doesn't have one of these tax-deferred accounts has only $2,500 saved for his or her golden years. Similarly, the average older worker (ages 50 to 64) who invests through either an

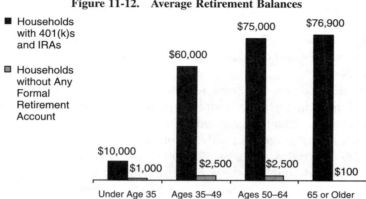

Figure 11-12. Average Retirement Balances

- ■ Households with 401(k)s and IRAs
- ☐ Households without Any Formal Retirement Account

	Under Age 35	Ages 35–49	Ages 50–64	65 or Older
With 401(k)s and IRAs	$10,000	$60,000	$75,000	$76,900
Without Any Formal Retirement Account	$1,000	$2,500	$2,500	$100

Source: Investment Company Institute

IRA or 401(k) has $75,000 saved. Meanwhile, older workers without either an IRA or a 401(k) have amassed just $2,500, on average. See Figure 11-12.

How They Work

A traditional IRA is very similar to a traditional 401(k), except that you can establish the account without the assistance of an employer. As with traditional 401(k)s, money invested in a deductible traditional IRA is funded with pretax dollars. In other words, if you invest $4,000 a year into these accounts, you will reduce your taxable income by that amount. So that's one way these accounts are tax-advantaged. Another way traditional deductible IRAs are tax-advantaged is that money invested through these accounts is allowed to grow tax-deferred until you retire. Then, at retirement, after age $59\frac{1}{2}$, money withdrawn will be taxed as ordinary income.

Eligibility

There are a couple of big sticking points when it comes to traditional IRAs. For starters, you can only contribute up to $4,000 a year in 2006 and 2007. This annual cap will rise to $5,000 in 2008, and starting in 2009 will be adjusted higher based on the rate of inflation. Moreover, while older workers are permitted to make catch-up contributions to their IRAs, the amount older workers can stuff into these plans is not nearly as large as the catch-up limits for 401(k)s. In 2006, workers 50 and older could only contribute an additional $1,000 into these tax-deferred vehicles, over and above the normal contribution caps.

The other problem with traditional IRAs is that not everyone is permitted to open these accounts. For starters, you have to be under age $70^1/_2$ and have earned income during the tax year to qualify for a traditional IRA. Moreover, your annual $4,000 contributions will only be tax deductible under certain circumstances.

For example, your contributions will be deductible if you work, but do not actively participate in a qualified employer-sponsored retirement account, such as a 401(k). If you do participate in an employer-sponsored plan, you can still deduct your full IRA contributions, but only if your modified adjusted-gross income is below $50,000 if you're single or $75,000 if you're married and filing jointly. If you're single and your income is between $50,000 and $60,000, you may be permitted to deduct only a portion of that $4,000 contribution. The same goes for a married worker filing jointly and earning between $75,000 and $85,000. Meanwhile, singles earnings more than $60,000 or a married worker earning more than $85,000 cannot deduct any of his or her IRA contributions.

Of course, if you earn too much to qualify for a deductible IRA, you can still participate in an IRA. The only difference is that your IRA would be classified as a *non-deductible individual retirement account.* In this case, your contributions would be made with after-tax money. Once inside the account, your money would be allowed to grow tax deferred. At retirement, your original contributions would be tax free, since you already paid taxes on your principal before making the contribution. But the gains that those contributions earned while inside the IRA would be taxable as ordinary income. Obviously, the tax advantage of traditional deductible IRAs make these accounts a more popular choice than nondeductible IRAs. But in many cases, a nondeductible IRA is still preferred—thanks to its tax deferral—than investing through a taxable account.

Why They're Appealing

Unlike 401(k)s, where your employer decides how many investment options to provide and which investment choices to offer, an IRA will allow contributors to put their money into any number of investment vehicles. This is because IRAs can be established at virtually any bank, brokerage, mutual fund company, or other financial services firm of your choosing.

This means that you can invest IRA money in stocks, bonds, mutual funds, CDs, T-bills, or even hard assets such as art or collectibles. If you already have a relationship with Fidelity Investments, for instance, and you're happy with that relationship, you can choose to open your IRA there. Or, if you have a long-standing history with a full-service broker like Merrill Lynch, that firm could establish your IRA for you. See Figure 11-13.

Figure 11-13.   Market Share of IRA Business

Aside from being able to open an IRA virtually anywhere—while being able to invest in virtually any asset of your choosing—tax deferral is a big reason to consider an IRA. Within your long-term financial portfolio, you will find any number of investments that are solid choices from a risk-reward standpoint but that are detrimental when it comes to taxes. High-yield bonds, for instance, which generate a sizeable amount of income, would be a good asset to shelter from taxes in an IRA. And because bonds do not enjoy favorable tax treatment under current law, fixed-income securities in general would be good to hold in an IRA. This is especially true of zero-coupon bonds, such as the Treasury STRIPS we spoke of in Chapter 6.

Yet another type of investment that may belong in an IRA is a REIT. As we discussed in Chapter 7, real estate investment trusts throw off large amounts of income, similar to a bond. But because REIT dividends are not classified as qualified corporate dividends, they will be taxed as ordinary income, not at the beneficial 15 percent dividend rate. So by investing in them through a tax-advantaged IRA, you can avoid a big tax hit while still taking advantage of a high-tax investment.

Variable Annuities

Don't confuse an individual retirement account with a variable annuity. Like a traditional IRA, variable annuities allow households to invest money tax-deferred. And like a traditional IRA, withdrawals from a variable annuity will be taxed.

Moreover, these retirement accounts give investors a dozen or so different invest-ment options to choose from. In a variable annuity, these are typically mutual fund-like investments called *subaccounts.*

But a variable annuity is really an insurance product. Think of it as a bunch of mutual funds that are wrapped in a layer of insurance. The insurance typically offers a surviving family member assurance that the account will retain a certain value, even if the account owner dies before retirement. But this death benefit often comes with a steep price. In general, the average variable annuity charges fees well in excess of a typical mutual fund. And depending on the fees, it could well take a decade or more of tax deferral before a variable annuity owner breaks even on the higher fees.

This is why many financials recommend variable annuities as a tax-deferred retirement account of last resort. First, take full advantage of at least your 401(k) match. Then take full advantage of your other retirement accounts, such as IRAs and Roth IRAs if you're eligible to participate. Then—and only then—should workers who still need additional retirement assets consider a variable annuity, financial planners argue. But if you do choose to use one of the vehicles, invest-ment experts recommend going with a low-fee variable annuity. Many low-cost mutual funds offer such plans, including Vanguard.

ROTH IRAs

A Roth IRA is similar to a traditional IRA in terms of investment flexibility, annual contribution limits, and tax deferral. But these accounts, which grew in popularity in the late 1990s, offer the reverse scenario of a traditional deductible IRA. See Figure 11-14.

Instead of using pretax dollars to fund these accounts, Roth IRA investors will contribute after-tax money into these tax-deferred accounts. Again, this means there is no up-front tax deduction for participating in a Roth. But at retirement, investors will be compensated because withdrawals from a Roth, including capital gains, will come out completely tax free.

The advantages and disadvantages between Roth IRAs and traditional IRAs are similar to the choice between Roth 401(k)s and traditional 401(k)s. The younger you are, the more time you give yourself to make up for the up-front tax hit you're likely to take with a Roth IRA. And so long as you contribute to a Roth when you're in a low tax bracket and then withdraw money at a higher bracket, you're likely to do better in a Roth IRA than a traditional account.

Roth IRAs do come with slightly different income restrictions than traditional accounts. For example, in 2006 you could only contribute the maximum amount,

Figure 11-14.   Growth in Assets in Roth IRAs (in Billions)

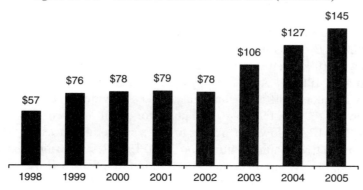

$4,000 each year, to a Roth if you were single and earned less than $95,000 in modified adjusted gross income, or if you were married filing jointly and earned less than $150,000. If you were single and earned between $95,000 and $110,000, you could still participate, but you weren't able to contribute the full $4,000 a year. The same went for married couples filing jointly and earning between $150,000 and $160,000. If you earned higher than those thresholds, you were not allowed to contribute to a Roth in 2006.

SMALL BUSINESS IRAs

In addition to individual retirement accounts geared for workers, the government has created a couple of IRA options for small businesses to take care of their owners and employees.

For starters, there's the *SEP IRA,* which stands for simplified employee pension plans. Small business owners or sole proprietors of firms of any size are allowed to establish SEP IRAs through banks, brokers, or mutual fund companies. These plans are particularly popular among small business owners who want to maximize their own retirement savings. This is because SEPs allow owners to sock away as much as 25 percent of their earnings into these tax-deferred investment accounts, up to a maximum of $44,000 a year (based on the 2006 tax year). So the ceiling for annual contributions to these plans is quite high. Moreover, you are not required to make contributions to a SEP every year, so you can determine how business is going on a year-to-year basis and fund as much as $44,000 or as little as zero.

But there's a catch. If you're the business owner and you contribute any money toward your own SEP account in a particular year, the same percentage of compensation must be contributed to the SEP accounts of every one of your employees

that year. This means a SEP may not be ideal for a business owner with a large number of employees.

For larger small businesses, a so-called *SIMPLE IRA* may be a better choice. The term *SIMPLE* stands for savings incentive match plan for employees. Small businesses with 100 or fewer employees earning at least $5,000 a year are allowed to establish a SIMPLE IRA. These low-cost and low-hassle plans can be created through any number of different financial services providers and are often referred to as the low-cost alternative to 401(k) plans for small business.

While a SEP IRA allows an owner to set aside as much as $44,000 a year toward retirement, the annual limits on SIMPLE IRA contributions are much lower. In 2006, the maximum annual contribution to a SIMPLE was just $10,000 (in 2006). And older workers could throw in another $2,500 in the form of catch-up contributions, for a grand total of $12,500 for workers 50 and older.

On the other hand, SIMPLE plans don't require big contributions to workers' accounts. Indeed, employers using a SIMPLE IRA need only make matching contributions to employees' accounts up to 3 percent of salary deferral.

Quiz for Chapter 11

1. According to academic research, workers who earn $30,000 to $90,000 a year will need to replace what percentage of their current incomes to maintain their lifestyles in retirement?

   a. Less than 80 percent

   b. 74 percent to 87 percent

   c. About 100 percent

2. What is considered a safe withdrawal rate from your retirement accounts?

   a. 4 percent

   b. 6 percent

   c. 8 percent

3. As a result of recently reduced federal taxes on income, capital gains, and dividends, investors don't need to invest as much through their 401(k) retirement plans.

   a. True

   b. False

4. A 401(k) is unique among other types of retirement accounts in that it offers...

   a. an up-front tax deduction.

   b. tax-free withdrawals on gains.

   c. a company matching contribution.

5. In a 401(k), all eligible workers can contribute as much as $15,000 a year.

   a. True

   b. False

6. The difference between a Roth IRA and a traditional deductible IRA is that

   a. Roth accounts are funded with pretax dollars while traditional deductible IRAs are funded with after-tax money.

   b. Roth withdrawals are taxed as ordinary income while withdrawals from traditional IRAs are tax free.

   c. Roths are funded with after-tax money while traditional deductible IRAs can be funded with pretax dollars.

7. Roth 401(k)s and Roth IRAs are best suited for workers...
   a. who are in a high tax bracket today and expect to stay there throughout their careers.
   b. who are in a low tax bracket today and expect to stay there throughout their careers.
   c. Who are in a low tax bracket today but expect to be in a higher tax bracket at retirement.

8. All retirement investors should consider putting money into a variable annuity.
   a. True
   b. False

9. Which of the following types of retirement accounts have the highest annual contribution limits?
   a. Roth IRA
   b. Roth 401(k)
   c. SEP IRA

10. Catch-up contributions are allowed for workers...
    a. 65 and older.
    b. 50 and older.
    c. 55 and older.

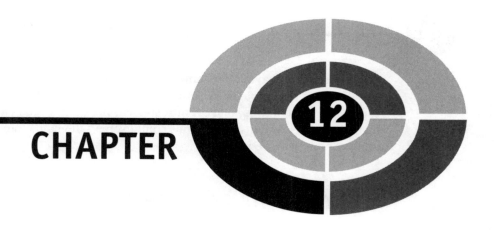

CHAPTER 12

Safeguarding Your Financial Plan

A Checklist for Your Financial Plan

As we've discussed throughout this book, creating a financial plan is the first step to achieving your financial goals. Study after study shows that whenever households sit down to literally map out their financial journey, they tend to get to where they want to go. This is probably because those people who map out their plans begin to see that it's not so hard to get from point A to point B.

But creating a financial plan is only half the battle. Once you start down the road to financial independence, you have to constantly check and recheck that you're still on the right path. Too often, savers and investors begin the journey to meeting their financial goals, only to get diverted and rerouted by last-minute emergencies or unexpected events in their lives.

It doesn't even have to be something big. Many times, life simply gets in the way. You may go through weeks and months where family obligations or work responsibilities build up, and all of a sudden, inertia has retaken control of your finances. This is why it's important to build some safeguards into your plan. Let's discuss some of those ideas.

ALWAYS PAY YOURSELF FIRST

As we discussed in Chapter 1, a huge obstacle to any financial plan is debt—in particular, bad forms of debt such as credit card balances. Data from the Federal Reserve show that the vast majority of households maintain some credit card balances at all times. Yet high-interest-rate credit card debt, as we discussed, can literally send your financial plan in reverse. What's the point of starting a savings and investing plan with the goal of earning, say, 8 percent annually when you've got thousands of dollars in credit card balances growing at an annual rate of 29 percent a year?

The best way to tackle debt, and then to start a positive savings regimen, is to literally pay yourself first. Often, when we sit down and go through our monthly finances, we start off with the big tickets items we owe, such as our mortgage obligations, car loans, student loans, utilities, and food. Then many households simply cover the minimum monthly payments on their card balances, or some fraction of what they owe. And after that, it's time to shop. Then, whatever money is left over is put into savings.

But try reversing the order. Ask yourself how much could you really save if you absolutely had to. Then set aside that amount off the top of your obligations each month. If you decide that you could save, say, an additional $250 a month, over and above what you are currently saving, start off each month by writing a check for $250 to yourself. Put the money into a separate account that's earmarked solely for paying down debt and jump-starting your savings.

By setting aside this money before you get to your other obligations, you ensure that you won't spend it on discretionary purchases. Now, if you are carrying credit card balances, keep paying your cards with your primary checking account. Then use this additional account that you've set up to make "extra" payments to your card issuers, in order to speed up your repayment process.

Once your bad debts are completely paid off, you're probably going to be able to set aside even more money every month to pay yourself first. After all, when you owe nothing on your credit cards, you won't owe any monthly checks to your credit card issuers. If that's the case, write yourself an even bigger

check each month. After the debts are paid off, use this account to make "extra" contributions to your savings and investing plans.

ESTABLISH AN ASSET ALLOCATION PLAN

As we discussed in Chapter 3, how you invest your money between stocks, bonds, and other assets will probably make more difference in your long-term investing plan than the individual stocks and bonds you select. Indeed, recent studies indicate that your *asset allocation strategy* will likely be the single-biggest determinant of your portfolio's performance and risk.

In a study published in 2003, the mutual fund giant Vanguard examined 40 years' worth of investment data and concluded that your mix of stocks and bonds will account for nearly 77 percent of the variability in your investment returns over time. A separate study published by Yale University finance professor Roger Ibbotson in 2000 showed that over long periods of time, nearly 100 percent of a portfolio's long-term returns can be explained by its mix of stocks and bonds, not its individual holdings.

Yet surveys show that the vast majority of Americans haven't established an affirmative asset allocation strategy that governs all their investment accounts. Instead, many of us often select individual stocks and mutual funds indiscriminately and allow those individual securities to haphazardly make up our asset allocation plan for us.

So before you get too far along in your financial plan, sit down and determine which asset allocation strategy suits your time horizon and risk tolerance. See Figure 12-1 for the long-term track records of various asset allocation strategies.

Figure 12-1. Asset Allocation Matters (Based on stock and bond market performance between 1960 and 2005)

Asset Mix	Worst Calendar Year Loss	Average Annual Returns
100% Stocks and 0% Bonds	−28.41%	10.5%
80% Stocks and 20% Bonds	−22.8%	10.0%
70% Stocks and 30% Bonds	−20.0%	9.8%
60% Stocks and 40% Bonds	−17.2%	9.5%
50% Stocks and 50% Bonds	−14.4%	9.1%
40% Stocks and 60% Bonds	−11.5%	8.8%
30% Stocks and 70% Bonds	−8.6%	8.4%
20% Stocks and 80% Bonds	−8.2%	8.0%
100% Bonds and 0% Stocks	−8.1%	7.1%

Source: Vanguard

It shows the average annual returns achieved and also how these various hypothetical portfolios have performed in their worst years.

Vanguard's research shows that a hypothetical portfolio consisting of 80 percent stocks and 20 percent bonds returned 10 percent a year on average between 1960 and 2005. By historical terms, that's a great track record. But in its worst calendar year—during the bear market of 1974—such a strategy lost nearly 23 percent of its value.

If you feel you can stomach such a steep one-time drop because your time horizon may be another 30 or 40 years, then this might be an asset allocation strategy for you. On the other hand, if you know that you won't be able to sleep at night knowing that there's a possibility that your investment portfolio could lose one-fourth of its value in a single year, you might consider reducing your risk. For example, a 50 percent stock and 50 percent bond allocation has returned slightly less than an 80–20 mix—a still respectable 9.1 percent a year between 1960 and 2005. But in its worst year, this more conservative strategy lost only around 14 percent of its value.

The fact is, determining your asset allocation strategy is more art than science, since a great many factors and subjective variables (such as your age, your time horizon, your tolerance for risk, your confidence in your abilities as an investor, and your confidence in your future income) can have a huge impact on the appropriateness of your mix of stocks and bonds.

The good news is that there are many sources for assistance. If you have a full-service broker or a financial planner, chances are he or she would have helped you formulate an asset allocation plan already.

If you're a direct investor, you also have access to help. Many online brokers such Charles Schwab (www.schwab.com) and mutual fund companies like Fidelity (www.fidelity.com), Vanguard (www.vanguard.com), and T. Rowe Price (www.troweprice.com) offer investors free asset allocation tools that should help you get started. And many financial Web sites, such as www.morningstar.com or www.mfea.com (the Mutual Fund Education Alliance), will also provide investors with templates that offer model portfolios that in most cases will suit your needs.

REBALANCE YOUR ACCOUNTS AT LEAST ONCE A YEAR

Once you set your asset allocation strategy in motion, you must revisit it at least once or twice a year. Why? Remember, certain assets in a portfolio tend to grow at a faster rate than others. And if an investment plan is left alone for years, the faster-growing assets will swamp the slower-growing assets and will eventually play a disproportionately large role in influencing the performance of your portfolio.

For example, say you start off with a 50 percent stock and 50 percent-bond allocation, based on an intermediate time horizon and a modest tolerance for risk. Assuming a $100,000 account, this means you might put $50,000 into a broadly diversified stock mutual fund and the other $50,000 in a bond fund.

Now let's assume that once you get this portfolio going, you leave it alone for 10 years. If the stock fund gains 10 percent annually, while the bond fund goes up 5 percent a year, what do you think the odds are that in 10 years your portfolio will still be 50–50 stocks and bonds? The answer is nil.

That's because in 10 years, that original $50,000 in the stock fund would have grown to $130,000, based on its 10 percent annual returns. Meanwhile, the $50,000 you put into the bond fund would have grown to around $81,000, based on a 5 percent annual return. This means that after a decade of investing, you would have turned a portfolio that was 50 percent stocks and 50 percent bonds into a 62 percent stock and 38 percent bond portfolio simply by leaving it alone.

This illustration highlights the need for all investors to revisit their portfolios and *rebalance* them back to your original asset allocation strategy. *Rebalancing* is a technical term that simply refers to resetting your mix of stocks and bonds so that they're held in an appropriate mix based on your needs and desires.

Rebalancing can be undertaken in a couple of ways. You could simply use new money to buy more of an underperforming asset. In our example, you might choose to simply buy more shares of the bond fund each year. Or, you could rebalance by selling some of your winning investments and using those proceeds to purchase more of the underperforming asset. In this sense, rebalancing is the essence of sound investing: by selling some of your winners to buy more losers in an effort to rebalance your asset allocation, you are literally buying low and selling high. While rebalancing won't guarantee you the absolute best returns, it is a strategy through which you can ensure that your investment portfolio will never be too risky for your own good.

What's the harm in letting the market dictate your allocation? After all, the example above shows that you made money over that decade. Well, for starters, in this example, by letting your portfolio grow unchecked, you would have dramatically increased your equity exposure just as you were getting older and closer to your financial goals. And as we discussed earlier on, as you move closer to achieving your long-term financial goals, it's necessary to shift your mindset from capital appreciation to capital preservation.

But the real problems arise during so-called inflection points in the investment markets, when things that are doing well stop doing well, and when investments that are doing poorly start to catch on fire. For example, consider what occurred during the late 1990s bull market in technology stocks, when investors were letting all their growth stocks and technology investments ride without any rebalancing.

Figure 12-2.   Power of Rebalancing

Portfolio That Was Not Rebalanced

Date	Stocks	Bonds	Cash	Value
12/31/1994	60%	30%	10%	$100,000
3/31/2000	78%	17%	5%	$271,000
7/31/2002	69%	25%	7%	$203,800

Rebalanced Portfolio

Date	Stocks	Bonds	Cash	Value
12/31/1994	60%	30%	10%	$100,000
3/31/2000	58%	31%	11%	$255,300
7/31/2002	56%	33%	11%	$215,200

Source: T. Rowe Price

T. Rowe Price went back to that time period and discovered that had investors not rebalanced periodically between 1995 and 2000, they would have done quite well by March 2000. But by not rebalancing, these investors entered the bear market of 2000 with an enormous position in equities. This ended up hurting them tremendously during the downturn, and by the summer of 2002, investors who chose not to rebalance wound up trailing those investors who had rebalanced year in and year out throughout the 1990s. Consider the example in Figure 12-2.

The moral of this story: In the long run, you will eventually end up doing better by constantly buying low and selling high.

Conventional wisdom says investors should rebalance their mix of stocks and bonds and cash once a year, perhaps at the end of the year so that you'll be reminded to do so. But you may want to revisit your plan twice a year, just to see if your portfolio has changed dramatically.

THINK ABOUT ESTABLISHING A WILL

A will is a document that details how you want your assets distributed after your death. In this sense, a will is the ultimate act of financial planning, since it outlines how you would like the fruits of your long-term savings and investment plans to be distributed among your family members and loved ones.

Yet according to recent surveys, an estimated 70 percent of Americans don't have a will. In the absence of this document, which must signed by you and a witness and which requires you to appoint an executor, the state will simply decide how your property and other assets are to be divided among your relatives, according to the law. This means if you have any specific intent—for instance, if you want to leave money for a favorite charity or friend—it may not happen without a will.

The good news is, writing a will can be a lot simpler than you think, especially if you have a basic estate with traditional assets. In fact, you can write your own will by downloading template documents from the Internet or by purchasing legal software such as Quicken's WillMaker program. Or, you could simply hire an estate planning lawyer to draw up a will for you.

Bear in mind that after your death, your will is subject to probate, meaning it will go through the court system and become a public record. This process could take several months as your executor goes to court, vouches for the validity of your will, pays debts and taxes on your estate, and distributes your assets among heirs.

DON'T FORGET BENEFICIARY DESIGNATIONS

Many savers and investors mistakenly believe that a will covers all their financial assets. It doesn't. Technically, your insurance policies and your retirement accounts, such as your 401(k)s, 403(b)s, and IRAs, will pass outside of your will and outside of probate. Why? All of these financial accounts come with a beneficiary designation in the contract, meaning the account owner is given the authority to designate to whom the assets in each account will pass in the event of one's death.

Typically, your spouse will be the beneficiary of your accounts if you fail to affirmatively make a designation. But what if you're not married? Or what if you don't want your spouse to get certain assets? In today's modern American family, it's not uncommon for retirement investors to have not just a spouse to consider but grown children from prior marriages.

As a result, it is in your best interest to ensure not only that all your beneficiary designations are made but that every year you revisit them and update them in case life circumstances change. For example, if you get divorced but fail to switch beneficiary designations, your ex-spouse could end up with the hard-earned assets in your 401(k). Or, if you want your kids from your first marriage to be the beneficiaries of a particular IRA and you fail to name them, your current spouse will obtain control over those funds after your death. And there is nothing preventing that spouse from using your money to benefit his or her kids from a prior marriage, rather than your kids with your first spouse.

THINK ABOUT ESTABLISHING A POWER OF ATTORNEY

A power of attorney is a legal document in which you give another person the authority to represent you and act on your behalf. The person you give this authority to can be anyone—your spouse, another relative, or a friend. But because of the enormity of this power, you should think hard about whom you can trust. The document must be signed by the two people involved, plus witnesses and a notary.

In general, there are four types of powers of attorney. The first is a *general power of attorney,* in which you give someone authority over a broad swath of your financial and personal matters, except medical decisions. Households should think long and hard before giving anyone such sweeping authority over their entire financial lives, since this person will have the power to pull money out of your accounts.

The next is a *limited power of attorney,* in which you give someone legal authority to make decisions on your behalf on a specific matter, such as a real estate transaction. This type of power of attorney can be useful if you cannot physically be at the site of a transaction, or if you feel that an attorney or financial professional is better suited to make decisions on a particular financial transaction.

There is also something called a *durable power of attorney,* which gives a loved one or professional the authority to make legal and financial decisions on your behalf if you are too sick or incapacitated. This is actually an important consideration. After all, what's the point of doing everything right when it comes to saving, paying off debts, and investing over the course of a lifetime, if one illness ruins your credit score because no one was around to pay your bills or to make financial transactions on your behalf while you were in the hospital?

There is also a subset within this category called a *durable medical power of attorney.* Sometimes, this is referred to as a health-care power of attorney or health-care proxy. This is a legal document in which you give someone else the power to make medical decisions on your behalf if you become incapacitated or too ill to make your own decisions. How is this different from a living will? In a living will, you have left instructions on how to handle your medical care; with a durable medical power of attorney, you would leave those decisions to someone else if you are too sick to make decisions.

Finally, there is something called a *springing power of attorney* which grants someone the power to represent your interest if—and only if—you become too ill to make financial and other decisions on your behalf.

To find out more about powers of attorney, go to www.findlaw.org and click on "Estate Planning," then "Sample Healthcare Power of Attorney." You can

also visit the Web site of the American Association of Retired Persons, or AARP (www.aarp.org), click on "Family, Home and Legal."

CONSIDER A LIVING WILL

A living will is a document that details medical treatment you want when you are sick. This piece of paper will not only spell out the medical procedures you want undertaken for your benefit (if you're too ill or incapacitated to communicate your wishes directly to your doctors), it will also detail those procedures that you don't approve of. A living will can vary from state to state. To get a free living will form from your state, go to www.freelegaldocs.com. And for more information on wills and living wills, visit AARP's Web site, www.aarp.org.

WRITE A LETTER OF INSTRUCTION

The average household maintains dozens of financial accounts and relationships, when you factor in bank accounts, brokerage accounts, mutual fund investments, credit cards, insurance contracts, annuities, and even wills and other estate planning documents. As a result, it's often difficult for your heirs to piece together your financial plans without a roadmap of their own.

That's sort of what a letter of instruction can provide. Technically, a letter of instruction is not a legal document, so much as it is a personal note written for one's heirs to find. Typically, this letter, which should be placed in a safe location accessible to at least one other family member, such as your spouse, can be used to cover details that aren't normally found in one's will. For example, a letter of instruction can provide details about desired funeral arrangements, or how you would like to be mourned. But in addition, letters of instruction are a great place to list the nature and location of all your financial accounts. This way, your heirs won't be surprised to find loan documents, insurance policies, or retirement accounts that they never knew existed.

LOOK INTO LONG-TERM CARE INSURANCE

Often times what upsets financial plans is the unexpected. This is why many financial planners recommend that retirees or those close to retiring purchase long-term care insurance as a safety net against having to pay for huge medical expenses on their own.

The fact is that unexpected health-care and health-care related costs can be astronomical. The average annual cost for staying at a nursing home, for example,

was $65,000 in 2005. Even if you don't expect to have to stay at a nursing home facility, chances are you'll need some type of assisted care in your old age. In fact, Americans 65 and over face a 40 percent risk of being in a nursing home, and 10 percent of those folks are likely to spend five years or more in such a facility. That's according to the Health Insurance Association of America.

Long-term care insurance pays for these types of catastrophic health care needs that aren't typically covered by your regular health insurance plan (and that are only partially covered by Medicaid or Medicare). These needs include: adult day care, paying for a home health-care worker, or living in a nursing home or assisted-care facility. As with all insurance, the premiums are lower when your risk of needing insurance is lower. That's why some people start buying long-term care insurance in their 50s; some plans even offer a discount if couples buy the insurance together.

Picking a long-term care insurance plan is similar to picking other insurance plans. There are a variety of plans out there at different price points depending on your age, where you live, and how much coverage you want. For example, the premium for a 60-year-old on a plan offered by AARP that covers nursing home, adult day care and assisted-facility expenses is about $110 a month (or $77 each per couple). The insurance offers a total benefit of $219,000 or $4,500 a month, which should last about four years.

In the event you never use your long-term care insurance, some plans will refund the remainder to your estate after your death. For more information, go to AARP's Web site, www.aarp.org. It offers a good explanation of how long-term care insurance works and offers its own plans. Another good source of information for long-term care coverage is the Kaiser Family Foundation. It foundation's site, www.kaiseredu.org, offers a series of free online audio tutorials, including one on long-term care insurance. Finally, you can visit the Web site of the American Association of Homes and Services, the trade group for nursing homes and adult-care facilities. Visit www.aahsa.org, and click under "Consumer Information." The section gives an overview on where to find a facility, how to choose one and how to pay for one.

DON'T BE ASHAMED TO SEEK PROFESSIONAL ADVICE

Maybe after reading this book, you've decided that managing your own finances just isn't for you. Not to worry: there are plenty of professional financial planners who are willing to help—for a price. Financial planners abound, and they can do as little or as much as you want them to. For example, they can simply develop financial goals and create a budget for you, or they can literally manage all your financial accounts and functions. This includes tracking your household income and expenses, giving you investment advice, and even making investment transactions on your behalf. Some planners also specialize, so you can pick one who works exclusively with retirement investors or divorced workers or young couples.

But before you start looking for financial planners, you must first understand how they are paid because that may ultimately help you decide whom to hire. The universe of financial planners can be divided among three basic groups. For starters, there are so-called *fee-only planners*. These professionals do not receive commissions for selling financial products. Instead, they are compensated through an hourly fee, a flat fee, or a fee based on a percentage of assets they manage for you. Next, there are *commission-only planners*. This group isn't compensated directly by their clients, but rather through commissions off the investment products they sell. For instance, if these advisers steer you into a certain mutual fund, the fund company will pay them a commission for the sale. Finally, there are *combination fee and commission planners* who charge clients fees for advice but who also earn commission on investment products sold.

Some households prefer fee-only planners because the adviser in this capacity does not have a built-in incentive—some might call it a conflict of interest—to sell you certain investments based on the commissions they can earn. Of course, there are plenty of reputable commission-based planners. So if you decide to go with a commission-based planner, just make sure to ask if there are any conflicts of interest in terms of investment recommendations he or she gives clients.

Where do you find financial planners? Like choosing a doctor, dentist or plumber, most people start with recommendations from their family, friends, or work colleagues. If you already have a tax accountant or a lawyer, you could also ask them because some work closely with financial planners and can provide contacts.

Short of that, the Financial Planning Association (www.fpanet.org) is a good place to start. This trade group for financial planners provides a directory of planners by area. Some planners you may notice have a Certified Financial Planner, or CFP, designation. That means the person has passed an exam and has three years of financial-planning related experience. In addition to CFPs, there are other specialized designations.

Keep in mind that financial planners for the most part are not regulated by the federal government. So doing research on prospective planners is critical. The association recommends that you interview at least three planners before settling on one. Face-to-face meetings are preferable because the relationship between you and your planner is as intimate as your relationship with your doctor. You must feel comfortable with the planner, after all he or she will be in charge of your financial health!

You may also consider asking for references, such as talking to current clients to see if they are satisfied with the planner's advice. The Financial Planning Association's Web site provides a comprehensive overview of professionals in your area. The site also provides a worksheet on questions to ask prospective planners to make sure he or she is the right one for you. You can also call the association's toll-free number at (800) 647-6340.

The National Association of Personal Financial Advisors, the trade group of fee-only planners, provides additional tips on its Web site (www.napfa.org). Click under "Consumer Services," where you can get advice on how to find a planner and where to find one. The Certified Financial Planner Board of Standards also provides a guide on how to pick a financial planner. Go to www.cfp.net and click on "Learn about Financial Planning." To find out if your financial planner has any disciplinary actions, you can type the planner's name in the search box. You can also call the CFP Board at (888) 237-6275.

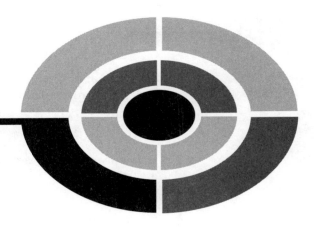

Final Exam

1. How much money should all households set aside in an emergency fund?
   a. At least 3 months' worth of expenses
   b. At least 3 months' worth of income
   c. At least 20 percent of their annual income

2. Which of the following accounts is an inappropriate place to stash your emergency fund?
   a. Stock mutual fund
   b. Bond mutual fund
   c. Bank certificate of deposit
   d. All of the above

3. All forms of borrowing represent "negative investing."
   a. True
   b. False

4. Which form of debt is not tax deductible?
   a. Credit card balances
   b. Mortgage debt
   c. Student loan debt

5. If you have a credit card you don't use, you should cancel it.
   a. True
   b. False

6. If you check your FICO score periodically, it is still necessary to check your credit bureau reports.
   a. True
   b. False

7. If your FICO score is 600, you are in the...
   a. top 10 percent of all American households in terms of credit-worthiness.
   b. top half of all American households in terms of credit worthiness.
   c. bottom third of all American households in terms of credit worthiness.

8. What is the biggest variable that makes up your credit score?
   a. Your track record in repaying your debts on schedule
   b. The total amount of debt you carry
   c. How many credit cards you have

9. Which of the following strategies is the most effective at improving your credit score?
   a. Getting a higher-paying job
   b. Paying your minimum monthly obligations faster than required
   c. Paying off all your debts on time

10. What are the three core assets that make up all financial portfolios?
    a. Stocks, bonds, and cash
    b. Stocks, bonds, and commodities
    c. Stocks, bonds, and real estate

11. What is the risk of not being invested in the stock market?
    a. There is no risk in not being in the stock market.
    b. Failing to outpace the negative effects of inflation over time.
    c. The chance of losing even more money in other assets like bonds or real estate.

12. If you invest in a broadly diversified collection of stocks, what are the odds of losing money over any 10-year period of time?
    a. 100 percent
    b. 10 percent
    c. 4 percent

13. Dollar cost averaging is a strategy that ...
    a. maximizes your investment returns.
    b. safeguards against any investment losses.
    c. diversifies when you purchase your investments.

14. Bonds provide ballast to an investment portfolio because ...
    a. they tend to zig when stocks zag.
    b. they are a guaranteed form of investing.
    c. they never lose money, while stocks often lose ground in short periods of time.

15. Corporate bonds expose investors to which of the following risks:
    a. Credit risk
    b. Interest rate risk
    c. Inflation risk
    d. All of the above

16. Which of the following forms of risk do U.S. Treasury bonds shield investors from?
    a. Credit risk
    b. Interest rate risk
    c. Inflation risk
    d. None of the above

17. AAA-rated corporate bonds never default.
    a. True
    b. False

18. Money market mutual funds protect investors from the following risks:
    a. Inflation risk
    b. Interest rate risk
    c. Credit risk
    d. None of the above

19. The average stock mutual fund invests in roughly how many different securities?
    a. 75

    b. 125

    c. 175

20. The reason to go with an actively managed mutual fund is because professional mutual fund managers have a good track record beating the broad market.
    a. True

    b. False

21. If you plan to dollar cost average into the stock market, you're best off going with...
    a. a mutual fund

    b. an exchange-traded fund

    c. direct stock ownership through a brokerage

22. Which assets provide investors with the greatest protection against inflation?
    a. Short-term government bonds

    b. Bank CDs

    c. Commodities

23. Investments in residential real estate are...
    a. just like bonds in that they rarely lose value.

    b. just like stocks in that they consistently produce double-digit annual gains.

    c. just as volatile as equities.

24. Why do some parents choose the Coverdell ESA over the 529 plan?
    a. The 529 plans can be used to pay for elementary and secondary school.

    b. There are more investment choices with Coverdell ESAs.

    c. There are no income restrictions with Coverdells.

25. To qualify for financial aid, it is best to keep your assets in the...
    a. child's name

    b. parents' name

26. Which of the following college savings vehicles is detrimental to qualifying for financial aid?
    a. Custodial accounts
    b. Prepaid college tuition plans
    c. 529 college savings accounts
    d. Coverdell education savings accounts

27. Roth 401(k)s and Roth IRAs are similar in that...
    a. they are both employer-sponsored retirement accounts.
    b. they are both tax-sheltered accounts that allow withdrawals to be made tax free.
    c. neither imposes any income restrictions on participation.

28. Households in certain income brackets may be prevented from funding all forms of individual retirement accounts.
    a. True
    b. False

29. It always makes sense to pay taxes up front in order to qualify for tax-free withdrawals at retirement.
    a. True
    b. False

30. At the very least, you should always take full advantage of your company match when it comes to your 401(k).
    a. True
    b. False

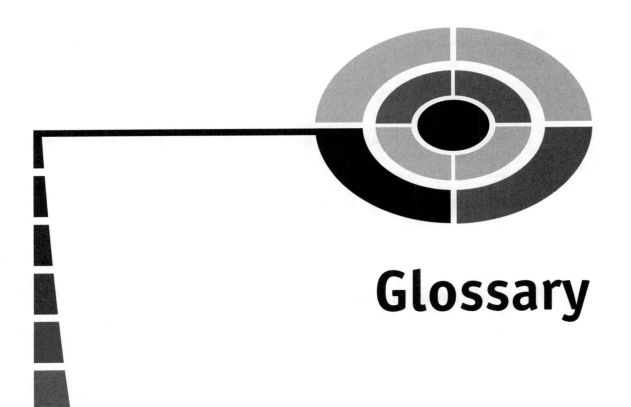

Glossary

American Depository Receipts, or ADRs. Allow individuals to invest directly in foreign companies, particularly in the stocks of developed markets. An ADR is a proxy of sorts that represents shares of a foreign company. The actual shares of that foreign stock are held by a bank in the United States, while the ADR itself, or the receipt of those shares, trades on the major U.S. stock exchanges, like the NYSE, Nasdaq, or American Stock Exchange.

Asset allocation. Refers to the amount of money, in percentage terms, that we invest in stocks, bonds, and cash in a portfolio. The vast majority of an investor's returns over time can be explained by his or her asset allocation strategy, rather than by stock selection.

Asset allocation funds. These are hybrid mutual funds that invest in a mix of stocks and bonds. A popular type of asset allocation fund is a so-called static-risk asset allocation portfolio. These usually come in one of three forms: conservative, moderate, and aggressive. Aggressive static-risk asset allocation funds typically invest around 80 percent of their assets in equities. Moderate risk funds tend to invest around 60 percent of their holdings in stocks. And conservative funds tend

to hold half or less of their assets in equities, with the remainder going to a mix of bonds and cash.

Automated savings plan. This is a savings program where a portion of your paycheck is automatically set aside each week or month and sent to a money market fund or some other savings vehicle.

Automated investment plan. This is a program where a portion of your paycheck is automatically set aside each week or month and sent to a brokerage, a stock mutual fund, or a bond mutual fund to dollar cost average into the market.

Balanced funds. Also known as *hybrid funds,* balanced portfolios are mutual funds that are allowed to invest in a mix of both stocks and bonds. Typically, the mix is set at around 60 percent equities and 40 percent bonds, but that can fluctuate.

Balance sheet. This is a financial statement that accounts for a company's assets and liabilities. It gauges a company's overall financial health at a particular point in time. The balance sheet is one of the three major financial statements that a publicly traded company must issue once a quarter.

Basic material stocks. These are shares of companies that produce, mine, or distribute commodities or other raw materials used in the manufacturing process. Basic materials stocks range from chemical companies to mining stocks to steel.

Beacon score. Refers to your FICO credit score based on your Equifax credit report.

Bear market. A major, sustained correction in the equity markets that causes stock values to fall more than 20 percent.

Beneficiary designations. Retirement accounts and insurance policies come with beneficiary designations that allow you to determine whom you want the proceeds of these financial accounts to go to in the event of your death.

Bond funds. A type of mutual fund that invests primarily in fixed-income securities. For smaller investors, this is the easiest—and cheapest—vehicle with which to gain bond exposure.

Glossary

Brokerage commission. This is the money paid to a broker or brokerage firm as compensation for placing and executing a transaction order.

Budget. A spending plan that factors in how much you earn, how much you need to spend on required items such as food and shelter, and how much you wish to save. An easy way to start a budget is to first assess how much you spend on all items in the course of a typical month.

Bull market. A major, sustained rally in the equity markets that causes stock values to rise more than 20 percent.

Callable bond. This is a bond that gives the issuer the right, under certain circumstances, to end the life of the contract sooner than expected.

Capital appreciation. Refers to investing with the goal of growing your principal through price appreciation over time.

Capital gains. Gains achieved in the underlying value of an investment. Upon sale, those capital gains are said to be *realized*. Prior to booking the profit, they are said to be *unrealized*.

Capital gains taxes. These are the taxes that must be paid upon realizing capital gains. At present, the federal tax rate on long-term capital gains—those held for more than a year—is 15 percent.

Capital preservation. Refers to investing with the goal of protecting the principal value of your investments by taking a conservative approach.

Cash drag. The negative impact on returns that large cash holdings have on a mutual fund's performance. Typically, cash drag occurs when funds are inundated with large cash flows, making it difficult for the fund manager to invest the money immediately in the stock market.

Catch-up contributions. These are additional contributions that workers 50 and older are allowed to make annually to their 401(k) retirement accounts and individual retirement accounts above other annual caps.

Certificates of Deposit, or CDs. Popular savings vehicles created by banks that allow savers to lock in interest rates. Like bonds, CDs come with maturity dates, typically ranging from as little as one month to as long as five years. During that

time, investors are largely restricted from having access to those funds. However, the interest rate at the time of purchase is guaranteed for the life of the CD.

Chicago Board Options Exchange. A leading exchange in futures and options contracts, which are complex financial instruments used by professionals to hedge their investment bets.

Chicago Mercantile Exchange. A leading commodities exchange that facilitates trading in a wide range of investments, from currencies, such as Eurodollars, to commodities like beef, dairy, fertilizer, and lumber.

Commodities. Any unfinished or unprocessed good that can be traded in bulk. They can range from agricultural products such as pork bellies, coffee, and cotton, to basic materials such as copper and silver.

Commodity futures. Financial contracts tied to the delivery of commodities, such as metals or agricultural products, at some point in the future. This can be a dangerous game. Investing in futures contracts is akin to betting more than investing.

Common stock. The most basic share of ownership of a business. As an owner of common stock, you will probably receive a portion of the firm's earnings back through dividend payments, which are typically made quarterly or semiannually.

Compound interest. The ability of your money to grow exponentially over time if allowed to grow unfettered. Compound interest refers to the fact that money invested will soon earn interest—and if left untouched, the interest your money earns will eventually earn interest of its own, and so on.

Correlation. Refers to the propensity of one asset to move in synch with another. The lower the correlation an asset has with other investments in your portfolio, the greater the diversification it offers to your holdings.

Coupon rate. This represents your interest rate if you purchased a bond at par. For example, if you bought a $1,000 Treasury bond with a 5 percent coupon for par value, you would earn $50 a year in interest on that bond.

Coverdell Education Savings Accounts. Previously known as Education IRAs, these educational savings plans allow parents to invest after-tax dollars in a tax-deferred account. Investment gains withdrawn from a Coverdell that are used for qualified educational expenses—such as tuition, room, and board—are free from federal taxes. Unlike a 529 college savings plan, though, money invested in a Coverdell can also be used to pay for educational costs at the K-12 level.

Credit Bureau. This term refers to one of the three major credit reporting agencies that maintain files on consumer borrowing activities. The three major credit bureaus are Equifax, Experian, and TransUnion.

Credit quality. Refers to the amount of credit risk to which a bond issuer exposes you. The highest quality bonds—with credit ratings of AAA from Standard & Poor's and Fitch, or an Aaa rating from Moody—expose investors to virtually no credit risk, due to their strong financial health.

Credit Reports. Files maintained by the three major credit bureaus that document our borrowing activities, as well as our track record in paying back our debts on time. These credit reports are then used by credit scoring agencies like Fair Isaac to come up with a credit score for each consumer. Because there are three major credit bureaus, each consumer has three separate credit reports, which could each contain slightly different information, due to errors or delays in reporting data.

Credit risk. Refers to the possibility that the bond issuer, despite its promises and best intentions, may default on its obligations to pay you a certain coupon or to return your principal to you at maturity.

Credit scores. These are quantitative assessments of the credit-worthiness of each consumer. Credit-scoring firms like Fair Isaac use information based in our credit reports to give us a three-digit score. The most common scoring system is called the FICO score, which ranges from 300 to 850. The higher the FICO score, the more credit-worthy a consumer is deemed to be.

Day traders. Investors who buy and sell stocks several times within a day, hoping to book quick intraday profits.

Default. The failure of a bond issuer to make good on its promise to pay the bond investor interest and to return the original principal investment back at an agreed-upon date.

Developed markets. This refers to the equity and fixed-income markets in leading industrial nations, such as the United States, Japan, Germany, the United Kingdom, France, and Italy.

Direct-sold funds. Also known as *no-load funds,* these are mutual funds bought and sold directly through fund companies. They do not come with commission charges.

Dividend payments. Refers to the occasional payouts that some publicly traded stocks make to their shareholders. These payouts represent a portion of the firm's earnings being returned to the owners of the business.

Dividend reinvestment plans, or DRIPs. Allow individuals to invest in stocks without having a brokerage account. With a DRIP, an investor can purchase stock directly from the publicly traded company itself.

Dividend yield. A measure of the amount of dividend income thrown off by a stock. The formula to calculate this is dividend income per share/current price per share = dividend yield.

Diversification. Refers to owning a mix of different assets—such as stocks, bonds, or cash—and different securities within those asset classes to minimize risk by spreading it out over numerous holdings.

Dollar cost averaging. This is a conservative investing approach that calls for putting small amounts of money to work each month, quarter, or at some other routine interval. By buying at intervals, you ensure that you will never be purchasing a security at the absolute worst possible time in the market. The idea is to diversify, or average out, based on when you purchase your securities.

Dow Jones Industrial Average. A benchmark stock index composed of 30 of the biggest companies in the U.S. market that reflects the industrial strength of the domestic economy. Companies are added or deleted from the DJIA by editors of the *Wall Street Journal.*

Earnings yield. Refers to the amount of corporate earnings an investor is purchasing for every $1 he or she is buying in equities. It is the inverse of a stock's price to earnings ratio. The formula to calculate earnings yield is earnings per share/price of security = earnings yield.

Emergency fund. A pot of money households should set aside before they invest in order to prepare for unexpected expenses. An emergency fund can be tapped to pay bills in the event you or your spouse lose a job. It can also be used to pay for unexpected bills, such as replacing a broken water heater or repairing a leaky roof. By setting aside at least three months' worth of expenses in a rainy-day fund, households won't be forced to go into debt or to tap their investments to cover emergency expenses.

Emerging market stocks. These are the stocks of companies—both large and small—headquartered in countries whose economies are relatively young and therefore are undeveloped, among them Brazil, China, Malaysia, Mexico, South Korea, South Africa, and Taiwan. Investment risks in these stocks include political instability, or in some cases even revolution, in the countries where these companies are based.

Empirica score. Refers to your FICO credit score based on your credit report maintained by TransUnion.

Equities. Another term for stock.

Experian/Fair Isaac Risk Model. Refers to your FICO credit score based on your credit report maintained by Experian.

Exchange-traded funds. These are baskets of securities that trade like a single stock on an exchange. Exchange-traded funds, or ETFs, are similar to index mutual funds. But unlike an index mutual fund, ETFs allow investors to make trades throughout the day.

FICO score. The letters stand for Fair, Isaac Co., a California company that assesses consumer credit-worthiness based on information found in credit reports maintained by the major credit bureaus TransUnion, Equifax, and Experian. FICO scores range from 300 to 850; the higher your score, the better your credit rating and the more likely you are to qualify for loans.

529 savings plan. A self-directed state-sponsored college savings plan that allows families to invest after-tax money tax-deferred. Investment gains withdrawn from a 529 that are used for qualified educational expenses—such as tuition, room, and board—are free from federal taxes.

529 prepaid tuition plans. These state-run plans allow parents to purchase future education credits at certain in-state public colleges based on today's prices. Recently, a new type of prepaid plan has been created that allows families to prepurchase credits at more than 250 participating private universities.

Unlike 529 savings plan assets, money used to buy prepaid credits is generally limited to paying for tuition and fees (not room and board).

Fixed-income instruments. Another term for bonds.

Fixed maturity date. Refers to the date at which a bond matures and the original principal value of the bond is to be returned in full to the investor.

Flight to quality. Refers to investors flocking to high-quality stocks (such as shares of big, blue-chip companies) and bonds (typically Treasury securities) during times of heightened economic or geopolitical risks.

401(k) plan. A self-directed company-sponsored retirement plan that allows workers to contribute pretax dollars and to invest the money tax-deferred. Typically, money held in a 401(k) is invested in mutual fund options.

403(b) plan. A self-directed retirement plan that allows teachers and workers at nonprofit organizations to contribute pretax dollars and to invest money tax-deferred.

457 plan. A retirement plan that allows state and municipal workers to contribute pretax dollars and to invest money tax-deferred.

Fund manager risk. Refers to the risk a mutual fund investor exposes him- or herself to by investing in an actively managed fund. While there is a possibility that your fund manager will outperform the market in any given year, there is also the risk that the same manager could have a bad year.

General equity funds. These funds invest in a cross section of different industries and sectors that make up the stock market.

General obligation bonds. These are a type of municipal bonds issued by states, counties, or cities for general purposes. Because they are issued by governments that have the authority to raise taxes, the perception is that these types of munis are relatively safe.

Gold stocks. Shares of companies whose core business is tied to the mining, processing, or distribution of gold.

Growth stocks. Shares of companies whose underlying profits and sales are growing faster than the overall market. Because of their growth characteristics, investors are often willing to pay higher prices for these shares, which leads growth stocks to have higher P/E ratios, in general, than value stocks.

High-yield bonds. Low-quality, or so-called junk bonds that are forced to pay higher interest rates to attract investors. High-yield bonds are typically issued by companies of questionable financial strength.

High-yield funds. Fixed-income mutual funds that focus on high-yield corporate debt.

Immediate fixed payout annuity. These insurance products allow retirees to convert a pile of money into a guaranteed income stream for life. Because payout annuities pool together the life expectancies of large groups of people, they can often provide investors with a greater income stream than can be generated through a collection of self-managed 401(k)s and IRAs.

Index. A benchmark of sorts that is used to gauge the performance of the stock or bond markets or a segment of them. Examples of leading indexes include the Dow Jones Industrial Average, the S&P 500 index of blue-chip stocks, and the Nasdaq composite index.

Index funds. Mutual funds that are passively managed and that simply attempt to mirror the holdings in an established stock or bond market index like the S&P 500. For example, an S&P 500 index fund simply buys and holds all 500 stocks in that index. Though these funds are not managed by a stock picker, historically they have performed quite well compared to the average stock fund. This is in large part due to the fact that index funds are among the lowest-cost portfolios around.

Individual retirement accounts. Commonly known as *IRAs,* these are self-directed retirement accounts an investor can voluntarily fund. Within them, money is tax-sheltered while it grows. An investor can choose any number of different stocks, bonds, or mutual funds to invest in. There are several different types of IRAs, among them traditional IRAs, which are funded with pretax dollars with the investor paying taxes on gains at withdrawal, and Roth IRAs, which are funded with after-tax dollars but where withdrawals are tax-free.

Intermediate-term bonds. Fixed-income securities that mature in 2 to 10 years.

Intermediate-term bond funds. Mutual funds that invest in intermediate-term debt.

Interest rate risk. Refers to the risk a bond investor faces should interest rates rise. A basic principle of investing is that bond prices move in the opposite direction of market interest rates. So, if market rates rise, bond prices would fall. And should bond prices fall more than the security yields, the investor's portfolio would face losses.

Intrinsic value. Gauges the true worth of a company by considering all the tangible and intangible value a firm possesses, including its perceived worth.

Investment-grade bonds. High-quality fixed-income securities issued by companies with strong credit histories and ratings, as graded by the major credit-rating agencies. These are the antithesis of high-yield bonds.

Large-cap stocks. Refers to companies whose market value is $10 billion or more. Also called blue-chip stocks because they are considered safer and more stable than shares of young start-ups.

Letter of instruction. This is a written communication to your heirs that spells out how you want to be mourned, but also where to find all of your personal and financial papers.

Leverage. Refers to the act of borrowing money to invest. By borrowing money, you can bolster or leverage your investment to even greater gains than you could otherwise afford on your own. A classic example of leverage is a home mortgage that allows households to invest in properties worth hundreds of thousands of dollars with little money down.

Life-cycle funds. These are hybrid mutual funds that invest in a mix of stocks and bonds. However, these funds are designed to gradually reduce the level of risk in your portfolio as you age. These funds are also referred to as *target-maturity funds*.

Liquidity. Refers to the ease with which investors can buy and sell an asset or security.

Living wills. Legal documents that spell out the precise medical treatment you want in the event you're too ill or incapacitated to communicate your wishes.

Load funds. A general term for mutual funds that are advisor-sold. As such, load funds charge investors a commission for the advice provided to purchase the fund.

Within the universe of load funds, there are *front-load, back-end load,* and *level load* funds.

Long-term bonds. These are bonds that mature in 10 years or more. They are regarded as more aggressive and risky from the standpoint of interest rate risk than short-term bonds.

Long-term care insurance. This is a form of health coverage that pays for big-ticket items that regular health insurance plans typically do not, such as adult day care, nursing home stays. and access to assisted-care facilities.

Market capitalization. Also called *market cap,* it refers to the company's total market value. It is calculated by multiplying the total number of shares a company has outstanding by the current price per share.

Market correction. A downturn in the markets. Among equities, a market correction refers to a loss of 10 percent or more in major stock indexes such as the Dow Jones Industrial Average or the S&P 500.

Market maker. Sometimes known as a *specialist,* a market maker is the middleman that facilitates trading in a given stock, in part by helping to match up buyers with sellers. Market makers are typically broker-dealer firms whose job, when there is an imbalance of buyers and sellers in the marketplace, is to facilitate trading in the security.

Market order. A transaction order for a security that requests immediate execution at the best possible price.

Market risk. The risk of potential losses investors face on their investments based on diminished prices.

Market value. Same as *market cap.* It refers to the value that Wall Street collectively assigns a company at any given moment in time, based on the company's stock price at that moment. The formula to calculate market value is current price per share $\times$ total shares outstanding $=$ market value.

Maturity date. The date when a bond issuer agrees to redeem the bondholder. It is also the date when the loan contract itself—the bond—expires.

Micro-cap stocks. Refers to tiny stocks, generally in firms with market capitalization of $250 million or less.

Mid-cap stocks. Refers to medium-size stocks, companies whose market values range between $1 and $10 billion.

Money market account. This is a type of savings account that places a few restrictions on the number of transactions one can make but in exchange will often pay noticeably higher yields than basic passbook accounts or checking accounts. Money market accounts are FDIC insured.

Money market mutual funds. These funds invest in extremely short-term debt and they are considered a cash vehicle. Money market funds sometimes pay out more in interest than money market accounts, but they are not FDIC insured.

Municipal bonds. Debt issued by states, counties, municipalities, local agencies, and school districts to pay for such things as construction projects, highways, or basic obligations.

Mutual fund. A popular investment vehicle that offers investors access to a pooled, diversified portfolio of stocks, bonds—or a combination—with relatively low minimum initial investment requirements. The majority of mutual funds also give investors access to professional management.

Mutual fund supermarkets. These are brokerage platforms that give investors access to thousands of different mutual funds run by hundreds of different mutual fund companies. Because fund supermarkets cater to self-directed investors, they tend to provide a large selection of no-load funds. Like food vendors dealing with grocery stores, the mutual fund companies themselves will often pay the fund supermarket for "shelf space" to sell their wares.

New York Board of Trade. A leading exchange that facilitates trading in commodities such as cocoa, coffee, cotton, ethanol, and sugar.

New York Mercantile Exchange. A leading exchange that facilitates trading in various commodities.

New York Stock Exchange. Sometimes referred to as *the Big Board,* the NYSE is the nation's leading stock exchange. It is where some of the leading stocks in the U.S. market are traded.

No-load funds. Also referred to as *direct-sold funds,* they are purchased and sold directly through fund companies and do not come with any commission charges.

No transaction fee funds. Within mutual fund supermarkets, these are lists of direct-sold funds that can be bought or sold without being assessed a brokerage commission by the brokerage platform itself. These are by definition no-load funds, so investors won't be assessed a load either.

Nondiscrimination tests. These are tests designed by the federal government to ensure that employer-sponsored 401(k) retirement accounts do not disproportionately benefit highly compensated workers. As a result of these tests, the amount of money that highly paid workers and managers can contribute annually to their 401(k) accounts is often determined by the rate of contributions of rank-and-file workers.

Opportunity costs. The potential gains investors could have earned in an alternative asset had they chosen to invest differently. All investors should consider the opportunity costs they are forgoing by choosing a particular asset.

Par value. Refers to the face value of a bond. Since bonds are typically sold in $1,000 increments, it's likely that the par value of your individual bond is going to be $1,000. One exception might be with municipal bonds, where par might be set at $5,000 per bond.

Power of attorney. This is a legal document through which you can give another person—be it an attorney, an accountant, or a loved one—the authority to represent you and act on your behalf.

Preferred stock. Represents an ownership unit of a company that is slightly less risky than common stock. Preferred stockholders typically receive bigger dividend payouts than common stock investors and are ahead of common stock investors in line to claim losses should the company file for bankruptcy. Typically, preferred shares do not give investors voting rights for the management of the underlying company.

Price appreciation. An increase in the underlying market value of a stock or other security. Combined with dividend income or yield, price appreciation represents a major component of an investment's total returns.

Publicly traded company. A compnay whose shares are not held exclusively by a single person or family, but rather, trade freely among members of the general public on an open exchange. A company must first go through an initial public offering to achieve publicly traded status.

R-squared. Refers to a mathematical estimation of how much of an investment's behavior can be explained by the movements of a benchmark. R-squared can be used by fund investors to gauge whether a portfolio is highly correlated to a market index, like the S&P 500, or if it diverges from that index.

Real Estate Investment Trust, or REIT. This is a publicly traded company whose purpose is to invest in real estate in some form or fashion. Some REITs specialize in commercial properties, while others focus on residential real estate. But at their core, REITs are companies set up to be landlords. Because of their focus on real estate, REITs are often considered an asset separate from equities. By law, they must pass along to shareholders the vast majority of the rental income derived from their investments; they are popular vehicles for income-oriented investors. However, REIT income is not considered qualified dividend income and therefore does not benefit from favorable tax treatment.

Rebalancing. Refers to the act of periodically resetting one's mix of stocks, bonds, and cash so market forces do not seriously upset a long-term strategic asset allocation plan. Typically, investors will rebalance once a quarter or once a year. Rebalancing is considered a strategy to reduce risk in a portfolio since it forces an investor to sell portions of an asset that have risen disproportionately in value and use those proceeds to purchase a competing asset that has not performed as well. That way, an investor books profits periodically and ensures that he or she buys low and sells high.

Redeem. Refers to the act of selling out of an investment in exchange for cash.

Revenue bonds. A type of municipal debt floated by an agency of a state or local government for a specific project. While revenue bondholders are typically paid from the receipts generated from these projects—like highway or tunnel tolls—there is no explicit promise that the state or municipality will bail out these bond issuers should the projects run into financial difficulties.

Reverse mortgage. A type of loan providing homeowners, often senior citizens, with a stream of income that is backed by their homes. Unlike a traditional mortgage, a reverse mortgage does not require you to pay back the loan, so long as you continue to live in the house against which the mortgage is applied. Upon sale of the home or death, the reverse mortgage is paid off by the proceeds of the home's liquidation. A reverse mortgage can be paid out in a lump sum, in monthly payments, or in some other form of routine installments.

Roth 401(k). An employer-sponsored self-directed retirement account funded with after-tax dollars. Once inside, investments in a Roth 401(k) are allowed to grow tax-sheltered. And at withdrawal, investment gains can be pulled out of these accounts tax-free, so long as the withdrawal meets certain requirements.

Roth IRA. A type of self-directed retirement account funded with after-tax dollars. Once inside, money in a Roth IRA can be invested in any number of vehicles and grows tax-sheltered. At withdrawal, investment gains can be pulled out of these accounts tax-free, so long as the withdrawal meets certain requirements.

S&P 500 Index. One of the three major stock indexes followed by U.S. investors. The S&P 500 is a benchmark that measures the performance of the 500 largest-capitalization stocks in the U.S. market. It is considered a better gauge of the broad domestic stock market than the Dow Jones Industrial Average, since the S&P measures the performance of 500 companies instead of the Dow's 30.

Sector funds. Also known as *specialty portfolios,* these are a type of mutual fund that specializes in a particular sector of the economy. For example, there are sector funds that primarily invest in technology, utilities, energy, or health care. Because of their niche, sector funds should not be used to make up one's core stock portfolio. Rather, they are useful to add some flavor to a diversified portfolio of stocks or stock funds.

Self-directed retirement accounts. These are tax-advantaged retirement plans, such 401(k)s and Roth IRAs, that force the investor to make all the investment decisions.

Senior bonds. A type of corporate debt higher up in the pecking order of claims in the event of a corporate bankruptcy. As a result of the greater assurance they provide, senior corporate debt does not necessarily have to offer as high an interest rate to pique an investor's attention.

SEP IRA. SEP is short for Simplified Employee Pension. Small business owners or sole proprietors of firms of any size are allowed to establish tax-deferred SEP IRAs through banks, brokers, or mutual fund companies. These accounts allow

small business owners to sock away as much as 25 percent of their salaries into these tax-deferred investment accounts, up to a maximum of $44,000 a year (based on the 2006 tax year).

Shareholder. An investor who owns a stake in a company or a mutual fund.

Short-term bonds. A form of debt that matures in only two or three years, meaning they are less susceptible to interest rate risk. There are short-term corporate and short-term government bonds.

Short-term bond funds. Mutual funds that specialize in investing in fixed-income securities that mature in about two or three years or less.

SIMPLE IRA. The term SIMPLE stands for Savings Incentive Match Plan for Employees. These tax-advantaged retirement accounts are considered a low-cost alternative to 401(k)s for small businesses.

Small-cap stocks. Shares of small companies with total market capitalization of $1 billion or less. Because of their size, small-cap stocks are considered a riskier bet than shares of big, blue-chip companies.

Standard deviation. A mathematical measure of an investment's volatility and risk. It compares a stock's or a fund's volatility to the average volatility of that same type of stock or fund over a particular period of time. A stock with a high standard deviation typically sees its price fluctuate wildly between high and low points.

Statement of cash flows. This is one of the three major financial statements that publicly traded companies must routinely provide to shareholders and regulators. It tracks the flow of money into and out of the company's coffers.

Stock. Sometimes referred to as *equities,* stocks represent partial ownership of a company. Stocks can be purchased directly by an investor through a brokerage account or indirectly through a mutual fund that in turn purchases these securities.

Stock-specific risk. The risk of potentially losing money in a stock investment—not because the overall market is shaky, but because of turmoil in the underlying business.

Subordinated bonds. A type of corporate debt whose investors must wait until other lenders are made whole before making claims against the firm, should it fall into financial trouble. As a result of having to take on more credit risk, owners of subordinated debt are often compensated with a slightly higher interest rate.

Swing traders. Investors who trade stock frequently and therefore have short holding periods. Unlike day traders, however, a swing trader may hang on to securities for days before selling, as opposed to hours.

Taxable bond funds. Mutual funds that invest in either corporate bonds, U.S. government debt, or a combination of the two. They are distinct from municipal bond funds, which invest in debt issued by states and municipalities and often come with tax advantages.

Tax-efficient stock funds. Mutual funds that attempt to minimize the tax liabilities of its shareholders through tactical purchases and sales and relatively low turnover.

Taxable-equivalent yield. A calculation that helps determine whether, on an after-tax basis, a tax-free municipal bond is more or less attractive than a taxable Treasury security. If the taxable equivalent yield of a muni is higher than the current yield of an equivalent Treasury, then a muni may be the better buy. The formula to determine it is muni bond yield/(1 − your tax bracket) = taxable equivalent yield.

Time horizon. Refers to the length of time an investor has before he or she needs to tap the money that is being invested. The longer the time horizon, the more aggressive an investor can—and should—be with an asset allocation strategy.

Time value of money. A key financial planning concept that says that money you possess today is worth more than the same amount of money you might earn in the future. This is because money you possess can work for you and earn interest of its own. Investors who take advantage of the time value of money can turn small amounts of money into large sums over long periods of time.

TIPS, or Treasury Inflation Protected Securities. This is a relatively new form of government bond whose principal value is adjusted to reflect the impact of inflation over time. Thus, unlike other bonds, TIPS do not suffer from inflation risk.

Total expense ratio. This ratio is composed of the annual fees that fund investors must pay every year to cover the management and administrative costs of the

fund. Expressed as a percentage of assets, the total expense ratio is deducted from your fund's returns.

Total return. The sum total of investment gains that an investor enjoys from a security. Within the realm of stocks, total return is calculated by adding a stock's capital appreciation to its dividend payout. Among bonds, total return is the yield plus or minus any changes in the bond's price.

Total sales. Also referred to as *revenues,* they reflect the amount of goods or services a company has sold in a particular period. It is listed on the income statement on a quarterly and/or annual basis.

Treasury bonds. Debt issued by the federal government that is backed by the full faith and credit of Uncle Sam. From the standpoint of credit risk, Treasury bonds are considered risk-free, since the Treasury Department can simply print more money to make an investor whole. However, Treasuries, like other bonds, are subject to interest rate risk.

Treasury bill, or T-bill. A short-term cash instrument issued by the federal government and backed by the full faith and credit of Uncle Sam. T-bills pay no direct interest, unlike Treasury notes or bonds, where you are paid interest along the way. However, T-bills are purchased at a discount to par value, and investors earn money when they recoup the par value at maturity. Along with money market accounts, CDs, and money market funds, these are a popular cash vehicle.

Ultra-short-term bond fund. A mutual fund that invests in extremely short-term debt that typically matures in about a year or two, or sometimes even less. While ultra-short-term bonds are sometimes used as a cash vehicle, they are still fixed-income assets that can lose value under certain circumstances.

UGMA accounts. Uniform Gifts to Minors Act accounts are a type of custodial account that allows parents to transfer cash, stocks and other securities to their children's name.

UTMA accounts. Uniform Transfers to Minors Act accounts are a type of custodial account that allows parents to transfer cash, stocks, art, collectibles and real estate to their children's name.

Value stock. Shares of companies that are undervalued or beaten down by investors, and therefore are considered a bargain by some investors.

Glossary

Vantage score. Refers to a new credit scoring system established by Equifax, Experian and TransUnion to compete against the FICO credit scoring system. Your vantage score is a three-digit figure ranging from 501 to 990. The higher your vantage score, the more credit-worthy you are deemed to be.

Variable annuities. Insurance products that serve as retirement savings vehicles. Variable annuities allow you to invest money tax deferred in a choice of mutual fund-like options. But because of the insurance wrapper, many of these products charge higher fees than traditional mutual funds.

Wills. Legal documents that detail exactly how you want your assets distributed, and to whom, after your death.

Wilshire 5000. A benchmark stock index that gauges the performance of the total U.S. stock market. Unlike the S&P 500, which only tracks the 500 largest stocks in the United States, the Wilshire 5000 tracks large-cap, mid-cap, and small-cap stocks.

Zero-coupon bonds. A type of bond that by design does not pay any interest to investors during its life. Instead, these bonds agree to pay the investor all of the money that would have accrued as interest over the life of the loan in a lump sum at maturity in addition to the principal investment that the investor is due back.

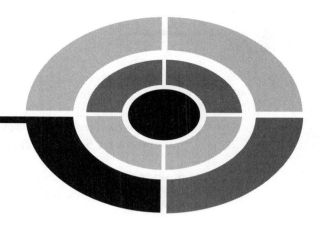

Resources for Additional Information

To learn more about savings and debt, visit the following Web sites:

www.choosetosave.org   This Web site, run by the American Council for Savings Education, offers several tutorials, savings calculators, and tips on how to get started saving. Check out the site's "Ballpark Estimate," a simple two-page worksheet designed to help households determine exactly how much they'll need to start setting aside to fund a comfortable retirement.

www.quicken.com   Quicken is a great resource for computerized budgeting tools. The software company's site helps you create a debt reduction plan.

And you might consider using Quicken's software programs to monitor your spending and finances.

http://moneycentral.msn.com MSN Money offers helpful tools to evaluate your current level of debt and strategies to start saving.

www.dinkytown.net This site offers a variety of savings, debt, mortgage, and investing calculators. It also offers data on how much you would save if you did little things—like skipping that $3 daily cup of coffee over a lifetime and investing that money.

www.mvelopes.com Personal mvelopes is an online budgeting site—think next-generation Quicken. Members pay monthly subscription fees that allow them to keep track of their expenses online and to get access to personal finance coaching.

www.consumercredit.com This site is run by American Consumer Credit Counseling, a nonprofit that aims to educate consumers about managing their own finances. The Web site offers live chats about money issues and variety of calculators and budget worksheets. One nifty calculator will tell you how much interest you're paying on your credit card if you only pay the minimum.

www.aba.com Visit the Web site of the American Bankers Association to learn more about savings and to take advantage of its savings calculators.

www.pearbudget.com This site offers a free downloadable Excel worksheet that helps you keep track of household expenses month by month.

www.moneychimp.com This is a great site to help you calculate compound interest. Click on "calculator" and start plugging numbers, interest rates, and number of years. The site also provides useful tips related to stocks, such as how to read a company's annual report.

To learn more about borrowing and credit, visit the following sites:

www.bankrate.com This comprehensive personal financial Web site offers up-to-the-minute data on interest rates being offered on savings vehicles such as CDs, money market accounts, and checking accounts. It also provides current data on interest rates being charged on various types of debt, including home mortgages, home-equity loans, credit cards, and auto loans.

www.annualcreditreport.com   By law, every consumer is eligible to receive one free credit report a year from each of the three major credit bureaus. Go to this central site run by all three bureaus to obtain your free report. The site also provides tips on how to protect your credit.

www.myfico.com   This is the consumer Web site run by the credit scoring company, Fair Isaac. Here, you can find out what goes into your credit score plus information on how you can improve your credit profile.

www.experian.com   This Web site, run by the credit bureau Experian, offers tools and tutorials on improving your credit.

www.transunion.com   This Web site, run by the credit bureau TransUnion, offers tools and tutorials on improving your credit.

www.equifax.com   This Web site, run by the credit bureau Equifax, offers tools and tutorials on improving your credit.

www.ftc.gov   This site, run by the Federal Trade Commission, gives the latest news and tips on checking and maintaining your credit. Click under "Consumers," then under "Credit."

To learn more about investing in stocks, visit the following sites:

www.morningstar.com   This Web site is run by Morningstar Inc., an independent research firm that tracks stocks, stock mutual funds, and stock market trends. The site offers stock tips and allows you to look up the best and worst performing stocks.

finance.yahoo.com   Yahoo's financial Web site offers up-to-the-minute stock quotes as well as news and commentary on market trends. Consumers can also access historical stock market data for free.

www.fool.com   Motley Fool's popular (and humorous) site aims to educate and amuse investors about equities. The site also offers stock news and tips.

www.marketwatch.com   This site, now owned by Dow Jones, is a great source of online financial news that features stories and blogs on the market.

www.cnnfn.com   This site, owned by Time Warner, is a great source of online financial news. It also features many articles published by Time Inc. magazines, including *Fortune* and *Money*.

www.schwab.com   This is the Web site of the online broker Charles Schwab. It also offers great tutorials and tools for equity investors.

www.fidelity.com   This is the Web site of the online broker Fidelity. While Fidelity is better known as a mutual fund company, this Web site offers great tutorials and tools for equity investors.

www.etrade.com   This is the Web site of the online broker E*Trade. It also offers great tutorials and tools for equity investors.

www.ameritrade.com   This is the Web site of the online broker Ameritrade. It also offers great tutorials and tools for equity investors.

To learn more about investing in bonds, visit the following sites:

www.investinginbonds.com   This Web site offered by the Bond Market Association provides news, tips, and strategies about the bond market.

www.pimco.com   PIMCO is among the world's best-known bond fund managers. Its Web site offers a plethora of information on fixed-income securities. The site also gives you news, tips, and strategies about the bond market.

www.americancentury.com   This Web site, which offers news and tips on investing in bonds, is run by American Century, another respected bond fund manager.

www.envisioncap.com   This Web site, which offers tutorials on bonds, is run by Envision Capital Management, an asset management firm that specializes in fixed-income investments.

www.schwab.com   Charles Schwab's Web site offers a good deal of information and data on bonds.

www.etrade.com   E*Trade's Web site offers a good deal of information and data on bonds in addition to other assets.

To learn more about investing in cash, visit the following sites:

www.bankrate.com   To learn about the best interest rates being offered locally or nationally on CDs, checking accounts, and money market accounts, go to bankrate.com.

www.imoneynet.com   This Web site, run by the financial research firm iMoneyNet, offers up-to-date data on money market mutual funds. It also offers a list of the highest-yielding money funds in various categories.

To learn more about investing in government securities, visit the following sites:

www.treasurydirect.gov   For more information on U.S. Treasury bonds, notes, and bills as well as savings bonds and Treasury inflation protected securities, visit the Treasury Department's public Web site. You can find out more about how various Treasury securities work, and you can open an account to purchase those securities directly from the federal government.

www.investinginbonds.com   In addition to tracking corporate securities, the Bond Market Association's Web site offers pricing and basic information on municipal bonds, Treasury bonds, and mortgage-backed securities.

To learn more about investing in real estate, visit the following sites:

www.realtor.com   This consumer-oriented Web site, run by the National Association of Realtors, offers would-be homebuyers and sellers a primer on real estate transactions. It also offers key listings on residential real estate, and helps consumers locate realtors in their regions.

www.realtor.org   This site, also run by the National Association of Realtors, offers key data on the health of the housing market, including home prices and sales trends in various metropolitan regions.

www.freddiemac.com   This Web site, run by Freddie Mac, a government sponsored mortgage company, offers consumers a glimpse of average mortgage rates being offered nationally. Freddie Mac also has a guide for prospective homebuyers.

www.bankrate.com   This financial Web site lists the lowest mortgage rates being offered nationally and regionally to consumers based on the type and length of the home loans they're seeking.

www.mbaa.org   The Web site of the Mortgage Bankers Association of America provides trends in mortgage interest rates as well as the various home loans available. Click under "Consumers" and then the "Home Loan Learning Center" tab.

www.zillow.com   This popular Web site calls public databases to estimate the value of homes.

www.mortgage101.com   For more information about mortgages, visit this Web site, which was established by the real estate industry.

www.nareit.com   To learn more about real estate investment trusts and how to invest in them. you can visit the Web site of the National Association of Real Estate Investment Trusts.

To learn more about investing in commodities, visit the following sites:

www.advfn.com   To keep track of commodity prices, visit the Advanced Financial Network (a UK stocks and shares Web site), which boasts robust information on commodity prices, charts, and news.

www.nymex.com   This is the Web site of the New York Mercantile Exchange.

www.cme.com   This is the Web site of the Chicago Mercantile Exchange.

www.cboe.com   This is the Web site of the Chicago Board Options Exchange.

www.cbot.com   The Web site of the Chicago Board of Trade.

To learn more about investing in mutual funds, visit the following sites:

www.morningstar.com   This site, run by the mutual fund tracker Morningstar, offers a comprehensive listing of mutual funds, including data on past performance, relative returns, and current holdings. You can also screen for funds based on various criteria through this site.

www.lipperweb.com   This site, run by the fund tracker Lipper Inc., allows investors to track their portfolio of funds and to screen for funds.

www.mfea.com   Investors interested in basic tutorials and information on how mutual funds work can visit the Mutual Fund Education Alliance (a not-for-profit trade association of the mutual fund industry) Web site, which is run by a consortium of no-load mutual fund companies.

www.ici.org   This is the Web site of the Investment Company Institute, the mutual fund industry's chief trade organization. Here, you can find various research reports on mutual fund ownership along with educational materials on the different types of funds, including exchange-traded funds.

www.fidelity.com   To learn more about funds offered by hundreds of different companies, you can visit the Web site of the mutual fund giant Fidelity, which operates a leading fund supermarket.

www.schwab.com   To learn more about funds offered by hundreds of different companies, you can visit the Web site of the brokerage giant Charles Schwab, which operates a leading fund supermarket.

www.etrade.com   To learn more about funds offered by hundreds of different companies, you can visit the Web site of the discount broker E*Trade, which operates a leading fund supermarket. E*Trade also offers a good deal of information on exchange traded funds.

www.ameritrade.com   To learn more about funds offered by hundreds of different companies, you can visit the Web site of the discount broker TD Ameritrade, which operates a leading fund supermarket. Ameritrade also offers a good deal of information on exchange traded funds.

To learn more about college costs and tax-advantaged college savings accounts, visit the following sites:

www.savingforcollege.com   This is a one-stop shop that provides free data and information on 529 college savings plans, 529 prepaid tuition plans, and Coverdell Education Savings Accounts. You can even compare the various state-run 529 plans side-by-side, including an analysis of each plan's investment options and fees.

www.collegesavings.org   This is the Web site of the College Savings Plan Network, a consortium of all the states that offer 529 college savings vehicles. This site details all the rules and regulations of each state's plan, as well as frequently asked questions on the pros and cons of using 529 plans.

www.independent529plan.com   This Web site is run by the Tuition Plan Consortium, a group of more than 250 private colleges and universities, which offers a 529 prepaid account to pay for private education.

www.finaid.org   This Web site offers comprehensive information on the federal financial aid system.

www.collegeboard.com   This site, run by the College Board—the firm that runs the nation's SAT testing system—provides valuable information on college costs, loans, and savings plans.

www.usnews.com   This Web site is run by *U.S. News & World Report* magazine, which annually ranks colleges and universities in a variety of categories. This site also provides valuable information on ways parents and students can pay for college. Simply click under the tab entitled "Best Colleges."

To learn more about retirement costs and tax-advantaged retirement savings accounts, visit the following sites:

www.ebri.org   This site is run by the Employee Benefit Research Institute, a research firm that annually tracks retirement savings and pension trends.

www.401k.com   This site is run by Fidelity Investments, which provides consumers with key information on how 401(k) plans work and their eligibility rules.

www.troweprice.com   This Web site is run by the mutual fund giant T. Rowe Price. It offers a plethora of information on retirement savings, as well as a retirement savings calculator and a tool that helps workers figure out how much they can safely withdraw from their 401(k)s and IRAs without running out of money prematurely.

www.financialengines.com   This Web site is run by a company called Financial Engines, which offers subscribers tools to figure out if they're on the right track when it comes to saving and investing for retirement. This site utilizes something called *Monte Carlo technology*, which uses historical data to predict the odds of being able to successfully meet your long-term retirement goals based on your current saving and investing strategy.

www.401kadvice.com   This educational site is run by the investment advisory firm Scarborough Group, which specializes in offering retirement planning advice for 401(k) participants.

www.403bwise.com   This Web site provides educational resources and tips about maximizing savings placed into 403(b) retirement accounts for teachers and workers at nonprofit firms.

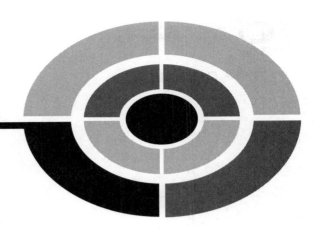

Answer Key

Chapter 1	Chapter 2	Chapter 3
1. B	1. B	1. A
2. C	2. B	2. B
3. B	3. B	3. A
4. A	4. B	4. C
5. B	5. D	5. C
6. C	6. C	6. B
7. C	7. B	7. C
8. A	8. D	8. B
9. A	9. A	9. C
10. C	10. B	10. C

Answer Key

Chapter 4	Chapter 5	Chapter 6
1. A	1. D	1. A
2. C	2. C	2. B
3. B	3. A	3. B
4. B	4. B	4. C
5. B	5. A	5. B
6. B	6. D	6. A
7. B	7. B	7. B
8. B	8. B	8. C
9. A	9. B	9. B
10. D	10. D	10. B

Chapter 7	Chapter 8	Chapter 9
1. B	1. B	1. B
2. A	2. A	2. B
3. C	3. C	3. B
4. C	4. A	4. A
5. A	5. A	5. B
6. B	6. B	6. B
7. B	7. A	7. A
8. B	8. B	8. B
9. B	9. B	9. C
10. C	10. C	10. A

Answer Key

Chapter 10

1. C
2. A
3. B
4. C
5. A
6. C
7. A
8. B
9. B
10. A

Chapter 11

1. A
2. A
3. B
4. C
5. B
6. C
7. C
8. B
9. C
10. B

Final Exam

1. A
2. D
3. B
4. A
5. B
6. A
7. C
8. A
9. C
10. A
11. B
12. C
13. C
14. A
15. D
16. A
17. B
18. D
19. C
20. B
21. A
22. C
23. C
24. B
25. B
26. A
27. B
28. B
29. B
30. A

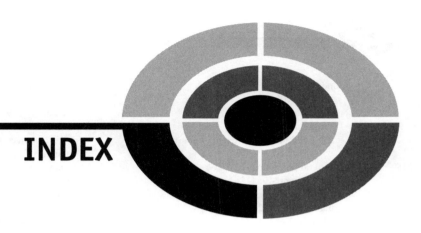

INDEX

Index

Index

Index

Index

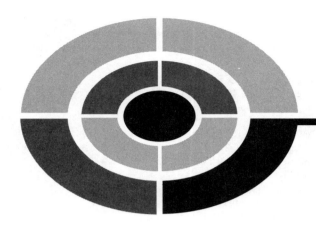

About the Author

Paul J. Lim is chief financial correspondent at *U.S. News & World Report* magazine, where he covers the markets and personal finance. Before joining *U.S. News*, he was a personal finance writer and mutual fund columnist for the *Los Angeles Times* in Los Angeles, as well as a staff writer at *Money* magazine in New York. Earlier in his career, he was twice named by the TJFR Group to its "30 Under 30 List" of the nation's top young financial journalists. He is also the author of *Money Mistakes You Can't Afford to Make: How to Solve Common Problems and Improve Your Personal Finances* and *Investing Demystified*.

A graduate of Princeton University and the University of Pennsylvania, Lim currently resides in Boston.